kins

73 TO 0

SUPER!

Next stop—
New Orleans

Chicago Sun-Times
25c CITY, SUBURBS 35c ELSEWHERE · MONDAY, JANUARY 6, 1986 · 5★ Sports Final

COLDER Page 2

GIANT STEP

Bring on the Rams!

MONDAY, OCTOBER 8, 1984 · PAGE 120

Bulls defeat Pacers; Irish scare Villanova
Stories, Page 102

Sun-Times
sports
104 · Wednesday, January 20, 1982

Sherrill leaves Pitt for Texas A & M job
Briefly, Page 101

MONDAY

ds, victory
yton, Bears

Ditka new Bears coach

Payton's feat
gets Reagan
on the line

Oldest McCaskey son will head Bears

MONSTER MASH!

LL TITLE

GIANT KILLERS!

g mark

BRING ON THE RAMS!

playoffs

SUPERMEN!

Bowl

BEARS CHAMPIONS, 14–10

73-0

CHICAGO SUN-TIMES · WEDNESDAY, NOVEMBER 2, 1983 · PAGE 120

Sports

Illinois No. 6
AP and UPI polls give Illini their top ranking since 1963 Rose Bowl-bound team.
Sports Digest, Page 114

NHL hits Lysiak
If court rejects appeal, the Hawks center will miss 20 games for tripping a linesman.
Page 119

Bears' Halas dies

THE BEARS

A 75-YEAR CELEBRATION
BY RICHARD WHITTINGHAM

INTRODUCTION BY
ED McCASKEY

FOREWORD BY
WALTER PAYTON

TAYLOR

TAYLOR PUBLISHING
FINE BOOKS DIVISION

Acknowledgments

A book of this scope involves the time, efforts and talents of many people. The author and publisher wish to extend their sincere thanks to all who helped in the creation of this celebration in words and pictures of the 75th anniversary of the Chicago Bears.

Foremost, the Chicago Bears themselves, especially CEO Mike McCaskey, Director of Marketing and Broadcasting Ken Valdiserri, Project Coordinator Brian McCaskey, Director of Public Relations Bryan Harlan and his assistant Doug Green, and Bear Editorial Consultant Bill McGrane as well all the others from the team's front office and coaching staff whose cooperation and aid were essential contributions.

We also wish to thank all the former Bears, loyal Bear fans and the members of the media who shared their reminiscences and insights with us which are engraved on the pages that follow.

Special appreciation is extended to authors Tony Hillerman, Jim Belshaw and John Coyne who penned their unique feelings about the Bears in exclusive articles for this book.

Photographer Bill Smith has been taking pictures of the Bears on the field and behind the scenes since 1975, and the great majority of photos of that era are his important contribution. Also noted with thanks are those taken by many other photographers over the 75 years of Bears history which are also included here.

Other valued contributors who deserve our thanks are: The Pro Football Hall of Fame in Canton, Ohio, notably Director Pete Elliott, Curator and Historian Joe Horrigan and his assistant Pete Fierle; the National Football League office; John Wiebusch and the staff of NFL Properties, Inc., Creative Services Division; and the *Chicago Tribune* and *Chicago Sun-Times*.

The Chicago Bears
    Brian McCaskey   Coordinator for the Chicago Bears
    Ken Valdiserri   Director, Marketing and Broadcasting
    Bill McGrane   Editorial Consultant for the Bears

Taylor Publishing Company
    Jack Smith   Publisher & Director, Fine Books
    Bob Snodgrass   Publishing Consultant

TD Media, Inc.
    Tony Seidl & Frank Coffey   Packaging and Editorial
    Robert Engle and Roger Greiner Design and Art Direction

Fiber Optic Photo   Wolf Photography and Chris Dennis
Contributing Photographers   Bill Smith, Chris Dennis, Tim Umphrey, Ron Nelson, Dave Maenza, Vernon Biever, Dan Hill, Don Lansu, Bill Hogan

Select photos courtesy Pro Football Hall of Fame, NFL Properties
Remaining photos courtesy of the Chicago Bears

Published by Taylor Publishing Company,
Dallas, Texas

ISBN: 0-87833-084-4 (Collectors)
ISBN: 0-87833-083-6 (Limited)
ISBN: 0-87833-082-8 (General)

INTRODUCTION

by Ed McCaskey

According to Webster's Dictionary, one use of the word celebration is "to observe an occasion with appropriate ceremony, festivity or merrymaking." As we celebrate the 75th year of the Chicago Bears football team, it is most fitting to celebrate the life and work of George S. Halas, who was truly a remarkable man.

In 1919, the Rose Bowl pitted Great Lakes Naval Training Center against the Mare Island Marines. Great Lakes won the game 17-0. The most valuable player was Great Lakes' end George Halas.

In April 1919, Halas was right fielder with the New York Yankees. Early on, the Yankees came to Chicago. The Chicago newspapers heralded the return of native son Halas even though he was wearing the uniform of the Yankees. Eddie Cicotte, pitcher for the White Sox, made short work of pinch hitter Halas in Comiskey Park with three curve balls. After the game, Halas and his .091 batting average were on their way to St. Paul. Offered a second season up there by the Yankees, Halas opted to return to Chicago and eventually a job with the A. E. Staley Company in Decatur, Illinois. Halas played baseball on the company team and also managed, coached and played on the company football team.

In 1921, the Staley Company decided to drop the football team. Mr. Staley offered George Halas $5,000 to take the team to Chicago. Halas accepted with alacrity.

In 1922, to link his team in the minds of sports fans with the Chicago Cubs—the Bears were playing their games in Wrigley Field—he changed the name of the Staleys to the Bears. A few years later, he broke pro football wide open by signing Red Grange and taking the Bears on a barnstorming trip across the country.

Professional football—and particularly Chicago Bears—football became the consuming passion of George Halas. Consequently, it also became a way of life for his wife, Min, and their two children, Virginia and George, Jr., who as an infant became known as "Mugs." In the wonderful and marvelous way that life unfolds, Virginia became my wife and Mugs my best friend. The entire Halas family was consumed with the Chicago Bears.

It was in 1941 when I met George Halas' daughter, Virginia, in Philadelphia where she was a student at Drexel Institute of Technology. Her uncle, Walter Halas, was the football coach at Drexel, and I was a student at the University of Pennsylvania. Virginia and I fell in love.

In 1942, the Bears were to play in Washington, D. C., against the Redskins for the championship of the NFL. George Halas flew in on leave from the naval station at Norman, Oklahoma. Virginia and I also traveled to Washington, where I had hoped to ask permission of her father to marry Virginia when we saw him after the game. The Bears were losing. As I looked over at Virginia, I saw tears streaming down her face. This is when I learned how much football meant to the Halas family.

I said to her, "What's the matter? It's just a football game."

She said, "Don't you realize my father will never let us get married if the Bears lose?"

The Bears did lose 14-6. But several months later, on February 2, 1943, George Halas' birthday, Virginia and I eloped. Everything worked out . . . later.

In February 1967, before I started working for the Bears, our great linebacker Bill George asked me to keep my eye on a "very special person." In September, my first day working for the Bears, Bill's "special person," Brian Piccolo, walked into my office and said, "Don't worry, Big Ed, I'll square you away with the players." That began a job I loved, functioning as the liaison among the owners, coaches and players. And Brian Piccolo, "special person" that he was, became like a son to Virginia and me.

Another thing happened my first day on the job: Mugs called into his office and asked me what I knew about the Bears. I replied that I knew they played football. Mugs then asked what I knew about the disaster plan. I said that I never heard of it. Mugs told me that because of the disaster plan I was never to fly on the team plane. He and his father would, but I would fly commercial. "If the team plane goes down, each of the other teams are required to give you three players," he told me, "but the week the plane goes down you will not be able to play. Now here's the important part, make certain that you make up that game at the end of the season."

In response, I said, "Mugs, suppose my plane goes down?" And without cracking a smile, he said, "Then we don't have a problem."

Mugs lived and died for the Bears and the NFL, just like his father. Football was a way of life for the Halases. And it became a way of life at the McCaskey home. It seems that only yesterday we were loading the station wagon to drive from Des Plaines to Wrigley Field, hoping and praying for a Bear victory. Win or lose, after every game, the children had a chance to hug their grandfather.

When the boys were little, they were ballboys at St. Joseph's College in Rensselaer, Indiana. So they were imbued with the same love for the Chicago Bears as their grandparents, their uncle Mugs and their mother, Virginia. Now, under Mike's leadership, they are striving to continue the proud traditions of the Bears.

In this book we celebrate the 75th anniversary of the Chicago Bears. A lot of people have teamed to capture the spirit and the story of George Halas and his Chicago Bears. What follows here is a six-day read. But on the seventh day, Game Day, I ask,

IN YOUR PRAYERS—REMEMBER THE BEARS.

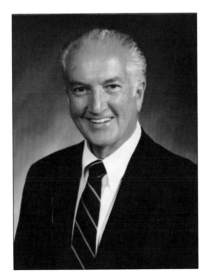

Ed McCaskey
Chairman of the Board
Chicago Bears

FOREWORD

by Walter Payton

Searching my mind and soul for the words to express my feeling about being a "Bear," I keep coming back to the famous farewell speech of Lou Gehrig. He was reflecting upon being a Yankee, and I too, share the same sentiments—I am the luckiest man alive. I am truly blessed.

The Chicago Bears are bigger than life. You come to realize this when you visit children in hospitals and see the sheer joy brought about because a "Bear" has come to see them. The same emotion is felt with elderly citizens when you hear them recall the days of Papa Bear, Red Grange, Bronko Nagurski, Gale Sayers and Mike Ditka, to name a few. The look in their eyes and the smile on their faces reflect the feeling and emotion they feel about the great memories and moments this organization has brought to their lives. I am living proof there is hope for a little boy born in Columbia, Mississippi to get an opportunity and fulfill his fondest dream.

Mr. Halas, I know you'll be reading this from high above with a lot of pride and honor. Again, I say thank you not only for giving me the opportunity but, for making the Bears the proud franchise they are today. This is and always will be your team.

To the friends of the Chicago Bears:

Welcome to this celebration—it could not have happened without you. It could not have happened without all of those who preceded you, all who have loved this football team for three-quarters of a century.

In the planning of this book, there was lively debate on the form it should take, the theme it should follow. After all, some of us argued, this story must begin...as does so much of professional football... with George Halas and the birth of the Decatur Staleys. This franchise, the argument went, is truly unique because it is his franchise. And so it is. But despite his towering presence and contribution, George Halas is not here today. Gone, too—from the field—are Grange and Nagurski, Luckman and Connor, Butkus and Sayers, Payton. Gone are hundreds and hundreds who have worn Bear Blue.

Worn it where, though?

In this game. The game—isn't that the constant? The game played on that worn field outside the Staley plant in Decatur is, at core, the same game we cheer today. We think Coach Halas would agree.

Accordingly, our Celebration begins with Game Day as the players know it today. Come with them, experience it. And then join us as we return to where it all began, as we meet George Halas and the giants of our history. Meet our people, our past, our present and our future.

When we set out to do this book, we wanted it to be "something special." We believe it is. We hope you do, too.

And thanks for being with us.

Mike McCaskey

250 NORTH WASHINGTON ROAD • LAKE FOREST, ILLINOIS 60045-2499 • PHONE (708) 295-6600 • FAX (708) 295-9514

THE CELEBRATION

GAME DAY

It actually begins the day before.

Saturday is when the Bear players and coaches begin drifting into the hotel down on Michigan Avenue. A mile away, at Soldier Field, staff members are getting everything ready, from the locker room to the press box to the field itself. For a road game, the cars of the players, coaches and staff begin pulling into a remote parking lot at O'Hare Airport. Their chartered jet waits out on the tarmac, far from the turmoil of the terminal, to whisk them off to Detroit or Dallas or Los Angeles or wherever they might be playing the following day.

At home or away the routine is much the same. The players, coaches and staff arrive at the hotel to find everything laid out for them on tables in advance—room assignment, room key, itinerary sheet. No long check-in lines here. The goal of all this is to remove the hassles, leaving the coaches and players free to focus only on the game at hand.

Their time is then their own until the offensive and defensive walk-throughs of the game plans, which are specified on the itinerary and carried out in conference rooms at the hotel. The mandatory team dinner is at 7:30 in another conference room.

Each player seems to have his own ritual leading up to a game. Some arrive early, others at the very last second. At home games, coach Dave Wannstedt's wife drives him in from the suburbs and they stop at Children's Memorial Hospital for an hour or two before she drops him at the hotel. He says it energizes him, talking to the kids, seeing their courage. It's refreshing for him before he immerses himself in the game that awaits the next day.

The team dinner is usually a relaxed affair, a lot of banter among coaches and players. Television sets around the room are tuned to catch the wrap-ups and results of the day's college games or other sports events that might be on. After the dinner, they go back to work.

"I'll talk to them first," Coach Wannstedt explains. "Give a little rehash of what we've been working on all week. Then we break up into groups. Special teams is the first meeting because it involves players from both the offense and defense. Then we split into offense and defense. The offensive and defensive coordinators will show films and call plays off the films and the players will interact with what's happening on the screen and make split-second decisions, game-day decisions. After the meetings, the team gathers for a light snack at 9:30. Lights are out at eleven o'clock."

And, yes, even though the great roisterers of the past like Bobby

Dave Wannstedt

1

Dante Jones . . . who faces the task of following in the footsteps of such Bear middle linebackers as Bulldog Turner, Bill George, Dick Butkus and Mike Singletary.

Noah Jackson, guard, 1975–1983

Mike Singletary.

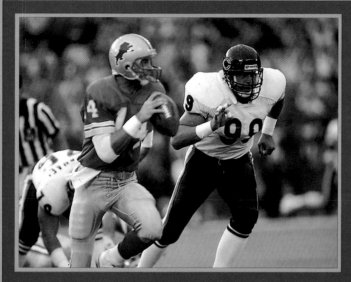

Dan Hampton converges on former Lion QB Erik Kramer, now a Bear.

Donnell Woolford snags a Packer running back, underneath it all is Dan Hampton (99).

Destroying the Rams in the 1985 playoffs. Gary Fencik (45) and Otis Wilson (55). In the vicinity, Dan Hampton (99), Wilber Marshall (58), Dave Duerson (22), and Mike Richardson (27).

Mike Richardson (27) returns an interception as Dave Duerson (22) looks to block.

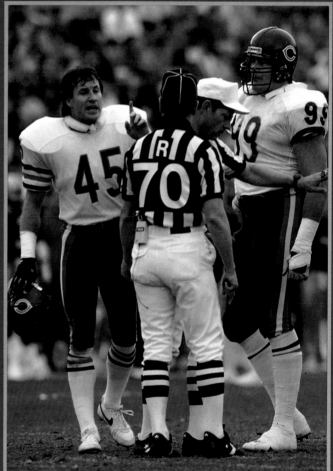

Gary Fencik (45), makes a point of expressing his disagreement with an official's call with Dan Hampton (99) lending his support.

Layne, Art Donovan, Doug Atkins, Paul Hornung, are gone from the game, replaced by those who accede to the big-business in which they are employed today, there is a bed check, conducted by the assistant coaches.

In the hotels, there are security people posted at the elevators on the floors on which the players are staying. There is a little irony here: in the old days, it was the coaches who tried to secure the place to keep the players in. Now it is security personnel working to keep out the auto-graph hounds and other overly curious fans.

The coaches do not have a bed check. After the snack with the players, they have their own meeting in Wannstedt's room which can go for several hours.

The next morning there is a Catholic mass followed by a nondenominational chapel service. Both are well-attended. All players and coaches are then required to be in attendance at the 8:00 a.m. pre-game meal served in a conference room at the hotel.

"I usually get up about 5:30," Coach Wannstedt explains, "because I often like to go for a run with some of the other coaches before the church service. Both help to clear the mind."

At the mandatory pregame meal the mood is alto-gether different from dinner the night before. The players are quiet now, withdrawn. Game faces are being donned, jittery stomachs are the norm, and con-centration is locking out table-talk.

For a noon game, everyone must be at the stadium by 10:00 a.m. On the road, buses take them over from the hotel; at home they drive themselves and park in the dark, musty area beneath the old north stands of Soldier Field. Some arrive much earlier than others, some come in with headsets blaring music that can range from rap to country. A few talk but not many; most are merely adrift in their own thoughts.

TENSIONS

Shaun Gayle, started as a cornerback after being drafted out of Ohio State in 1984, moved to safety the following year where he has played ever since. He sums up Game Day in a sentence:

"I don't feel comfortable at all until the first hit, then all the tensions just drain away and we get on with it."

Shaun Gayle brings down a Buc.

"It is all in the way each chooses to prepare him-self," CEO Mike McCaskey says, "and they are all unique in that."

"At this point," Wannstedt says, "everybody respects the privacy of the guy next to him. It is focus time."

The locker room is off to the right when you walk in through the double doors manned by a security guard. To the left is the training room. Straight back is the washroom, which will cater to the needs of the jittery stom-achs, and the shower room, draped with a curtain to allow players privacy from the reporters working in the locker room after a game.

There are tubs filled with Gatorade and soft drinks. A large container is filled with enough sticks of gum to car-pet a skybox. There are large pots of coffee and, in cold weather, beef bouillon. There are stacks of bags filled with ice which will be used to wrap injured body parts as well as to keep the soft drinks cold. Each team ordinarily goes through about 600 pounds of ice on game day. Buckets of fruit are on tables—oranges are big at halftime, their rinds scattered across the locker room floor like the leaves on the ground outside on an autumn day.

In the locker room, talking to the trainers and other staff are the physicians who will be on the sideline, three orthopedic surgeons and an internist. On call in the stands there will be an optometrist and podiatrist. A staffed X-ray room is across the hall from the dress-ing room. Paramedics man the ambulances which are parked under the stands

When the players begin to arrive, everything is in order. The equipment staff has been working since Saturday. The first thing that hits you is it doesn't smell like a locker room. The large, rectangular room with open locker stalls forming the walls on all four sides, carpeted in Bear navy blue, smells like a hotel lobby. Everything is spotless. The uniforms, pads, and hel-

On the road.

Time to get ready.

Before taking the field.

Halftime.

The media descends.

Aftermath.

Donnell Woolford returns one against the Lions.

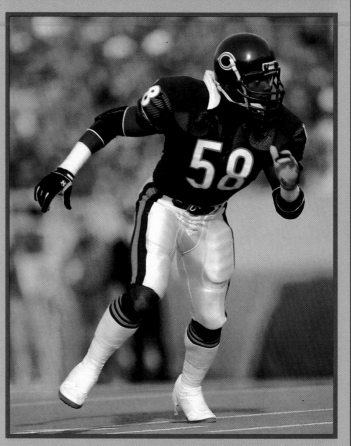

All-Pro linebacker Wilber Marshall.

Rosey Taylor, safety, 1961–1968

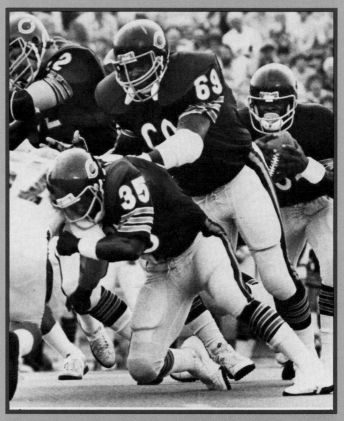

Walter Payton follows the blocks of Roland Harper (35)
and Revie Sorey (69).

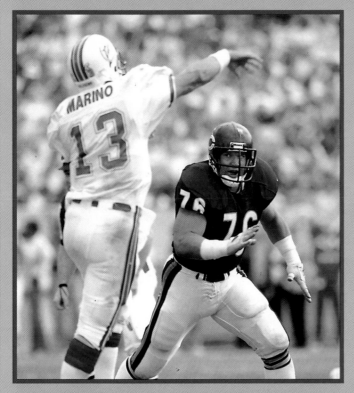

Steve McMichael pressures Miami quarterback Dan Marino.

Mike Hartenstine (73) rises to meet the occasion of a pass from Viking quarterback Tommy Kramer.

William Perry surges in for a touchdown against the Packers. On the ground is Keith Van Horne, behind Perry is Andy Frederick (71).

Ken Margerum grabs a Jim McMahon pass.

mets are hung in each locker neatly with the look of a Marine barracks. There are special things, like flak jackets for the quarterbacks, or other protective or specialized gear for players with specific bumps and bruises. New socks are on the bench, along with a game program. The shoes are neatly lined up in each stall, some so big you wonder if they were made for a Kodiak bear instead of a Chicago Bear. Almost all of those preparations had been done the day before, and a security man remained stationed in each team's locker room all night to ensure that nothing is disturbed. The blackboards haven't the trace of a chalk mark or a speck of dust, the plastic-lined garbage cans are empty.

Over the next few hours, that will all change.

The players begin drifting in, shedding street clothes, heading off to the training room to get taped and have assorted lingering injuries tended to. The training room shelves and cabinets are stocked with

WRIGLEY FIELD
Sunday Morning

Bob Kilcullen played tackle for the Bears from 1957 through 1966 in the twilight of the Bears' residence at Wrigley Field. He remembers game day this way:

"I can still smell and feel today the walk from the car across Waveland Avenue by the fire station to beautiful Wrigley Field on a Sunday morning. This was always a very unnatural walk. Sunday morning, in our society, is a time of calm, peace, rest and joy. For most people anyway.

"Instead, because God gave some of us the limited ability to run, move, hit, fall and get up from it, Sundays were a different thing. My stomach on one of those Sunday mornings was full of heat and turmoil. Everything was very uncertain. There was an itch all over my skin. There were aches in every joint of the body and the thoughts of more to come.

"It was a very different time as you walked through those big steel gates on a Sunday morning, thinking about what you were to face in the next few hours. You realized that in those few hours the results of your labors would be quickly realized, defined, whereas in most other endeavors in life it takes months or years to see them realized."

rolls of white adhesive tape, elastic bandages and pre-wraps. Jars of lubricant, band-aids, clear tape (for stocking tops), cotton swabs, ammonia caps, containers of aspirin, sun block, and even Maalox, for those churning stomachs, are neatly laid out. It does not smell like a hotel lobby in this room, analgesic balm is the overwhelming aroma here.

There are a lot of other things happening. The equipment manager and his staff are tending to individual player needs. The game balls, all brand-new, are being inflated to exactly 13 pounds and then taken to be approved by the officials. Wannstedt is in the head coach's dressing room; the assistant coaches in theirs—some of them are wandering around with a word or two for a player or two, encouragement for some, reminders to others.

Players are all different at this time.

Walter Payton used to isolate himself, covering up with towels and lying under a table. The usually loquacious Dan Hampton, according to Steve McMichael, "never said a single word before the game, but after it you couldn't shut him up." McMichael, for his part, liked to walk silently up to one of the concrete block walls, stare at it for a time, and then kick it. Actually he would raise his foot and slam it into the wall as if to burst a hole in the foot-thick concrete. He would keep at it until the foot-slams were head high. Then, for good measure,

Dan Hampton and Steve McMichael when Game Day is done.

he'd give the wall a resounding block or two with each shoulder.

Afterwards, he'd take a few deep-breaths and then walk out to check the field.

Former kicker Bob Thomas read the Bible. Jim Covert just looked furious. Mike Singletary laboriously taped each knuckle. Gary Campbell, another linebacker, read the Sunday sports pages after appropriating a donut from the locker room attendants. Jim McMahon went nowhere without a paper cup for his enormous dip of Copenhagen. Mark Bortz got red in the face while others looked ashen. Roland Harper prayed.

Doug Buffone, forearm pads taped into place and wearing gray shorts, would write the day's defensive formations on a chalkboard, then sit in front of it and study them, smoking cigarettes. No one smokes anymore.

Mike Ditka probably was more at ease before a game than at any other time during the week. Ditka enjoyed sitting in his little office in the locker room and visiting. He'd smoke a cigar and swap stories about "the old days."

In that same office/dressing room, Dave Wannstedt talks to two of the game officials, a standard procedure, regarding game captains, trick plays or "anything we should make them aware of that might transpire during the game, or they should let us in on." Then he takes some quiet time, "maybe a half-hour, if

JITTERS

George McAfee, Bear halfback of the 1940s and Pro Football Hall of Fame enshrinee has certain special memories of Game Day:

"We were always very nervous before a game. A lot of the players threw up. Joe Stydahar (Bear tackle who would also make it to the Hall of Fame), he always got sick to his stomach before a game. We'd be in the locker room and we'd hear from the bathroom someone in there heaving and we'd say, 'Well, Joe's ready.'

"I always got so keyed up during the ballgame that it was after it was over when I would get sick. It used to make me so darn mad because all the other guys would go out together after a game and have a big meal and a good time, and I couldn't even think of eating anything until maybe midnight."

I'm lucky, to review things in my own mind and to give some thought to what I'm going to say to the team just before we head out onto the field for the game—the pep talk, if you want to call it that."

Tensions continue to build in the locker room. The equipment men feel it as much as the players, especially with the task of slipping jerseys over linemen's shoulder pads. It's hard work, more like a skin-graft operation. Linemen don't want a jersey which an opponent can grasp, so their uniforms are skin-tight. It takes two equipment men to peel the jersey over pads and hard flesh. They struggle and grunt—but when they're done, any self-respecting skin specialist or plastic surgeon would be proud of the results.

The rest is timed to the minute. The pre-game time sheet reads:

11:00 A.M.	Field available to both teams for warm-ups
11:43 A.M.	Both teams clear the field
11:48 A.M.	Two-minute warning to visiting team
11:49 A.M.	Two-minute warning to Bears
11:51 A.M.	Bears leave dressing room
11:52 A.M.	Introduction of visiting starters
11:53 A.M.	Introduction of Bears' starters
11:56 A.M.	Singing of national anthem
11:59 A.M.	Coin toss
12:01 A.M.	KICKOFF

. . . and another Game Day, for the fans at least, has just begun.

HALAS AND HIS SWEATER

This game day story is told by Virginia McCaskey who, as the daughter of George Halas, watched him prepare for hundreds of Bear games:

"On a typical day of a game, my father tried—and let me emphasize tried—to be calm and as normal as on any other day. But he was intense. There was always this eagerness in him we could all sense. We knew how much he wanted to get going, get to the ballpark, to the game.

"On those Sundays we always went to church together as a family at St. Hilary's on the northwest side of Chicago. Then we would go back home for breakfast. My father would read all the newspapers during breakfast and afterwards until he would leave for the game.

"He was not really superstitious, but things had to be done in certain ways. He, of course, always wore a coat and tie to the games, but what I remember is a navy blue sleeveless sweater he would wear. To him, it was a good luck charm, and when one was wearing out my mother would go out to get a replacement because it had to be there. Sometimes she had to go all over town to find just the right one. If it was a little different, it wouldn't do. She always succeeded.

"The night before a game, I remember all the cardboard sheets he would go through. In those earlier days, Dad had to have other business interests to keep us all going. He was a part owner of the White Bear Laundry, and he would bring home a stack of the white cardboards they used for shirts. He would diagram plays on the cardboards and would have a big stack of them on the dining room table. He would go through them one-by-one the night before, then take them down to give to the coaches on Sunday.

"Besides going through the plays, he was always answering the telephone calls about passes for the game the next day. I can still hear him saying, 'Well, yeah, I'll leave two at the pass gate.'

"My mother used to say to him, shaking her head, 'Why can't these people pay to get in?'

"He would nod and say, 'They will, one of these days, don't you worry.'

"He would leave and we always felt a kind of excitement when he did. That was what he gave to us. We would go to the game later, my mother, Mugs and myself, and we would bring along that same excitement.

"After the game, he would talk to the team, then go up to the Pink Poodle in Wrigley Field and meet with the press and dignitaries who might have been there that day. Then he would come home and we would have a late Sunday night dinner. My mother usually made a wonderful chicken stew, one of his favorites. And then game day was over—for that week anyway."

Going for a loose ball: Doug Plank (46), Ron Rydalch (76), and Gary Fencik (45).

Game Day 1994
Alonzo Spellman leads the defense onto Soldier Field.

Ronnie Bull breaks away against the Packers in 1968.

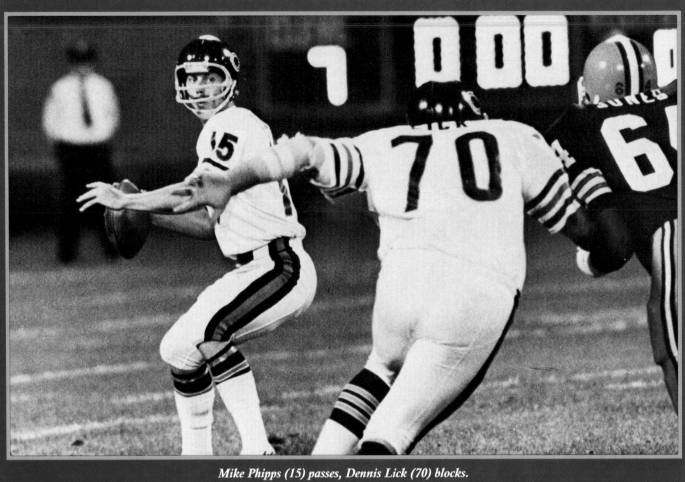

Mike Phipps (15) passes, Dennis Lick (70) blocks.

Payton's incredible balance gets the extra yard.

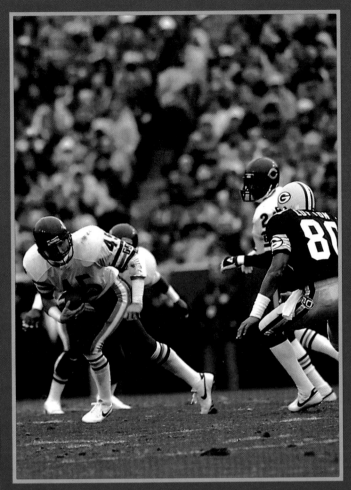

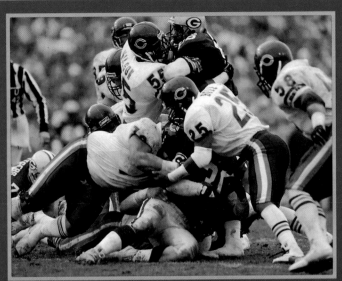

In the trench with Green Bay, William Perry, along with Otis Wilson (55), Todd Bell (25), and Wilber Marshall (58).

Gary Fencik starts back with one of his 38 career interceptions, the most in Bear history, this one against the Packers.

Walter Payton broke Jim Brown's NFL all-time rushing record on this play against the Saints, October 7, 1984.

Ready: Mike Hartenstine and Mike Singletary (50).

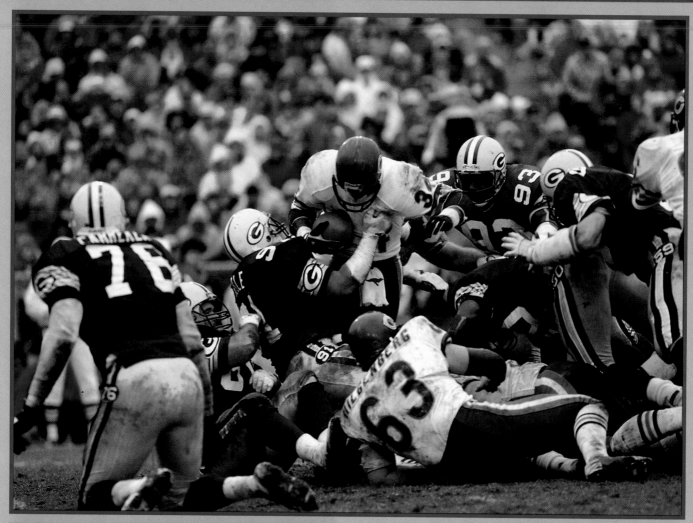

Payton vaults in for a touchdown against Green Bay. On the ground is Bear All-Pro center Jay Hilgenberg.

Dave Whitsell (23) returns an interception in the championship year of 1963. Other Bears are Joe Fortunato (31), Larry Morris (33), Bill George (61), Bennie McRae (26).

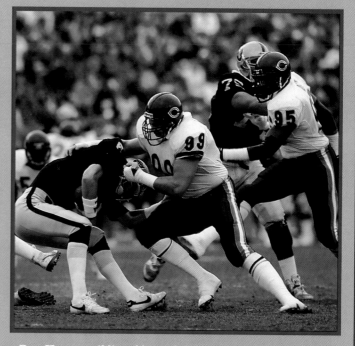

Dan Hampton (99) tackles with Richard Dent (95) coming on.

Ed Sprinkle (lower right) cuts down a 49er back.
Lunging in is George Blanda (22); No. 58 is Ed Neal.

Trace Armstrong does battle with a Green Bay blocker.

Hello. Mike Singletary loses his helmet stopping a Lion.

The first team.

"I could not believe such good fortune . . .
A team of my own . . . I (said) I'll do it . . . ."
—George Halas

WHERE IT ALL BEGAN

Not in Chicago.

Not even with a team called the Bears.

The Bears were born in Decatur, a small town in central Illinois, in 1920, and the name on the birth certificate was the Staleys.

Their reason for being was because a corn products' manufacturer by the name of A. E. Staley was a great sports fan as well a successful businessman. And he had been outfoxed.

Staley had a thriving business in rural Illinois, buying up corn from local farmers and processing it into products like corn starch and then shipping them out to cities throughout the country. His factory was in Decatur, a town about thirty miles west of Champaign, where the University of Illinois is located, and thirty miles east of Springfield, the state capital.

Sports, especially baseball and football, were the great entertainment preoccupation in the days just after World War I. To keep his army of employees happy, Staley subsidized teams. His employees played on the teams, and those who didn't came and brought their families to watch the games. He

George Halas (r) with Paddy Driscoll (l) and Jim McMillen (c) of the Great Lakes Rose Bowl championship team of 1919.

enticed a former major league baseball player, Joe "Iron Man" McGinnity, who had played for the Brooklyn Dodgers and the New York Giants in the years before the war—well enough to later earn his way into the National Baseball Hall of Fame—to come to Decatur and organize his baseball program.

Staley wanted to oversee the football program himself but enlisted the help of his general superintendent, George Chamberlain, to get it started. They fielded a team of employees who were pretty good. Early in the autumn of 1919 they entertained a team from the town of Arcola on the field adjacent to Staley's company and whipped them 41-0. The humiliated Arcolans went back home and decided to do something about it.

At the time, town-pride and wagering on these games were just as serious as the games themselves. So the people of Arcola decided to avenge their honor and make a few bucks on the side. They scheduled a rematch, this time to be played in Arcola.

The businessmen and farmers from Arcola pooled their money for the bets and launched their plan.

It was simple. By far the best football players

of the day were playing for the colleges. One Arcola resident was a conductor on the Illinois Central Railroad who traveled regularly through Illinois and northern Indiana. He was given the job of recruiting the best players from the universities of Illinois, Indiana, Purdue and Notre Dame for the Arcola eleven that would host—and destroy—the Decatur Staleys.

One of the first people he contacted was Ed "Dutch" Sternaman, the top back and kicker for the Fighting Illini. Sternaman agreed to help him put together a team. As a result of the combined efforts of Sternaman and the itinerant railroad conductor, a team of the best college talent of the region was organized, one that even included the fabled George Gipp of Notre Dame, to represent the town of Arcola in its upcoming confrontation with the Staleys.

The game was scheduled for November 30, 1919. Posters and handbills were printed, and the bets were placed.

The college players descended on Arcola a few days before to practice together (Gipp did not because he was ill, according to Sternaman, but he sent along a wager anyway).

A. E. Staley, however, found out about Arcola's new team. He knew he had been taken and he did not

A. E. Staley,
the man who started it all.

want to embarrass himself or his employee-players. To insure against that embarrassment, the Staleys didn't show up.

Ultimately, though, this game that never was became the genesis of the Chicago Bears.

Staley, always the astute businessman, decided to turn the advantage to Decatur. He contacted young Sternaman and told him that he wanted to put together a team with the same kind of talent that Sternaman and his conductor-friend from Arcola had brought together. Sternaman told him he still had to finish his education, another semester, at Illinois so he could not put the whole thing together. Sternaman suggested, however, that Staley talk to a young man he considered a hero, "a guy named George Halas who had been a top-notch football player and baseball player that Illinois was really proud of."

Staley did. . . and all the rest is history.

It was in March of the year which ushered in the decade of speakeasies and flappers, known as the "Roaring 20s," that Mr. Staley picked up one of those old black stand-up telephones and dialed the number that belonged to young George Halas.

Staley offered the 25-year-old Halas a job in the plant, a position on the baseball team and the commission to build a football team capable of competing with any team that Arcola or any other rival city might field.

Halas, whose great love was sports, also needed a job. He had no trouble accepting Staley's offer.

When the school year was over in June, Sternaman was hired by Staley, too, and joined Halas in Decatur. The two then set about putting together a football team. They proved to be fine recruiters. Among the employee-players they brought aboard were end Guy Chamberlin from Nebraska, who would go on to become one of the pro game's greatest early players and a member of the Hall of Fame, and center George Trafton of Notre Dame, who would also earn his way into the Hall. At quarterback they signed Charlie Dressen, a fine football player but who would later make a bigger name in baseball as manager of the Brooklyn Dodgers. They added halfback Jimmy Conzelman who had played on the Great Lakes Naval Training Center team with Halas that won the Rose Bowl in 1919. Conzelman would also

Paddy Driscoll.

be inducted into the Hall of Fame as a player and a coach. A millwright from the plant was also put into uniform and given the additional duty of team trainer. His name was Andy Lotshaw and he would go on to become a legend in Chicago tending to the aches and ailments of both Chicago Bears and Chicago Cubs over the next four decades.

Tackle Hugh Blacklock (1920–1925), center George Trafton (1920–1932), and guard Bill Fleckenstein (1925–1930).

At the same time, there was talk elsewhere of organizing a professional football league. For years there had been semipro and pro teams, especially in the steel mill and mining towns of eastern Ohio and western Pennsylvania, places like Canton and Massilon and Pottsville, but also in cities closer to Decatur like Hammond and, yes, Chicago (two, in fact, the Tigers and the Cardinals).

Halas and Sternaman were convinced that if this proposed league ever got off the ground they should be a part of it.

The idea to organize a league was the brainchild of Ralph Hay who owned the Canton, Ohio, Bulldogs, one of the better teams of that era. He also owned a Hupmobile auto agency in that city and that is where, as history has well recorded, the gentlemen from various midwestern cities convened to form a professional football organization which would later become known as the National Football League.

George Halas was designated to represent the Decatur Staleys at the meeting which took place on September 17, 1920. He boarded a train in Decatur which took him, ironically through Chicago, to Canton. In his words, "That meeting in Hay's showroom must have been the most informal on record. The showroom was big enough for four cars—Hupmobiles and Jordans—and occupied the ground floor of the three-story brick Odd-Fellows building. Chairs were few. Most of us lounged around on fenders and running boards and talked things over."

The meeting lasted only a little over two hours, but brought results. There were a total of ten teams represented at that now famous meeting. Besides Canton and Decatur, they hailed from Chicago (the Cardinals); Akron, Cleveland, and Dayton in Ohio; Rochester, New York; Muncie and Hammond, Indiana; and Rock Island, Illinois.

The ten teams founded the American Professional Football Association (APFA) and named the most famous athlete of the day, Jim Thorpe (who was also the star back and coach of the Canton Bulldogs), as its president. The Sac and Fox Indian superstar of track and field, baseball and football was an administrator in name only, but everyone at the meeting felt the name would give substance to the new league.

"To give the new organization an appearance of financial stability," Halas recalled, "we announced that the membership fee for individual clubs had been set at $100. However, I can testify that no money changed hands. Why I doubt if there was a hundred bucks in the whole room."

NFL CHARTER MEMBERS 1920

Akron Pros
Buffalo All-Americans
Canton Bulldogs
Chicago Cardinals
Chicago Tigers
Cleveland Tigers
Columbus Panhandles
Dayton Triangles
Decatur Staleys
Detroit Heralds
Hammond Pros
Muncie Flyers
Rochester Jeffersons
Rock Island Independents

The official minutes of the meeting are spare, typed under the AKRON PROFESSIONAL FOOTBALL TEAM letterhead. But the league was formally launched that September afternoon in 1920.

Halas returned to Decatur and attended to the duty of turning out a team for A. E. Staley to play in the loosely-knit new league. There were no schedules drawn up, no plans for official records, and only one rule or regulation of note which had to do with tampering with any player who had been signed by another team in the league. Each team was on its own. As Ralph Hay said, "We just have to keep in touch."

The teams of 1920 ordinarily consisted of 15 to 18 players. The games were scheduled for Sundays so as not to compete with the college games that were traditionally played on Saturdays, although that was a relatively meaningless concession because a college game

involving the University of Illinois or Chicago or Ohio State or Notre Dame would draw tens of thousands into their stadiums in 1920 and a pro game would be lucky to entice 1,000 spectators into the bleachers or onto the standing areas around the field where they played.

Schedules were based on the proximity of teams because the cost of travel was a major factor in a time when ticket prices ranged from 50 cents to $1 to watch a professional football game.

About two weeks after George Halas returned from Canton, the Decatur Staleys, a full-fledged member of the APFA, played their first game. The date was Sunday October 3, 1920. The team they faced was the Moline Tractors who had traveled over from the Quad Cities area on the Mississippi River and their confrontation was on Staley Field. Moline was not a

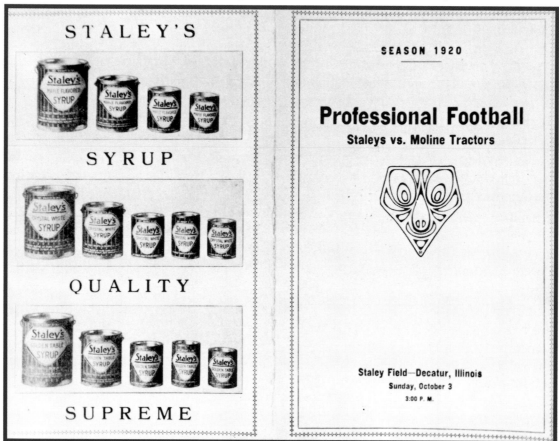

member of the APFA, but that did not matter in those days. They were paid to play and recognized as an independent pro team and this was what has been recorded as the Decatur Staleys/Chicago Bears very first professional football game. In 1993, on Sunday, October 3, the Bears—in a remarkable coincidence—would play their 1,000th game.

The Staleys defeated Moline that Sunday, October 3, 1920, by a score of 20-0. One thousand games later, on Sunday, October 3, 1993, the Bears also won in a shutout, beating the Atlanta Falcons 6-0.

The Staleys scheduled seven league games in 1920. All but one was on the road, although geographically they roamed no further than a 125-mile radius of Decatur. They traveled to Chicago four times to play both the Cardinals and the Tigers, and twice to meet the Independents in Rock Island. They entertained only the Hammond Pros down in Decatur and soundly whipped them 28-7.

The Staleys had only two touchdowns scored on them in those seven games. One resulted in their only loss, a 7-6 defeat at the hands of the Chicago Cardinals.

With a league record of 5-1-1, the Staleys were in second place at the end of the year behind the unde-feated Akron Pros (6-0-2). The ever-competitive Halas, discontent at not being on top, contacted the owner of the Akron team and arranged for the two teams to meet. Halas suggested a neutral site, Wrigley Field in Chicago, in what was billed as: *The Game to Decide the Pro Football Championship of the World.*

THE FIRST LOSS

In their first season, 1920, the Decatur Staleys, lost only one game—to the Chicago Cardinals who would become an archrival over the next four decades, until 1960 when they moved to St. Louis.

It was a questionable loss.

This is how the story was told:

The game was played at Normal Park on Chicago's south side, the Cards' home field. A crowd of about five or six hundred people showed up, and was certainly prejudicial to the Chicago eleven and opposed to the interlopers from down-state Decatur.

With the Cardinals losing 6-0 near the end of the game, one of their receivers caught a pass thrown by tailback Paddy Driscoll. The receiver ran to the sidelines and was about to be tackled but found refuge in the middle of a group of partisan specta-tors who had edged their way out onto the field.

Halas said later, "The guy used them for block-ers and went in for a touchdown." The referee, more afraid of the suddenly jubilant Cardinal fans than the wrath of Halas and Sternaman and assorted other Staley players, allowed the touch-down to stand. Driscoll drop-kicked the extra point and the Staleys suffered their first and only loss of the season.

Some years later, Halas was quoted as saying in regard to the incident, "It taught me officials are human and can make mistakes. Since then, I have always tried to assist officials in order that they might make correct calls."

It didn't. They played to a scoreless tie before a crowd estimated at 10,000, by far the largest of any pro game that year. All seats were priced at 50 cents. Halas also managed to breach the league's only rule for that game by enticing Chicago Cardinal tailback and future Hall of Famer Paddy Driscoll to suit up for the Bears, although he did not help. And so Akron ended up with a record of 6-0-3 and the Staleys 5-1-2.

Thus ended the first NFL season, even though it was known then as the first APFA season.

Professional football on an organized basis had established itself on the American sports scene and it was here to stay.

The Staleys, however, were not going to stay in Decatur. Business was not good at A. E. Staley's company in 1921, the country was in a recession and the effects reached all the way to little Decatur, Illinois. One of the easiest ways to cut costs was to cut the newfound football team. Staley called Halas into his office and said, "I know you're more inter-ested in football than you are in the starch business, and I want you to know I can't underwrite the foot-ball expenses anymore."

Halas was, in his own words, "flabbergasted . . . dumbfounded." Staley went on to suggest that Halas and Sternaman could move the team up to Chicago. "Decatur can't support a team," he said. "Professional teams need a big city base. Chicago is a good sports city." And he offered a deal.

Staley was a benevolent man and he liked both Halas and Sternaman and wanted to honor the com-mitment he had made to them. He offered them

(continued on page 26)

The Great Barnstorming Tours of 1925–1926

It began on an August evening down in Champaign, Illinois, in 1925. That night All-American halfback Harold "Red" Grange walked into the Virginia Theater and sat down with his running mate at the University of Illinois, fullback Earl Britton, to watch Harold Lloyd in the silent film comedy *The Freshman*.

That same night the theater owner, C. C. Pyle—a dapper dreamer who was most comfortable dressed in spats, a three-piece suit, diamond stick pin, homburg hat and brandishing a silver-handled walking stick—asked Grange to step into his office (a sportswriter once suggested Pyle's initials stood for Cash and Carry). Pyle then asked the young superstar, "How would you like to make a hundred thousand dollars, Red . . . maybe a million?"

Grange was leery. The amount was astronomical to a 21-year-old who had been working his summers lugging hundred-pound blocks of ice from an ice-wagon to people's backdoors on a home-delivery route in Wheaton, Illinois. And there was always the specter of gambler's dirty money. "How?" Grange asked with suspicion.

"Playing football, my boy," Pyle said, "just playing football." He then went on to explain his plan.

Grange was one of the biggest names in sports in 1925, right up there on the same marquee with Babe Ruth and Jack Dempsey. Crowds of 60,000 and more jammed stadiums to watch the "Galloping Ghost," as legendary sportswriter Grantland Rice had dubbed him.

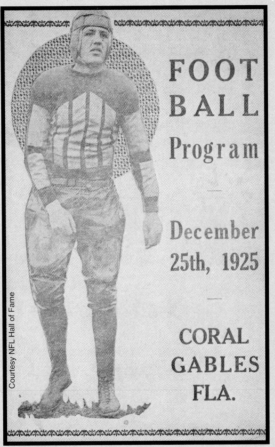

FOOT BALL Program

December 25th, 1925 —

CORAL GABLES FLA.

Courtesy NFL Hall of Fame

With his college career coming to an end the Saturday before Thanksgiving, Grange, according to Pyle's plan, would immediately sign with the Chicago Bears and make his debut as a pro. Then Grange and the Bears would go on two national barnstorming tours, bringing "the legendary Grange and pro football to millions of eager fans."

Grange said he would think about it. After all, playing football for money was frowned upon in 1925. Amos Alonzo Stagg, the grand old man of the college game and head coach at the University of Chicago, had condemned it as "a serious menace, possibly greater than all other (gambling, crooked coaches, and overzealous alumni and friends)." Grange's own coach at Illinois, Bob Zuppke, had counseled against it, "Football isn't meant to be played for money," he said. "Tainted" money is in fact the way he described it.

In the meantime, Pyle began making covert arrangements with George Halas and Dutch Sternaman, who were most interested in putting the star-spangled name of Red Grange on the Bear roster.

The college and pro seasons of 1925 rolled on. The Bears drew anywhere from 5,000 to 10,000 a game while the University of Illinois and Grange entertained throngs as large as 70,000.

Clandestine meetings and off-the-record talks went back and forth, between Grange and Pyle, Pyle and the Bears.

The result was that Grange finally agreed to

Pyle's deal. He later told his coach, "You get paid for coaching, Zup. Why should it be wrong for me to get paid for playing?" Zuppke would not speak to Grange for several years after the Galloping Ghost decided to join the pro ranks although eventually the two would reconcile their differences.

The Bears also agreed, reluctantly but with little choice, to Pyle's plan and the general terms he outlined, a 50-50 split of the gates, with the Bears to pay all team expenses out of their 50 percent.

The meetings between Pyle and the Bears were held secretly during the autumn of 1925 because of an NFL rule against tampering with college players. So it was agreed final financial details would not be settled until after Grange's last college game, nor would any announcement be made by parties on either side. Rumors of Grange turning pro, however, were all over the nation's sports pages.

Grange made his last collegiate appearance in Columbus, Ohio, on November 21, 1925, before a crowd estimated in excess of 70,000 where the Illini defeated Ohio State 14-9. Immediately after the game Grange announced he was turning pro. The next day he signed formal contracts.

The following Thursday Red Grange made his professional debut when the Bears faced their crosstown rivals, the Cardinals. More than 36,000, a standing-room only crowd at Wrigley Field in those days, paid for tickets that Thanksgiving afternoon, not to watch a mere pro football game but to observe the fabled Red Grange play as a pro.

They were disappointed as the game ended in a scoreless tie, and the Galloping Ghost gained only 36 yards on 16 carries. The result didn't dampen the enthusiasm of the Grange-Pyle-Bears consortium. The tours were to go on as scheduled with

everyone relying on Pyle's P. T. Barnum merchandising instinct and Grange's name.

From the outset, it was clear that Pyle had not been a football player. He scheduled eight games in eight different cities in twelve days.

The first tour kicked off on a Wednesday, December 2, 1925 in St. Louis. After barnstorming the east, it concluded in Chicago on December 13.

Pyle would not let the holidays interfere with the second tour as the first game was held on Christmas Day in Florida. The Grange/Bears, traveling in a special Pullman car and with a personal porter, played through Florida, New Orleans, and up and down the west coast. The schedule was more relaxed this time, often allowing a week between games. It ended in Seattle on January 31, 1926. The Bears returned to Chicago while Grange and Pyle went to Hollywood where Pyle had struck a deal for Grange to star in three motion pictures.

When the two tours were over, it was estimated that Pyle and Grange split about $250,000 and the Bears netted approximately $100,000. As George Halas said later, "it was the first financial cushion we'd managed to accumulate." The other Bear players earned between $100 and $200 a game and expenses. But as the team's quarterback, Joey Sternaman said, "It was still quite something. We saw the nightlife of New Orleans and a lot of the stars in Hollywood. I even had my first airplane ride. It was an experience."

The tour also served to popularize the game of professional football in America, giving it a respectability and a national following it had not experienced before, and proved to be one of the truly important landmarks in the history of the National Football League.

CHICAGO BEARS v.s. LOS ANGELES TIGERS

Jan 15, 1926

Courtesy NFL Hall of Fame

DWARD ST. AMAN   GEORGE HALAS   HAROLD 'RED' GRANGE   C. C. PYLE

"RED" SIGNS HIS FIRST PRO CONTRACT, NOVEMBER 1925.

IN NEW YORK . . . DAMON RUNYON OBSERVES

Then sportswriter Damon Runyon recorded the historic first meeting between the Chicago Bears and the New York Giants, the game that saved the New York franchise and brought the game of pro football to the nation's headlines:

"I here preach from the old familiar text: It pays to advertise!

"There gathered at the Polo Grounds in Harlem this afternoon the largest crowd that ever witnessed a football game on the island of Manhattan, drawn by the publicity that has been given one individual—Red Harold Grange, late of the University of Illinois.

"Seventy thousand men, women and children were in the stands, blocking the aisles and the runways. Twenty thousand more were perched on Coogan's Bluff and the roofs of apartment houses overlooking the baseball home of McGraw's club, content with just an occasional glimpse of the whirling mass of players on the field far below and wondering which was Red Grange."

In the press box with Runyon that memorable afternoon were also such celebrated sportswriters of the time as Ring Lardner, Grantland Rice, Paul Gallico, Westbrook Pegler and Ford Frick.

QUOTES OF NOTE FROM THE BEARS/GRANGE TOURS

Babe Ruth, visiting Red Grange in the Astor Hotel in New York offered these tidbits of advice:
"Kid, don't believe anything they write about you . . .
Get the dough while the getting's good, but don't break your heart trying to get it . . .
And don't pick up too many checks."

C. C. Pyle to George Halas, who was bemoaning the state
of the rain-drenched, mud-covered uniforms after their game
in Philadelphia and the fact that they had another game
to play the following day in New York:
"This tour will make you so wealthy, Halas,
that next year you'll be able to afford two sets of uniforms."

Don Maxwell of the Chicago Tribune:
"It's not long since the definition of a pro football player was a
'tough guy.' Now the pro is a 'star' who draws more money
in one day than a coach makes in a year."

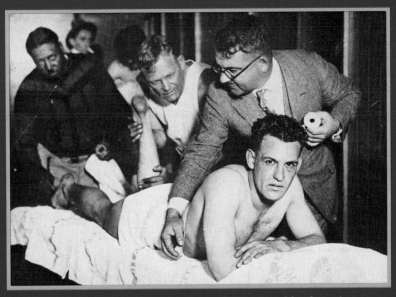

Red Grange, a little worse for wear, being treated by the trainers.

Halas as an end in the early 1920s.

$5,000 seed money and ownership of the franchise; asking that they maintain the name Staleys for at least one year and provide him some free advertising in the game programs.

As Halas later explained, "I could not believe such good fortune . . . A team of my own . . . I'll do it . . . ." Actually it wasn't a team of his own since Dutch Sternaman owned half. But the team was moving to Chicago, and the first part of the phrase Chicago Bears was established.

Halas and Sternaman met with William L. Veeck, an owner and the CEO of the Chicago Cubs, about playing their games in Cubs Park, which was later re-named Wrigley Field. A deal was made. Veeck was not greedy and wanted to be helpful. He said the two new pro football franchise owners would pay 15 percent of gross

IN WASHINGTON . . . MEETING THE PRESIDENT

On the tour, in the nation's capital, a visit to the White House was set up. Red Grange himself explains it best:

"We went to Washington . . . . The senator from Illinois, McKinley I believe it was, arranged for us to meet the president, Calvin Coolidge. We were taken in and I was there with George Halas. The senator introduced me as 'Red Grange, who plays with the Bears.'

"Coolidge shook my hand and said, 'Nice to meet you, young man. I've always liked animal acts.'"

receipts for use of the stadium, although they could only use it after the baseball season. When gross receipts of the team exceeded $10,000, the rate would escalate to 20 percent. The Staleys could keep the profits from all concessions and programs. Needless to say, Halas and Sternaman were thrilled. "The negotiations took all of seventy-five seconds," said Halas.

So the Staleys moved to Chicago. They opened at Cubs Park against a semipro team from Waukegan and demolished them 35-0. Then, as an additional concession to A. E. Staley, they went back to Decatur to play the first league game of the season at Staley Field. They defeated the Rock Island Independents before a crowd of about 4,000 by the score of 14-10.

In Chicago, they took on all comers and they came from Buffalo and Rochester, New York; Detroit; Dayton and Canton, Ohio; and Green Bay, Wisconsin,

Grange in his newly-earned raccoon coat shakes hands with younger brother Gardie who would later play end for the Bears, 1929-31.

IN JACKSONVILLE . . . STRIKING THE DEAL

In an article in Liberty magazine, the meeting between C. C. Pyle and erstwhile promoter John S. O'Brien regarding the upcoming game in Jacksonville, Florida was duly recorded. O'Brien was representing the great Stanford fullback Ernie Nevers, the most famous college football player of the day after Grange, who was to star on his Jacksonville All-Star team.

"It should be the battle of the century, Mr. Pyle," said O'Brien. "I aim to cover the South with announcements that no red-blooded man should miss the titanic struggle between the Galloping Ghost and the Lion of the Sierras—Red and Ernie. It will be a sell-out with lamentable numbers turned away at the gate."

"I'm glad to hear it," said Mr. Pyle, "because you will now read with less pain our contract, which, I regret to say, has embarrassed other managers. . . ."

whose Packer team decided to join the league that year.

The Staleys won nine games, lost one to the Buffalo All-Americans and played to a scoreless tie with the Cardinals in the last game of the year out at Normal Park on Chicago's south side. It was the Staley's only "away" game besides the opener in Decatur. They were acclaimed the league champion, and the Bears had their first NFL title, even if they were the Staleys and the crown bore the name APFA.

The following year, Halas and Sternaman changed the team's name to the Chicago Bears, and the American Professional Football Association changed its name to the National Football League.

"On a typical day of a game, my father tried—and let me emphasize tried—to be calm and as normal as on any other day."
Virginia Halas McCaskey

PAPA BEAR

Legendary Green Bay Packer coach Vince Lombardi said, "There is only one man I embrace when we meet. And only one I call Coach—George Halas."

Babe Ruth and Joe DiMaggio were Yankees, Bob Cousy and Bill Russell Celtics, Bobby Hull and Stan Mikita Blackhawks. George Halas was a Bear. All these men were uniquely the embodiment of the teams with which they were associated. But no one in the history of American sports had greater impact on his game than George Halas had on professional football.

Papa Bear was there from the inception of the National Football League in 1920, and was instrumental in many milestone moments during its 75-year evolution. Halas was present at the first organizational meeting in Canton, Ohio, in 1920. He brought aboard the college legend Red Grange in 1925 and with a barnstorming tour that criss-crossed the country from Boston to San Diego, from Miami to Seattle, firmly established the game as a legitimate and exciting sport on the American scene. With the T formation/man-in-motion offense, he revolutionized the game in 1940. In the 1950s, he played a crucial role in bringing together the sport of pro football and the medium of television. In the 60s, he was one of the pivotal figures in bringing about the merger of the NFL and the AFL, thereby providing football fans everywhere with all the wonderfully exciting playoff and Super Bowl weekends that have grown over the past three decades.

George Halas played in the NFL for ten years,

1920–29, and was selected on the Pro Football Hall of Fame's All-Decade team as an end. He coached for 40 years and held the record for the most victories as a head coach until Don Shula moved past him in 1993. He owned the team and was active in league affairs for 64 years until his death in 1983.

Papa Bear was one of a kind.

He was born on February 2, 1895, in a Bohemian neighborhood on the southwest side of Chicago. His father ran a small tailoring business and his mother did the buttonholes. "They were the best, people would say. She taught me a person has to pay attention to the smallest of details," said Halas.

His first introduction to sports was playing softball in the street near his house where manhole covers and flattened boxes served as bases. He took the streetcar to Cubs Park to watch the fabled infield trio of Tinker, Evers and Chance play.

Halas went to Crane Tech High School in his neighborhood in 1909 and graduated four years later, as he said, "at the hefty weight of 120 pounds." He played football, ran track, and played indoor baseball—the game of the times in Chicago.

In the fall of 1914, Halas enrolled at the University of Illinois in Champaign where his real sporting life began. He put on weight, made the football, basketball, and baseball teams, and lettered in all three sports. When he was not in school, he worked at the Western Electric Company to help pay for his education. There he met a girl named Min Bushing, who would eventually become his wife. He graduated in 1918 and joined the Navy, which enabled him to earn his first real piece of sports publicity.

In the years of World War I, college football, a major pastime in America, had sunk in priority. Therefore, the Rose Bowl game of 1919 was played between two service teams, the Great Lakes Naval Training Center from Illinois and the Mare Island Marines of California. Great Lakes had three future Pro Football Hall of Fame players on its roster: Halas, tailback Paddy Driscoll and halfback Jimmy Conzelman. Halas scored one touchdown on a pass

from Driscoll, and nearly had a second but was dragged down at the three-yard-line after his 77-yard inteception return. The sailors beat the marines on New Year's Day, 17-0, and Halas was named the game's Most Valuable Player.

After his tour of duty with the navy, Halas, who had been scouted in college by the New York Yankees, joined the team for spring training in Florida. He made it as a right fielder. In an exhibition game against the Brooklyn Dodgers, he doubled off future Hall of Fame pitcher Rube Marquard but tried to stretch it into a triple and injured his hip sliding into third base. That

Grange (left), with Halas behind him, 1925.

30

injury, along with an inability to hit a curve ball and a batting average of .091, helped him to decide that perhaps football was the sport for him to pursue.

Back in Chicago, Halas, who had majored in engineering at Illinois, took a job in the bridge design department of the Chicago & Burlington Railroad for $55 a week. On the weekends he played football for a semi-pro team in Hammond, Indiana. "I could not get out of my mind, the words Zup (his football coach at

George Halas in the 1930s.

RED GRANGE

on Halas and Creative Refereeing

They had a referee in the Twenties, Jim Durfee, who was a character. He and George were pretty good friends, but Durfee loved to penalize the Bears, especially right in front of their bench. When Halas was riding him pretty hard in a game one day, Jim began marching off a five-yard penalty.

Halas got really hot. "What's that for?" he hollered at Durfee.

"Coaching from the sideline," Jim yelled back. It was illegal in those days.

"Well," said George, "that just proves how dumb you are. That's a fifteen-yard penalty, not five."

"Yeah," said Jim, "but the penalty for your kind of coaching is only five yards."

Another day Jim was penalizing the Bears fifteen yards and Halas cupped his hands and yelled, "You stink!"

Durfee just marched off another fifteen yards, then turned and shouted, "How do I smell from here?"

Illinois, Bob Zuppke) had said to me," he later recalled. "He told me that just when he taught us really how to play football we graduated and he lost us. I thought that was a shame, we ought to play more." So he did. In Hammond, which he traveled to on the electric railroad, there was one practice a week, on Thursday night, and a game on Sunday.

Then came the offer he could not refuse. A. E. Staley, a corn products manufacturer in Decatur, Illinois, asked him to come to work for him, play baseball on the company team, and put together a football team that could compete with other pro and semi-pro teams in the midwest.

Halas went downstate and all the rest is documented history. Along with Ed "Dutch" Sternaman, another Illinois football player, he launched the Decatur

31

This Is Your Life, George Halas, 1950, from the famous television show of the era. From the left, front row: Phil Handler, Mugs Halas, George Halas, Min Halas, Virginia McCaskey, Ed McCaskey, Walter Halas, Hugh Blacklock, George Schultz, Luke Johnsos, Red Grange, Jack Brickhouse; back row: Eddie Edgar, Ed Sprinkle, Ralph Brizzolara, Paddy Driscoll, Frank Halas, Bob Zuppke, George McAfee, Howard Brundage, Bert Bell, Bill Osmanski, George Connor, Sid Luckman, Ed Healey, Fred Gillies, Milford Baum.

Staleys as a professional football team. However, despite a fine 1920 season, Staley could no longer afford to underwrite the football program. He suggested Halas and Sternaman move the team to Chicago and offered them $5,000 to keep the name Staleys for one year and provide the company free advertising in the game programs.

They moved to Chicago and played at Cubs Park, now known as Wrigley Field. The team "headquarters" was in the lobby of the old Hotel Planters in downtown Chicago because they could not afford to rent office space at the time.

Halas did everything in those infant days—played end, coached, handled the many and varied administrative details, wrote press releases and delivered them personally to the newspaper offices, saw to the laundry, kept the ledgers, hawked tickets, anything that needed to be done to keep the team going. His hard work paid off. They won the league championship that first year in Chicago, 1921, banked a few dollars, and made their presence known in the Windy City.

His favorite playing-day memory was in the game

ROZELLE ON HALAS

Pete Rozelle, NFL commissioner from 1960 through 1989, had many dealings with Halas over the years.

"My fondest memory dates back to the 1950s," Rozelle said. "I was employed by the Los Angeles Rams then, first as publicity director and then general manager."

I recall watching George Halas during those games when he brought his Bears out to play us. He would patrol the sideline with his arms flailing as he urged his players to perform. I was struck by the intense enthusiasm of a man his age. George would slam his hat to the turf if things didn't quite go his way, and he was never reluctant to let the game officials know when they, in his estimation, had made a mistake.

His competitiveness and fervor for the game of football were, to me, the personification of the league itself."

With the war over and football on their minds . . . Halas flanked by Admiral Chester Nimitz (left) and General Dwight D. Eisenhower.

against the Oorang Indians and their legendary back Jim Thorpe. It was a rainy day and the field was muddy and the much-rounder ball than the one used today was slippery. The Indians had the ball near the Chicago goal and appeared about to score. Thorpe took the snap and headed toward the goalline. Somehow he fumbled, and

THE FIRE

Chuck Mather, a Bear assistant coach, was there with George Halas the day that a fire raged through the Bears' offices on Madison Street in 1961.

"It was the most devastating thing in his life," Mather recalled. "All the memorabilia he had stored in that venerable office building was being destroyed. Mr. Halas was a great saver of mementos; pertinent, valuable papers, football plays, and statistics."

"I stood with him across the street and watched the fire shooting out of all the building's openings, and it was quite obvious that the result would be total destruction. For conversation, I said, 'Coach, this is really terrible.'

After a slight pause, he turned to me and unemotionally said, "The hell with it! Let's get a drink."

He never mentioned the fire again."

the football ended up in the hands of Halas at the two-yard-line. He started back up the field, and as Halas recalled, "I heard an angry roar. It was Thorpe coming after me. I ran faster and faster but I sensed he was gaining. I could hear the squishing of his shoes in the mud as he narrowed the gap. I zigged, I zagged, and just short of the goal Thorpe threw himself at me and down I went into a pool of water—but at the same time I slid over the goal line."

The 98-yard fumble-return touchdown was an NFL record which lasted for 50 years. As Halas said, "They recorded it as 98 yards. I think I ran 198 yards trying to stay away from Thorpe."

In those days of 50-cent tickets and 10-cent programs, the Bears were lucky to draw 5,000 fans—and quite a few of them were not paying spectators. But Halas saw the team through those fledgling years and was an instrumental figure at all league meetings when the NFL mainly consisted of teams from such towns as Canton, Ohio; Rock Island, Illinois; and Duluth, Minnesota.

The world of professional football picked up after the Bears/Red Grange tours of 1925-26, but then came the Great Depression and then World War II. Halas, however, met every challenge and the Bears weathered every storm.

In 1933, after the team lost $18,000 the previous season and a rift between he and co-owner Dutch

Sternaman had grown to unmanageable proportions, Halas offered to buy out Sternaman's share. This occurred during the era of the Great Depression and Halas did not have the $38,000 he needed to make the purchase. He came up with most of the money. He dug into whatever was in his pocket, borrowed some from a bank, persuaded his mother and a couple of players—Bear greats George Trafton and Jim McMillen among them—to invest. Friends Ralph Bizzolara, who would later become the Bears' business manager, and Charles Bidwill, who would later buy the cross-town rival Cardinals, came up with more money, but Halas was still $5,000 short.

There was a provision in the buy-out contract that if Halas failed to make complete payment by August 9, 1933, all stock in the Bears would revert to Sternaman. As Halas later explained, "August 9th came; I was desperate. At noon I would lose my Bears. Years of effort would be lost. I had tried everything. About 11 o'clock, a banker in Antioch, Illinois, C. K. Anderson, called and said he had heard I needed $5,000 urgently. He said he would lend me the money I needed.

"They had an office in Chicago. I raced out the door from my office on Washington Street to their office at Randolph and LaSalle Streets just a few blocks away. I collected the check, then ran to the lawyers' office down the street. It was ten minutes to twelve when I handed over the final payment."

The adoption papers were signed—George Halas was now truly Papa Bear.

He gave up the coaching reins several times over the years, and left the organization only once, to serve three years in the Navy during World War II. But he built the team into a dynasty in the 1930s and through most of the 1940s.

During his long career, he was the game's most significant innovator. Besides all his contributions to rules changes and league restructuring over the years, he was the first to. . .

• Conduct daily practices
• Set up a pre-season training camp
• Use a coach to work from the press box
• Take game films for later study
• Create a pro team fight song
• Have games broadcast on the radio
• Lay down a tarpaulin to protect the playing field
• Employ a field announcer
• Publish and distribute a team newspaper
• Organize a club alumni association

• Honor his former players at a "Homecoming Game" and dinner each year.

Over the 40 years he strode the sidelines as head coach and the many years when he ran the organization from the front office, stories of him abounded—some true, some apocryphal, some false. He had a plaque on one of the walls of his office that read "Never Go To Bed A Loser." He had a pet line, "I'm getting older . . . not old." Halas retired from coaching after the 1967 season, the winningest coach, at the time, in NFL history. He said, "I knew it was time to quit when I was chewing out an official and he walked off the penalty faster than I could keep up with him."

Some said he was stingy, others knew he was generous. He could reduce a 250-pound player to a quivering mass of jelly with the fire of his words and glare if he felt it was earned, then spur another on to do things on a football field that the player never thought he could do. He could clap a desolate player on the shoulder after a heartbreaker, when that was deserved. Harlon Hill, the Bears' great end of the 1950s remembers that very well, telling the story of when he was near the end of his career. It was a game against the Rams and he dropped a sure touchdown pass in the last few seconds that could have been a game-winner. In the locker room afterwards, Halas walked over to him, put a hand under his chin and lifted his head, looked him in the eye, and said, "Hey, kid! I'll forget that one, but the ones you've caught to help win all those other games, those are the ones I'll remember."

He battled assistant coach George Allen over the breach of his contract when Allen wanted to move on to a head coaching job. Halas won the case in court, said all he really wanted to do was prove the importance and validity of a signed contract and then released Allen from the contract so he could go on to a fine head coaching career. He lived with the outrageous antics of Doug Atkins, but controlled him enough to enable the gargantuan defensive end to earn a place in the Pro Football Hall of Fame. He reacted to a letter from a former disgruntled player of his who had become known as a hot-tempered, clipboard-throwing assistant coach with the Dallas Cowboys, Mike Ditka. The letter-writer wanted a job, a big one. He wanted to be head coach of the Chicago Bears.

Halas hired him because, as he later said, they shared the same pride in the Bears and the same sense of the way the game should be played.

(continued on page 38)

Halas gives a little kick to help things along from the sideline. Charlie Bivins is number 49.

FROM ONE LEGEND
TO ANOTHER

Red Grange, immortal as a running back and the first of the Bears' great ones, always held George Halas in special esteem.

"George was a great football coach. He never backed away from any kind of challenge. Even when he was having a tough time making enough money to keep the Bears together in the early days of professional football, he'd face the challenge and work it out.

While I was playing professional football George would call me into his office in the spring following the football season and ask me how much money I wanted to play for the coming season. He always paid me what I thought I was entitled to . . . never an argument.

Like Bob Zuppke, who coached both of us at Illinois, George had an instinctive feel about each of his players. He was an outstanding strategist and an untiring worker, with the rare gift of being able to get the most out of his players.

The National Football League wouldn't exist today if it weren't for the perseverance and dedication of George Halas."

The Coach speaks . . . and draws some grins.

Senator John F. Kennedy, at a Gridiron Club dinner in Washington, D.C., accepting an award presented by Halas:

"You have always been one of my heroes. The way you have run the Chicago Bears, the way you have helped guide the National Football League. It is inspiring. . . ."

To which Halas responded,

"Thank you, senator. Now it's your job to get the government running as well as professional football."

(above)
Papa Bear, Hizzoner Richard J. Daley, mayor of Chicago.

(below)
The Coach with President Reagan and First Lady Nancy.

(above)
With Pittsburgh Steeler owner and longtime friend Art Rooney.

(below)
With President Gerald Ford. Ford played in the second College All-Star game in 1934 in which his fellow collegiate all-stars lost to Halas's Bears, 5–0.

George Halas was controversial and cantankerous, innovative and motivational, a businessman with a soft touch . . . a man of so many facets.

But football was his life. A story that truly confirms that fact occurred in 1980, when at 85 Halas and some friends, had gone to see a performance of the gorgeous and great torch singer, Lena Horne. "It was an evening

Coach Halas with his offensive arsenal of the 1950s, Rick Casares (35) and Harlon Hill (87).

I will never forget," Halas stated afterwards.

"Spectacular, this young lady could stay up there for at least an hour and a half and pour out such energy. You could see the perspiration on her bare back, trickling off the tip of her beautiful nose . . . I only wish our players had half her stamina and spirit and dedication. I am going to talk to them about it."

Legendary coaches, George Halas and Vince Lombardi.

Bob Hope, was introduced as the main speaker at a banquet in Chicago by Halas. Papa Bear, in so doing, told a few of his own stories, at the podium. Hope took the microphone and said with a coy smile:

"Don't ever invite me to follow him again!"

Back to baseball, throwing out the first ball at Wrigley Field.

George Halas Drive in Canton, Ohio.

Bob Newhart, at a roast of George Halas:

"Coach Halas wants his players to resemble Catholic priests. He wants them all to have the vows of poverty, chastity, and obedience."

THE FRUGAL HALAS

Ookie Miller, the Bear center from 1932 through 1937, always remembered this Halas story.

It was in 1933 and Bronko Nagurski was playing for us. He had a sore hip, and I had a charley horse. When we arrived in Brooklyn to play the Dodgers, Halas arranged for the man who had been the trainer of the boxer Jack Dempsey to work on us before the game.

Halas bought a bottle of Absorbine Jr. to use on our injuries, which actually turned out to be beneficial. Riding back on the train to Chicago, Halas was paying me off in cash, wages for the game, as was customary in those days. After he got done, I said, "George, you are a dollar short."

Halas said, "That's for the bottle of Absorbine Jr."

"Hey," I said, "but it was also used on the Bronk."

"Yeah, but you kept the bottle," Halas said.

COACH

by Bill McGrane

SINCE 1920 . . . .

It was September 17, and he met with the rest of them in an automobile agency in Canton, Ohio. They formed the American Professional Football Association. Of course, the rest of them are gone, now.

Hornsby won his first batting title that year; hit .370 at St. Louis.

Nice, warm fall day. The blue Lincoln purrs regretfully to a halt at a red light. There's a beer truck in the next lane and the driver grins and hollers.

"Hey, Coach! You guys gonna win Sunday?"

"We'll murder 'em!"

"All right! Good seeing you, Coach!"

"Okay, pal. Say, how about a free beer?"

SINCE 1920 . . . .

The League of Nations was formed in Geneva and Carpentier was the light-heavyweight king.

He works six days a week in the office and is gentleman enough to hide his disappointment that no one will go in with him to work on Sundays. So, Sundays, he sits in his apartment looking over Lake Michigan and makes notes on matters that must be attended to in the upcoming week.

He eats bran flakes for breakfast and has a cup of soup at his desk at noon.

He rides an Exer-Cycle morning and evening and pumps dumbells during the day. In the office, he exchanges his suit coat for a comfortable old windbreaker and wears slippers when he's seated at the desk and you can't see his feet. Normally, he is at his desk by

10 in the morning and he doesn't lock it up again much before 7 at night.

SINCE 1920 . . . .

In Mexico, the revolutionary, Zapata, had been dead only a year, shot from ambush.

Once a club official was noting dourly to fellow-workers that he'd had speaking engagements the last three nights in succession.

The Coach happened by just then. He said, "Where are you speaking tonight?"

"I don't have one tonight, Coach."

"Oh, really? That's a shame."

SINCE 1920 . . . .

Hemingway was in Paris and the VII Olympic Games were in Antwerp.

Walking through the office, he paused to look at a portrait of the 1933 championship team taken at the Washington Monument. Big, good-looking kid in the middle of that picture, had a square jaw and shoulders wide as a hay bale. The kid hadn't influenced opponents, he had terrified them. His name was Nagurski.

The coach looked at the picture for a good long while and his face softened.

"God, what a man he was."

SINCE 1920 . . . .

A couple of years ago, when his team was being retooled and refitted and most of the faces were new, he stood in the rain at Soldier Field and watched night practice before the home opener.

After a while, a rookie nodded toward him, standing

40

George Halas with Bobby Layne, 1948. In the background, from left: George Connor, Bulldog Turner and Sid Luckman.

41

The Bears celebrate their 1940 Championship.

there in the rain. He turned to a veteran defensive back and said "Who's the old man over there?"

The veteran looked, grinned, and raised a hand. The Coach waved in return.

The veteran said to the rookie, "I don't see no old man. I see the Coach."

Then he trotted over and shook the huge hand.

"Good to see you again, Coach Halas."

The Coach smiled. "All right, kiddo. Now let's get after 'em tomorrow!"

42

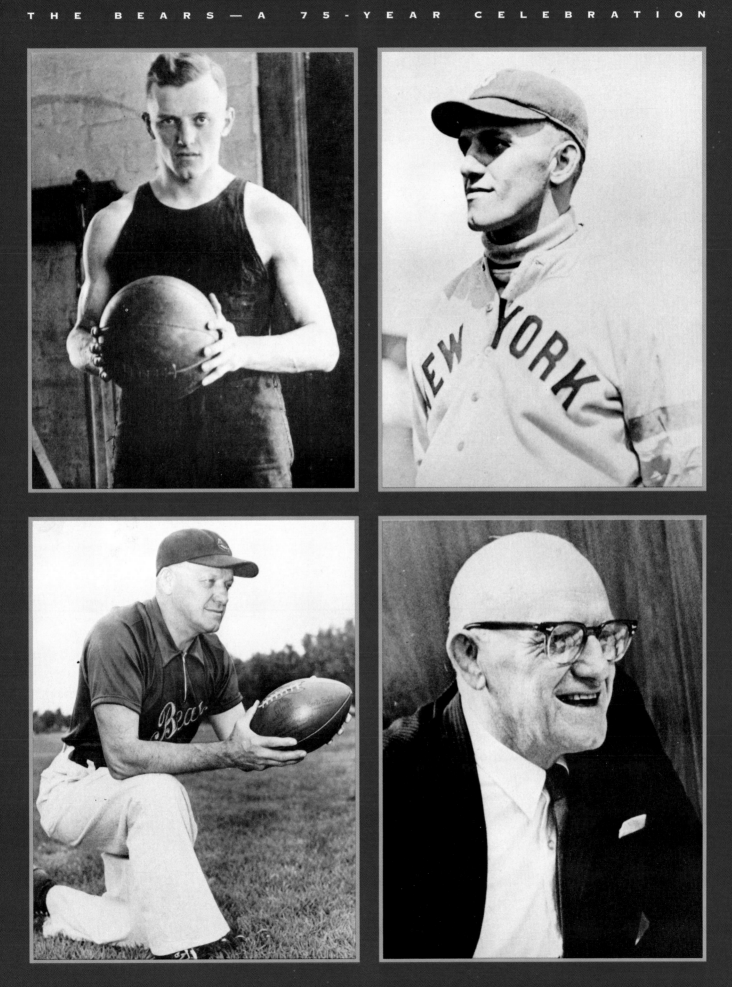

FROM THE PRESS BOX

CONDON ON HALAS

Dave Condon, former columnist for the
Chicago Tribune and longtime Bear reporter.

I was in awe of George Halas:

For his tenacity in fighting for his beliefs. For the practice of his religion.

For his dedication to Chicago, and for service to his country in two World Wars.

For a humility that prompted him to decline hundreds of honors. For his philanthropy, so much of it anonymous (and, with that, the way he shrugged off the insult when the unknowing called him a skinflint).

For broad shoulders that enabled him to laugh when he, and his teams, were roasted by the media or on the banquet circuit.

In the early days, there were no press boxes. There weren't even sportswriters at the games. In the early 1920s, George Halas would write a summary up after each game, while his partner Dutch Sternaman was paying the players. Then Halas and Sternaman would personally deliver those handwritten press releases downtown to the Chicago's major newspapers in the hope of getting some coverage in the Monday editions.

"In time I decided the Bears deserved a professional reporter," Halas later explained. "I hired a writer with the Chicago Evening Post for $25 a game. He was probably professional football's first public relations man."

Today armies of reporters fill the press boxes. Television and radio broadcast the games on a scale that is going global and each autumn or winter Sunday night and Monday morning millions of people have heard or read about Chicago Bear games.

The following are some notes, quotes and anecdotes from those covering the Bears in recent years. . . .

Irv Kupcinet
Columnist, *Chicago Sun-Times*, and former Bear broadcaster

I remember especially in the earlier days my dinners with George Halas on Monday nights after a game. We would get together at the Tavern Club—George, Don Maxwell of the *Tribune,* Joel Goldblatt, Henry Crown, Wilfred Smith and sometimes others. We would talk about the game, the team and, of course, other things.

I was an official in those days as well as a writer.

On Sunday, when I was on the field and he was on the sideline, he would use every swear-word in talking to me—better, shouting at me—but on Monday night we were friends and everything was as cordial as if we had been at a happy wedding the day before. That was the way Halas was — he was so determined to win and when he stalked the sideline he truly stalked it, like nobody else. Away from it, he was smiles and stories and good times.

He always liked to tell a story about me and, let me say, it was an invention of his, but one he got a lot of mileage out of:

A game against Green Bay back in the '40s. It was an important play, fourth-down-and-one for the Bears. Luckman handed off to Osmanski and he hit the line. It was close and I, as the head linesman, rushed in to make the spot and measure it. According to George, I raised my hands in the air and shouted, "We made it! We made it!"

Hub Arkush
Publisher of *Pro Football Weekly* and current Bear radio broadcaster

Most unforgettable? One had to be the Fog Bowl, the Bears—Eagles playoff game in 1988.

We broadcast the first half with little problem. In fact the sun was shining and the Bears were winning at halftime 17-9. Then we got a report from our network meteorologist that there was a big fog moving in. It started as a little mist and then suddenly it became so dense we couldn't even see the field.

In the fourth quarter, all television coverage was from field-level cameras, trying as best they could to get something from under the fog. We could catch snatches through the fog but not much and most of the time we were just guessing at what was happening down on the field. Finally Jim Hart, who was doing color then, was so fed up he kicked off his shoes, propped his feet against the wall, and said to us, "Let me know how it all turns out."

The climactic play came in the final period and we couldn't see it. We heard a roar from the fans in the southeast corner of the field and we knew something momentous had happened. Philadelphia had the ball and was moving at the time when we saw defensive back Mo Douglass come to the sideline with the ball, high-fiving everybody in sight. We realized he had

intercepted a pass (he had intercepted a Randall Cunningham pass and returned it 47 yards).

Wayne Larrivee and I agreed afterwards: "It was the greatest game we never saw."

Fred Mitchell
Sports reporter for the *Chicago Tribune*

Dealing with Mike Ditka was always an experience.

But one evening in Platteville in 1990, I saw a side to him he rarely revealed to the media. About four of us writers went out to dinner after the day at training camp was done. The dining room was full so we went to the bar. Ditka was there with somebody else from the Bears and I, not by choice exactly, ended up sitting next to him. Ditka acknowledged us and just started talking about the day's practice, the injuries he was worried about, the team in general, and then he began talking about his past and his youth.

It was very interesting and it revealed a side of him that he was not known to show, at least to us. They told us our table was ready but we opted instead to just eat there at the bar and continue talking.

Ditka told about a baseball game in Aliquippa, Pennsylvania, when he was a kid. His brother, Ashley, was pitching on their team and gave up a final-inning home run. Mike chased him off the field, down the street, jumped over a fence and finally caught him in front of an auto body parts shop, and proceeded to beat on him until his teammates caught up and pulled him off.

We talked about growing up in towns like that—I grew up in Gary, another laborers' town. He talked about how strict his homelife was and the expectations everyone had for him and he had for himself.

There was none of the harshness or animosity that he often displayed when he was on guard. When he finished waxing nostalgic, he smiled . . . and he picked up the check for all of us.

Dan Pompei
Sportswriter, *Chicago Sun-Times*

Two players come to mind when I think of unique Bear moments, William Perry and Jim Harbaugh.

I always remember Perry up in Platteville after the Super Bowl season. We'd get out there early for practice and the Fridge was always either the first or among the first on the field. We'd find him out there by himself, sitting under the broiling sun on his helmet or just standing and looking around at the emptiness and all of a sudden, he would let out this great bellow: "Oh, what a happy day!" It was aimed at no one in particular and he did it every day. You could probably have heard it ten farms away.

Harbaugh was tough. As a rookie, he got into something with both Hampton and Dent after one play in a practice session. They were supposed to go easy on the quarterback, but he was getting a little initiation, I guess. He got up and started shoving back. These two monstrous, Super Bowl stars were as surprised as could be at the rookie, looked at each other and then went for him, but nothing came of it. On another occasion in his rookie year he underthrew Dennis McKinnon who came back to the huddle and proceeded to curse him up and down. Harbaugh just walked up and punched him in the jaw and knocked him down.

Johnny Morris
Television sports broadcaster

I had the interesting experience of observing the Bears from two different perspectives, as a player and a broadcaster. I was a member of the family, so to speak, when I was a player, but when you become a member of the media you are an adversary.

It wasn't necessarily that way with Mike Ditka because we had played together for six years in Chicago and went through the '63 championship season with the Bears, but we still had some slam-bang sessions on the air. Mike never changed from player to coach, he never lost the ferocity. Mike was never concerned about saying the safe thing. He would always manage to come up with something controversial. It was always a challenge working with him and you never knew how things might come out. That's what made those 11 years of his coaching in Chicago so memorable.

We had a rapport that went all the way back to 1961 when he joined the Bears. But I best remember the night in 1964 when we were at a banquet. At the time there was a quarterback controversy with the Bears—who should start, Bill Wade or Rudy Bukich. We were at the head table and one of the guests got up and asked who we, being two starting

receivers, thought should be the starter. We didn't think much about it because we didn't know anyone from the press was there. So we both said we thought it ought to be Bukich and gave our reasons.

The next day the headline in the sports section of the *Sun-Times* read: Morris and Ditka Say: Bukich Should Be Quarterback

Ditka got the first call that morning, from George Halas. It woke him up in fact. I got one fifteen minutes later. He told us both to get over to his office, immediately. We did. And he went through the roof. "You betrayed the team," he roared. "You are going to apologize to the entire team before practice today."

Later, in the locker room, he called on both of us to stand up. "These two said some things last night that were taken out of context." Halas said. "I believe they want to make an apology to all of you."

I said something about we were just at a banquet, talking, and we didn't really mean it the way it came out. I tried to make it sound like we were sorry.

Halas then gestured to Mike, "And?" he said.

Mike said, "I don't have any apology. Forget it."

Don Pierson,
Sportswriter, *Chicago Tribune*

I remember Abe Gibron's cook-outs down in Rensselaer. He would even interrupt practice sometimes to check to be sure whoever was getting the food got enough of it—the corn from the nearby cornfields, the lambs or whatever to roast. Gibron was one of a kind, from the old breed. He would have you come to his room to talk. He would take you out to dinner and order an enormous meal for you and, if you couldn't finish it, he would.

Walter Payton, who stood out above everyone because of his relentless play. He was as elusive to pin down to talk to as he was to tackle on the field. After 13 years of covering him, I still had to make 22 phone calls to get an interview at the end of his career. At the same time, he always made himself available after losing games because he was very sensitive about taking the pressure off his teammates.

Jim McMahon, who had such a great rapport with his teammates but virtually none with the media. I remember how careful and objective you had to be in dealing with him, but you always had to respect his great ability to lead.

Mike Singletary. He seemed more like a head coach after the game, so mature, standing there fielding questions, making more sense than the coaches.

The great game Bobby Douglass played in Detroit in 1971 which was lost in the tragic on-field death by heart attack of Lion wide receiver Chuck Hughes. Douglass had his finest day ever as a Bear quarterback, bringing them back three times from deficits to win 28-23. After the game, in the Bear locker room, despite the win, the comebacks, and Douglass' great performance there was only anxiety and gloom over the fate of a fellow football player.

So many memories.

Jack Brickhouse
Former Bear broadcaster

George Halas, on the night before a game, was a portrait of concentration. He had what I always called the "head-coach glaze" in his eyes. You could talk to him but you knew his mind was somewhere else. I tested my theory once. Halas had gotten sandbagged into going to this social event the night before a Green Bay game in Chicago. I was there, too, and I saw him nodding at the conversation going on around him. He had that glaze in his eyes, he looked edgy, ready to get out of there. I walked up to him and said, "George, we were just talking over there and someone said your grandfather was a horse thief."

George looked at me, and nodded, "Yeah, sure, sure, but if we can score first tomorrow, we're going to win. The thing is, we've got to score first."

Cooper Rollow
Former sports editor and writer,
Chicago Tribune

The beginning of the 1964 season, that was a real memory. The Bears were coming off a hard-fought championship and everyone was predicting Willie Galimore was en route to his greatest season. He seemed to be over the injuries that had plagued him before and was having a great training camp . . . everyone was excited for him.

But on that terrible night down in Rensselaer he and Bo Farrington were hurrying back to camp so as not to miss curfew. Their car missed a curve and they were both killed. The curve sign that was ordi-

narily there as a warning had blown down or somehow had been taken out and, as a result, their little Volkswagen went plummeting off the road and crashed into a cornfield.

I was in my room and heard a knock on the door. It was Joe Stydahar, the Bears' defensive coach, who said, "We just lost a couple of our kids."

I had no idea what he meant and said, :What're you talking about?"

He said, "Galimore and Farrington were just killed in an accident." Then he added, "Don't tell the old man, I told you. He'll want to tell you himself."

I drove down to the little coroner's office and waited until Halas came out with the coroner and the sheriff. He confirmed the tragedy. I called the *Trib* late that night and dictated the story. It was a scoop but not the kind of one you were happy to have.

The next morning was just terrible, the shock of it all. I remember George Halas leading the team down past the cornfields to the practice field before breakfast and getting everyone down on their knees and leading them in a prayer.

On another note, there was a game I was covering which did not, at least directly, involve the Bears. It was the Dallas-Philadelphia playoff game in 1981. Mike Ditka was an assistant with Dallas then and I was talking with him.

He told me he wanted to be a head coach. With the Chicago Bears. Neill Armstrong was the head coach then and the Bears had just come off two losing seasons. Ditka said, "I don't mean anything against Neill Armstrong, I'd just like the job."

I said, "Chicago? The Bears? Halas? The man you said 'Throws nickels around like manhole covers?'" He just said, "Yeah."

I thought there was a good story there for Chicago. So I called George Halas and told him what Ditka had said. Halas said, "Ditka, huh. Well, that's something." There was a long pause and then he added, "Maybe it's something we should keep in mind for the future."

He hired Ditka one year later.

Chet Coppock
Sports broadcaster

I go back with the Bears a long way, my father much longer. He came to Chicago in 1929 and with the exception of four years in the Navy during World War II, he never missed a Bear home game until he passed away after the 1974 season. My father became good friends with George Halas and Red Grange and was so devoted to the Bears that in those days, when season tickets were readily available, he ending up amassing 180—and he never scalped a single one.

The Bears won their first game with the Packers in 1963, which made the rematch even that much more crucial. The Bears were in the heat of the fight for the division title and the Packers were the defending NFL champions. The game was at Wrigley Field and the hype was incredible. My father had at least 200 calls for tickets—everything was sold out for this one.

As the day of the game drew closer, Halas had received a request for some tickets from some Navy brass who were going to be in town for the game. Papa Bear could not come up with the extra tickets. He called my father who was able to take care of him.

That game, which I had the privilege of attending, was one of the greatest spectacles in Bears' history. At Wrigley, the air was thick with tension and anticipation an hour or two before the game. The build-up was something I had never seen before, nor since. The noise level in the ballpark that day was extraordinary. Never in Soldier Field could it reach such a crescendo.

It helped, I'm sure, because the Bears overran the Packers that day 26-7 and solidified their march to the NFL championship.

The other Green Bay game which is indelible occurred on November 3, 1968. Everyone remembers the magnificent day Gale Sayers, as a rookie in 1965, had scored six touchdowns, a tremendous feat. But the game he played in Green Bay against the Packers on a frozen turf, when he gained 205 yards rushing, was a classic. It was what any ordinary runner would consider a terrible day for carrying the ball, but weather conditions never seemed to stop him. He set the Bear all-time single game rushing record at the time.

And to make it a perfect day, it had an ending written in Hollywood. The score was tied 10-10 and Green Bay had to punt from its own end zone with not too many seconds remaining. Cecil Turner was back to receive and the ball twisted in the air, but he signaled for a fair catch and then dove for it and caught it. Immediately my father was on his feet shouting "Free kick . . . Free kick. . . " Abe Gibron, on the sideline, rushed over to Jim Dooley. He was shouting something, which I'm sure was the same thing my father had been shouting.

Jim Dooley, whether or not he heard them or just made the choice himself, sent Mac Percival out. The players just stood around, helpless, and watched as Percival teed up the ball and booted it through for a game winning field goal, 13-10 Bears in that never-ending rivalry.

Mike Conklin
Columnist, *Chicago Tribune*

A favorite story. It's about the quarterback who is no longer with the Bears, Jim Harbaugh.

It was in December 1992 and Harbaugh made one of those-spend-an-hour-pick-up-a-check-for-$1,000-and-leave appearances that are so common with Chicago's pro athletes. This time the location was a sports pub in Oak Lawn. Now, Harbaugh never had been a clock-watcher at these events. He once made an appearance with chicken pox and warned any parents in the crowd not to get close to him. On this night, Jim signed everything in sight and taking the time to chat with fans, stayed well past the hour.

Finally the line was down to a solitary person who had been waiting patiently on the side. He brought a football to Jim to autograph and, in an apologetic way, asked him to personalize the message to his son. In the course of their conversation, Harbaugh was told the youth was hospitalized with leukemia. The quarterback had a better idea: Why didn't the two of them, Jim following the father's car, go to the boy's room and deliver the football?

You can imagine what it must have been like for the boy: Late at night, he wakes up to one of his heroes standing above him. The parties involved, including Harbaugh, requested no publicity at the time.

I heard later the youth didn't make it. At the very least, his stay in a hospital was made a lot brighter one night by an athlete's thoughtfulness.

I remember being down in my stance before the ball was snapped the first time, and this thought just flew through my head: "Jim, Dick Butkus is playing right behind you. Dick Butkus! He's a legend." I wanted to pinch myself. Then the ball was snapped and bodies started flying and then it was just football.
— Jim Osborne

FIVE

ON BEING A BEAR

DICK BUTKUS
MIDDLE LINEBACKER, 1965–1973

Everybody gets the wrong impression about me. They think I hate everybody and that I eat my meat raw. But I can talk and read and write like ordinary people do, and actually I like to have my meat cooked.

Dick Butkus

BOB SNYDER
PLACEKICKER/QUARTERBACK, 1939–1941, 1943

Many people who did not know Coach Halas had him pictured as a tough, selfish man who underpaid his players and would do most anything to win. The following incident happened at 4 a.m. in the morning of our game against Green Bay in 1939.

I received a call from my wife telling me that Bobbie, our 8-day-old son had suddenly passed away. She advised me to stay and play the game and come home after it. Ray Nolting, my roommate, was the only one who knew of the tragedy. I played and we won the game, 30-27, and I kicked the winning field goal, which helped ease the pain.

When the season was over, I went to the Bears' office to sign for the 1940 season. Coach gave me an envelope and after I left the office I looked inside and there was a check for $1,000. I did not have a bonus in my contract so I went back in and asked Halas about it.

He said that would help bury my son. We both started to cry a bit, hugged each other, and I left.

BOB MACLEOD
HALFBACK, 1939–1940

As a '39 rookie from Dartmouth, I took a hefty dose of disdain about the quality of Ivy League football despite the fact that several teams the year before, including my own, were ranked in the top ten.

Cornell, the Ivy League champion, was scheduled to play the Big Ten champion, Ohio State, in

Columbus on the Saturday before our match-up with Green Bay at Wrigley Field. . . . The needling was nonstop. I offered to take all bets (no points). There was a stampede to my locker to get a piece of the action. It was a gold rush frenzy to put in chits along with derogatory comments . . . "Massacre . . . Easy money . . . Bring your wallet!"

Ohio State scored two touchdowns in the first quarter, but Cornell won the game 27-14.

The following day in the clubhouse, I couldn't wait. I arrived early, set up a table at the locker room door, and had a sign on my hat:

Pay Here. No checks, Cash only.

None of us were making a bundle in those depression days, but the poverty excuses I heard were masterpieces of pathos. The I.O.U.s outdistanced the cash.

George Halas appeared. All hat, coat, and full-out intensity! He promptly fined me $100 for "disturbing the pre-game atmosphere." Fortunately we beat Green Bay 30-27

P.S. George rescinded the fine. Typical George.

P.P.S. I still hold most of the I.O.U.s.

STAN JONES
GUARD/DEFENSIVE TACKLE, 1954–1965

George Blanda was our quarterback and a nervous kind of guy. One of the funniest things I remember from those days was when we were breaking the huddle and lining up one game, and all of a sudden I feel George behind me. I was the right guard, and he's there behind me, his hands under me, and he starts calling the signals.

Larry Strickland, the center, who's got the ball, looked over at me with this strange expression on his face, trying to figure out what the hell George was doing with his hands under the guard instead of the center.

Another time George and his nerves damn near got me fired. It was nearing the end of the half, and he was a little frantic with time running out, and he told me to fake an injury—you know, to buy some time, which you were sometimes able to get away with in those days.

Well, I did, and I was lying there. But they didn't stop the clock. So George now starts yelling "Get up! Get up! We got time."

This Jack Manders (10) field goal assured a 10-9 Bear victory over the Giants in 1934.
Other Bears pictured are "Ookie" Miller (76), Zuck Carlson (20) and Carl Brumbaugh (8).

Rick Casares (35) finds a hole in the Colt defense as John Hoffman (89) leads the blocking in a 1956 game.

So I started to get back up, but by the time I did the gun went off. Halas met me about 20 yards from the sideline and kicked me all the way to the dugout there in Wrigley Field.

OOKIE MILLER
CENTER, 1932–1936

My first trip to New York as a Bear was in 1932, a memorable one. A team member asked me to complete a foursome for a night on the town before the game. We went to the Cotton Club in Harlem to see Cab Calloway.

When I returned at 3 o'clock in the morning, pasted on my door was a message.

> Ookie,
> When you get in, come see me.
> George Halas

I called my friend and said, "We're in trouble," and told him about the note.

He said, "We're in trouble? I didn't get any note."

When I saw Halas the next day, he said, "Hey, Ookie, did you have a good time last night?" I explained that this was my first trip to New York City and George said, "Don't worry about it, kid, it will only cost you a hundred dollars."

I told my teammates that if I wasn't going to get paid I wasn't going to play. One of them told me he had had the same kind of experience and after he'd played a good game, Halas rescinded the fine.

So I said okay, I'd play, and I had a heckuva game. After the game Halas came down to where I was dressing in the locker room and said, "Ookie, I think I'll fine you $100 every game. You play better!"

I did not get a refund.

RICK CASARES
FULLBACK, 1955–1964

George Halas conducted a weigh-in every Thursday morning. Any player over his prescribed weight was fined $25 a pound.

Players over their weight would line up in front of the scale. On one side was Halas and on the other was Doug Atkins.

As the player stepped on the scale he would call out the weight he was supposed to make. Doug would deftly place two fingers under the player's butt and apply a delicate lift. It could knock off five or six pounds without making the scale jiggle all over the place.

It worked for about a month, but one morning Doug's fingers slipped when Earl Leggett was on the scale and suddenly the weight marker bobbed back and forth. From that time on Halas made everybody stand away from the scale, including Atkins. Halas knew he'd been had, but I don't think he was ever sure how it was done.

MATT SUHEY
FULLBACK, 1980–1989

The thing about being a Bear is you really are part of Chicago. I mean, the Bulls have had a had a great run, and the other teams have made marks of their own, but I still think this is a Bears' town.

It's hard to comprehend, if you didn't play but the excitement, the electricity there is in Chicago . . . it's something. It didn't matter if we were good or bad, or if it was cold and lousy outside or nice weather. The people were there.

I think the Bears, as I knew them, were indicative of Chicago, the toughness and the confidence and the strength. This town is about getting it done.

When people played us—when we were good and when we weren't—they knew they'd better bring their lunch because it was going to be an all-day affair. We had a great defense in 1985, going to the Super Bowl, but we had an offense, too. We weren't fancy . . . it wasn't a deal where opposing defenses had to go looking for us. We'd look them up. We'd get in their face.

*Matt Suhey signs autographs at
a military base in Wiesbaden, Germany.*

I have a strong love affair with this city. I think the people who made it special are all the working guys, the cops and the firemen and the laborers. The city and the team are a perfect fit for each other.

DOUG PLANK
SAFETY, 1975–1982

I had just completed my third year as a starting free safety. Since I was drafted in the 12th round, my salary qualified me for low-income housing. I was attempting to double my salary. After I submitted my initial offer to Jim Finks, he immediately countered with a 50% reduction in my increase.

Intimidated by his position and negotiating ability, I explained that I would have to discuss the offer with my wife before making a decision.

After my response, the room became very quiet and he stared into my eyes for what seemed like an eternity. He eventually responded by saying, "Doug, go home and talk to your wife, and I will go home and talk to my wife. I want to make certain that I did not offer too much.

Safeties Doug Plank (1975–1982) and Gary Fencik (1976–1987)

GARY FENCIK
SAFETY, 1976–1987

Ditka was volatile. I remember in 1983 when we lost two overtime games in a row. The second was in Baltimore. I had gotten hurt that game backpedaling—I hit the infield in the stadium and managed to rip my groin.

I wasn't the only casualty that day.

In the locker room after the game Mike came in and whacked one of those black traveling trunks we had. He hit it so hard it echoed through the locker room. He ordinarily led the team in prayer, but he turned to (Bear QB) Vince Evans and said, "Vinnie, you better lead the team."

Then, as he was walking down the hallway, I could hear him saying to Fred Caito, our trainer, "I think I broke my hand."

He wore a cast for a couple of days and then got rid of it. I think he was a little embarrassed about it.

GEORGE CONNOR
TACKLE/LINEBACKER, 1948–1955

I got my initiation into the street-fighting arena, which is more commonly known as the pro football line of scrimmage, as a rookie with the Bears in 1948.

In the pre-season I was used as a back-up tackle for Fred Davis. He told me, "When I raise my hand coming out of the huddle, kid, that means I need a rest. You come in on the next play."

I watched. When I saw his arm go up, I grabbed my helmet and when the play was over raced out onto the field. As soon as the ball was snapped on the next play, my face ran smack into the fist of the lineman I was opposing. It was an especially unpleasant greeting in those days before facemasks were routinely worn.

I was startled but thought that maybe this was the typical welcome a rookie got to the brutal game I'd heard that the pros play.

Later, in the same game, Davis raised his hand again and I replaced him on the next play. This time I was lined up opposite a different lineman. But the reaction was the same. When play began, this line-man smashed me square in the face, too.

After the game, I tried to figure out why it was happening to me. Perhaps they resented all the publicity I'd gotten for a rookie, or maybe it was because I came from Notre Dame—a lot of the pro players were less than fond of the Fighting Irish alumni in those days. I even asked a few other linemen about this so-called special greeting. They agreed that work in the line was violent as hell, but what was occurring to me did seem a bit extraordinary to them.

It went on for several weeks. Then one Sunday it all became crystal clear. This time, when Davis raised his hand, I kept my eyes on him rather than on the play itself. When the ball was snapped, I saw Davis lunge across the line, punch the opposing lineman in the face, and then trot off toward our bench.

For the rest of that year, I announced myself to whoever the opposing lineman was when I lined up after coming into the game for Davis: "Connor in, Davis out!" It made my life a lot easier.

MARK BORTZ
GUARD, 1983–1994

I didn't play much when I was a rookie, and I remember standing on the sideline watching Walter Payton run. I'd never seen a runner like him. He'd be running near the sideline and guys would come over to give him their best shot, but he'd end up being the guy who gave the shot. He'd hit people with those forearms and shoulders and just jack them up.

When he broke Jim Brown's rushing record, it was special, but it really didn't seem that big. The play he

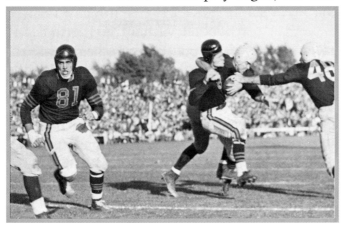

Hall of Famer George Connor (81) zeros in on a Packer while Bear halfback Jim Canady is neck-tied in a 1949 game at City Stadium in Green Bay.

Neal Anderson follows the block of Mark Bortz through a hole in the Tampa Bay line.

ranks of a running back. I saw stars. I was dazed. The one thing I did see though was Dick Butkus leaping over me and slugging one of the two linebackers. Then a huge brawl broke out on top of me.

I literally crawled out from under the melee and made it to the sidelines where our punter, Bobby Joe Green, was watching and laughing uproariously at me.

DAN HAMPTON
DEFENSIVE END/TACKLE, 1979–1990

I remember one game in 1984, after somebody wrecked us . . . just beat us like bad dogs. We came into the locker room and everybody sat down, dejected.

Steve McMichael, or Ming as I called him, walks in last and yells, "Quick, close the door, the sons of bitches are coming in after us!"

Dan Hampton, defensive tackle/end, 1979–1990.

BOB THOMAS
KICKER, 1975–1984

In 1977 we played the New York Giants in what some called the "Ice Bowl." The frozen, snow-covered turf at the Meadowlands was very difficult to stand on, let alone block, run or kick.

We were in a sudden-death overtime, the score knot-

Bob Thomas, placekicker, 1975–1984

ted at 9 apiece and we needed to win to get into the playoffs as a wildcard entry, and the Bears had not been to the playoffs for 14 years. There was only one overtime period because this was a regular season game, and a tie would do us no good. The pressure was mounting.

As Bob Avellini and Walter Payton engineered our final drive, my teammates on the sideline were offering all kinds of words of encouragement. Bob Parsons, our punter, obviously not a psychology major at Penn State, told me if I didn't make the kick he would personally break my neck.

We got close and time was running out and we did not have any time-outs left. I remember Walter Payton and Roland Harper appeared to be making angels in the snow out there to clear a spot for me to kick. And to me it seemed like I never stopped moving from the time our coach, Jack Pardee, pushed me onto the field until my foot propelled the winning field goal through the uprights with just a few seconds left to play.

Avellini, my holder, raised his fist in jubilation. Parsons and center Dan Neal were rolling on the tundra like polar bear cubs. I was hoisted onto my teammates shoulders in a state which could only be described as a mixture of shock and euphoria.

What a wonderful memory. For the Bears I think it was a turning point for the NFL's greatest franchise.

RALPH KUREK
RUNNING BACK, 1965–1970

My first game as a starting fullback came in 1966 against the Los Angeles Rams. At the time they had the famous defensive line known as the "Fearsome Foursome": Lamar Lundy, Rosey Grier, Merlin Olsen and Deacon Jones.

Jones was 6'5" and about 285 pounds. Our game plan was to run at Deacon the first couple series and make him play his area. On the right side was Mike Ditka, our tight end, and Bob Wetoska our right tackle. We were hoping to take away Deacon's ability to pursue down the line and break up the play from behind.

It was Wetoska's task to block Jones whichever way he started to go, and I was to double-team Deacon if the linebacker wasn't filling the hole. Gale Sayers was to read our blocks and pick his hole accordingly.

Now Ditka had a way of talking across the line to the opposition—this was Mike's way of getting his level of play up, firing himself up. On this particular day he chose to let Deacon know what he thought of him—the team he played for—the town he came from—and I think he may have even brought some of Deacon's family members into the comments.

Needless to say, Deacon responded in the All Pro fashion he was capable of. He stopped Sayers in our backfield for two consecutive losses.

After the second, on the way back to the huddle, Wetoska turned to Ditka and said, "Mike, I hope you're fired up enough by now because Deacon doesn't need any more help. I've got to block the guy all afternoon and the way it's going, it may be the longest afternoon of my life."

JIM COVERT
TACKLE, 1983–1990

When I was a kid in Pennsylvania, my dad would take me to Latrobe to watch the Steelers in training camp. There were thousands of fans there . . . that's when the Steelers were great, and I can remember thinking that professional football was great, and that someday I was going be a pro football player.

I was surprised when the Bears drafted me in 1983 because they had not been in contact with me. About the only things I knew about the Bears were that they had Walter Payton and they weren't very good. I held out for a couple of days at the start of training camp. When I finally went in, Willie Gault, the Bears' other

first-round pick that year, was still holding out, so I figured I'd kind of be the big noise with the fans.

Camp was in Lake Forest then, and the day I arrived I was a little late, and the team was already on the field. The only person in the locker room was Ray Earley, the equipment manager. Ray said, "What's your jersey number, kid?"

I said it was 75.

"That's taken," Ray said. "A veteran's got it and a rook never gets a veteran's number."

"What about 74?" he said. I said that would be great. He went to look for the jersey but then came back and told me he didn't have a 74. He would have to get one made and sent up to camp. So he handed me one with 77 on it. Ray told me that was Red Grange's number, the legendary 77. Grange's number was retired, but, he

Jim Covert, tackle, 1983–1990

said, I could wear it for a day or two.

As I was getting dressed in the locker room that first day, I remembered what it was like in Latrobe, all those thousands of fans out there to greet the Super Bowl Steelers. I was feeling pretty good. After all, I was the number one draft choice and here I was, taking the field for the first time.

I went out the back door and up the hill to the practice field, like Ray Earley had directed me. Practice had already started. Ray had warned me to take a lap as soon as I hit the field, so I took the lap.

There were two fans in the stands, not thousands . . . two! One of them was smoking a cigarette and he pointed a finger at me and burst out laughing. "Look," he hollered, "here comes Red Grange. He's making a comeback!"

I got brought back to reality real quick.

STEVE WRIGHT
TACKLE, 1971

Washington had traded me to the Bears in 1971 and we were playing them at Soldier Field that year. The Redskins had a real good shot at winning their division and we were playing them very well that day.

We were winning by one point with just a little time left and the Redskins had a shot at a field goal.

I was out there and I started yelling at the top of my voice, "Odin! Odin!," invoking the Viking god of weather. "Blow you sonofabitch, blow!"

George Allen, their coach, swore after the game that there was no wind at all until Curt Knight's kick took off for the goal posts and just then a gust came rushing in off Lake Michigan and blew it off course.

And we won 16-15.

GLEN KOZLOWSKI
WIDE RECEIVER, 1987–1992

Once you're a Bear, you're always a Bear.

My brother Mike played for the Miami Dolphins for 11 years and I'm sure he's proud of the association, but I don't think it's the same thing.

For one thing, Mike Ditka did a great job instilling that pride in his players, the feeling that being a Bear is special. And a lot of it has to do with George Halas. I know the first time I walked in the door at Halas Hall, I felt like he was there, sizing me up. His presence always seems to sort of loom through the organization.

I lived my fantasy. I played in the National Football League, yet it didn't turn out the way I had planned. I came into the league thinking I'd be this hotshot receiver and catch a million passes. Didn't work, though—my knee was hurt so bad I never could cut any more, and run the patterns I needed to run. I had a choice. I could adjust and find out what I could do in football, or I could go do something else. I adjusted, and I found out I could play special teams.

Everything did work out, and it enabled me to live my fantasy. I am a Bear . . . I walk down the street and people stop and they want to talk about the team. They don't think of me as being retired. To the fans, I'm still a Bear. I'm very proud of that.

ROSS MONTGOMERY
RUNNING BACK, 1969–1970

In 1970 we were playing the Lions in Detroit. As a running back my job on this one play was to block Alex Karras, Detroit's All-Pro defensive tackle. Alex was about six feet tall and weighed about 250. Blocking him was like blocking a fireplug.

The first time I did, I hooked him, which is an illegal block . . . but very effective if you don't get caught. I was lying on the ground after the play and Alex rolled over and put his knee on my chest and proceeded to tell me that if I ever did that again he was personally going to kick my bleeping head in.

Three plays later, Jack Concannon called the same play, and I had to make a decision. Did I want my head kicked in by Alex or my butt chewed out by our coaches for missing a block? Common sense told me I did not want either. When the play started I hooked Alex and took him to the ground . . . and then jumped up and ran like hell. I ended up ahead of the ballcarrier downfield and blocked the safety.

The next Tuesday when we were watching game films the coaches ran that play over and over to show everyone what a "great effort" I had given on that play. All I was trying to do was keep from getting my bleeping head kicked in.

ALLAN ELLIS
CORNERBACK, 1973–1979

I just played football, never thought about much else. I grew up in Los Angeles, played high school sports there and football at UCLA. I never thought much about being a pro or being rich. I played because I liked to compete and I just loved the game.

I remember the rough times. We played Miami in 1975 when we weren't very good, and they were. Howard Twilley had a big day against me. It seemed like every time they threw to him he caught it. I just felt sick. I wanted to run off the field and hide. But that's part of playing corner . . . happens to everybody.

After that I got better. I believe I became a good corner. Then I got hurt, and not having been hurt before that was pretty tough. I was used to seeing other guys go down and saying, "Hey, you'll be back . . . it'll be alright."

It was in 1979, and I thought I'll rehab, I'll make it back. But I couldn't. The hardest part was the loneliness, not being a part of the team anymore. They

Allan Ellis, cornerback, 1973–1979

moved on and I wasn't part of it.

And I had to move on. And I did. But it was great while it lasted.

MARTY AMSLER
DEFENSIVE END 1967–1968

Mr. Halas and coach Jim Dooley had faith enough to sign me as a free agent in 1967. The one moment I remember so well took place when we were playing the Dolphins in an exhibition game down at the Orange Bowl in Miami.

Miami called a running play which didn't work too well, a fumble, and there was a huge pile-up at the line of scrimmage. Out of it I heard a blood-curdling yell. It seems that one of the officials was looking for the ball in the pile. In doing so he apparently stuck his finger through Dick Butkus' face mask who, in turn, promptly bit the finger that was protruding into the "no-finger-zone."

CRAIG CLEMONS
SAFETY, 1972–1977

It feels wonderful to have been a Bear. George Halas and Craig Clemons had similar temperaments. Self-disciplined individuals, a strong tendency toward self-determination, confident in our abilities, and very aggressive

George Halas was a man of continual motion with

activity that was well-planned and meaningful. I've always believed that the coach or the leader sets the standard by which his house operates. George Halas set high standards for his family and his football team. He surrounded himself with people of like mind and behavior.

I was drafted by the Bears in the first round, and shortly afterwards received an invitation to a birthday party that year, scheduled for February 2, 1972. The party was for George Halas and was given by Sid Luckman at the Standard Club in downtown Chicago. That experience was a great thrill in my life.

I am grateful and proud that George Halas chose me to be a part of his team . . . but it was God's will for me to be a Bear.

SHAUN GAYLE
SAFETY, 1984–1994

Tough, we always played that way. I remember Mike Singletary in the course of a very important game against the Vikings, getting up after a tackle and saying to me something about his thumb hurting. I pulled his glove off and took one look and almost fell over . . . the top third of his thumb was almost completely severed . . . about to fall off, I thought.

Mike went out of the game but the next thing I knew he was back out there with his hand all taped up, same intensity, like nothing ever happened. It made me realize a true competitor simply blocks out pain and injury or any other element that might interfere with what you want to accomplish on the field.

ED O'BRADOVICH
DEFENSIVE END, 1962–1971

The "Big Guy," Doug Atkins, was late for practice the first day of training camp at Rensselaer in 1963. After about 45 minutes, out he comes. He had on shorts, a T-shirt and a helmet with no chin strap and no face guard. He looked like Captain Video.

He started out about a hundred yards from us and ran right by like we weren't even there. He ran down to the end of the field, walked about a hundred yards and then ran another three or four hundred yards. Then he just walked around the perimeter of the field. Finally he came right by us again but didn't say anything, right by the old man, Halas, and right back into the locker room. Didn't say a word to anybody.

When I caught up to him in the lunchroom later, I said, "Doug, what the hell were you doing out there?

Ed O'Bradovich, defensive end, 1962–1971

Are you crazy?"

He said, "I was breaking in my helmet."

BRIAN BASCHNAGEL
WIDE RECEIVER, 1976–1984

There are two things I will never forget from my days as a Bear.

The first was my very first reception. It was in a game against the Redskins in 1976 at Soldier Field. I ran a post pattern and Bob Avellini, our quarterback, overthrew the ball. I leaped, actually dove and ended up with my body parallel to the ground. I caught it on my fingertips.

What made it so special to me was that with it I realized a dream I'd had since I was a little kid. In 1963, when I was nine years old, my father took me to a Giants game that year and I remember seeing Frank Gifford make this spectacular diving catch. When we got home after the game, I ran into the house and got a football and had my dad throw passes to me. I asked him to overthrow them so I could dive for them, so I could emulate Frank Gifford.

Well, when I made that catch in '76, and when I heard the sixty-some thousand fans cheering, the first thing I thought of was Gifford's diving catch and I

realized my little kid dream had become real.

The other moment was not as gratifying. It was in 1979 in the wild card playoff game against the Eagles. We were on a roll that year—in the first half of the season we were 3-5 and in the second half we won seven of our eight games. We had a lot of momentum, a lot of confidence when we went to Philadelphia. We were up 17-10 at the half.

In the second half, we were deep in our own territory. We called a play where Walter (Payton) was to take a pitchout from Mike Phipps and go around right end. I was to go in motion and beyond our tight end then crackback block their outside linebacker, which I did. Walter ran 84 yards with the ball, the longest run of his career, all the way to about the one-foot line at the other end of the field.

The play was called back, however, because of a flag. I had no idea what the penalty was and then I found out the official had called it on me, illegal motion. I was astonished because I didn't think I did it, but he did, and that's all that matters on the field.

If that play had stood up, I know we would have scored and the game would probably have been ours. After the game I was very emotional. I went home with my family rather than on the team plane. But before we left, Walter came up and put his arm around me, consoling me. He didn't say anything, he didn't have to, you always knew how much Walter cared about his teammates. And the next day I got a call from our coach, Neill Armstrong. He said, "Brian, I want to tell you that last night I went back to the office and I watched that play over and over again and it was simply a bad call." He knew how bad I felt and he just wanted to tell me that. It was a very thoughtful thing to do, but then he was always a very thoughtful man.

TONY MCGEE
DEFENSIVE END, 1971–1973

My first year with the Bears, I guess, I was kind of mesmerized, stunned by the fact that I really was in pro football.

My career really started one day against the Washington Redskins. I hadn't been playing much. Somebody got hurt and Abe Gibron, who was the defensive coach then, was going to put in Dave Hale. Dick Butkus called a time-out. He went over to Gibron and said, "Put in that McGee." They put me in.

It was late in the game and the Redskins were driving on us. We were ahead by one point (16-15). I remember Washington only needed to gain maybe five yards or so on third down to get their field goal kicker within decent range. I busted through on a pass rush and jumped up and knocked the ball down. Their kicker, Curt Knight, just barely missed, maybe a yard short, and we won the game. Next day a newspaper headline said:

GOOD KNIGHT! McGEE SAVES GAME!

The best blocker I ever went against was George Kunz of Atlanta and later the Colts—he was so quick off the ball, and I never had a tackle hit me as hard as he did. The toughest players I ever saw? There were a number of them. On the Bears, I'd say they were Dick Butkus and Willie Holman. People don't know much about Willie, but he was one tough guy. He'd play hurt, but he'd always get it done.

And Butkus! We were playing New Orleans once and somebody cheap-shotted me. Butkus called a defense where I'd have a shot at that guy, then Dick jumped offside at the snap. I didn't jump though. Dick was furious in the huddle. He said, "Why the hell didn't you nail that guy? I set it up for you!"

MIKE SINGLETARY
MIDDLE LINEBACKER, 1981–1992

Being a Bear? I think of George Halas, of tradition, of hard work, dedication, loyalty.

What was it like?

When I think about it, I see Soldier Field. It's a cold day. I'm on the field with a group of guys. There's blood on my jersey and on my pants . . . not much, but a little. The fans are cheering. It's third down and one and there isn't much time left. We're in the defensive huddle. I can see the guys, see their breath on the air. We know what we have to do and we know we're ready. We come out of the huddle and we're lined up . . . waiting. To me, that's what being a Bear was about.

Mike Singletary, middle linebacker 1981–1992

Kurt Becker, guard, 1982–1989

Bronko Nagurski, fullback/tackle, 1930–1937, 1943.

Willie Gault, wide receiver, 1983–1987, and friend

Gary Fencik, safety, 1976–1987

Ralph Jones, head coach, 1930–1932. Regular season record 23-10-7, and an NFL championship in 1932.

Maurice "Mo" Douglas, defensive back, 1986–1994

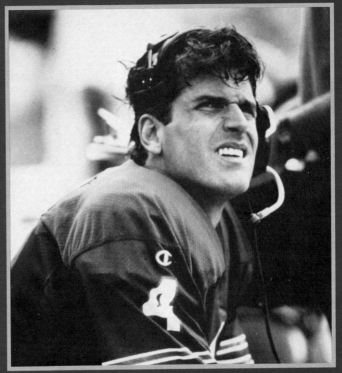

Jim Harbaugh, quarterback, 1987–1993.

Trace Armstrong, defensive end, 1989–1994

Chris Gardocki, punter/placekicker, 1991–1994

Jim McMahon, quarterback, 1982–1988

Fred Williams, tackle, 1952–1963

Mike Singletary, middle linebacker, 1981–1992

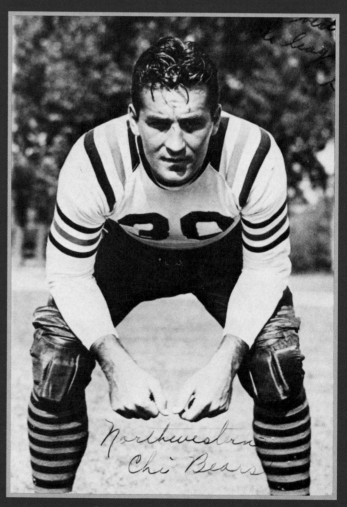

George Wilson, end, 1937–1946

Kevin Butler, kicker, 1985–1994

Richard Dent makes the acquaintance of an English bobby.

Doug Plank, safety, 1975–1982

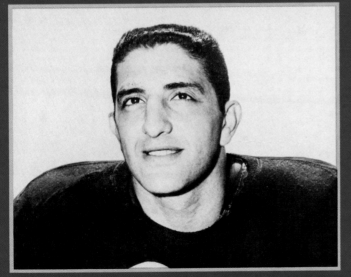

Bill George, middle linebacker, 1952–1965

Dennis McKinnon, wide receiver, 1983–1988

Quarterbacks Johnny Lujack (32), 1948–1951,
and Sid Luckman (42), 1939–1950.

William Perry, defensive tackle, 1985–1993

Abe Gibron, head coach, 1972-74, regular season record 11-30-1.

Bobby Douglass, quarterback, 1969–1975

Mark Carrier, safety, 1990–1994

Chris Zorich, defensive tackle, 1991–1994

Bob Parsons, punter, 1972–1982

Todd Bell, safety, 1981–1986

A pair of future Hall of Famers, Bear Doug Atkins (81), defensive end, 1955–1966 and Colt Johnny Unitas (19).

Bob Avellini, quarterback, 1975–1984

Dennis Gentry, wide receiver, 1982–1992

Willie Galimore runs behind the blocking of Jim Cadile (72).

Dave Duerson, safety, 1983–1988

Greg Latta, tight end, 1975–1980

Jay Hilgenberg, center, 1981–1991

Doug Buffone, linebacker, 1966–1979

Tandem running backs Roland Harper, 1975–1982, and Walter Payton, 1975–1987.

Alan Page, defensive tackle, 1978–1981

Mike Tomczak, quarterback, 1985–1990

Donnell Woolford, cornerback, 1989–1994.

Jack Pardee, head coach, 1975–1977, record 20-22 in
the regular season, and a trip to the playoffs in 1977.

Otis Wilson, linebacker, 1980–1987

Willie Galimore, halfback, 1957–1963

George McAfee, halfback, 1940–1941, 1945–1950

Matt Suhey, fullback, 1980–1989

Bobby Joe Green, punter, 1962–1973

Steve McMichael, defensive tackle, 1981–1993

Keith Van Horne, tackle, 1981–1993

Ed Sprinkle, end, 1944–1955

Revie Sorey, guard, 1975–1982

Wendell Davis, wide receiver, 1988–1993

*Doug Buffone (55), linebacker, 1966–1979 and
Dan Hampton (99), defensive tackle/end, 1979–1990.*

Neal Anderson, running back, 1986–1993

SIX

"PIC"

Running back Brian Piccolo joined the Bears as an undrafted free agent in 1965 after leading the nation in scoring and rushing at Wake Forest. After sitting out the first season with injuries, he then played four years, rushing 258 times for 927 yards and four touchdowns and catching 58 passes for 537 yards.

Warmly liked and respected by his teammates, Piccolo contracted cancer and died of embryonal cell carcinoma in 1970 at the age of 26, leaving his wife Joy and three daughters. The story of his heroic struggle against the disease and tragic death touched the heart of the nation and has been the subject of several books and a motion picture.

Doug Buffone remembers...

Brian and I arrived together as rookies in 1966 and became good friends.

In 1969, we were in Rensselaer at training camp and I got sick. So did Brian.

Brian Piccolo, 1966–1969

We were both quarantined to the dorm. I had the flu. Brian had a slight cough and just generally wasn't feeling good.

I got better, but he still didn't look too good even after we went up to Chicago for the regular season.

One day at Wrigley Field—my locker was right next to his—he was coughing, worse than when we were quarantined together back in Rensselaer. So I said, "Pic, you've got to get rid of that damn cough. Why don't you go see a doctor or something."

He looks at me and says, "I think I got cancer."

Now Pic was always a clown, loved to kid around. So I just shook it off because Pic was always that way. But then, a little later, down in Atlanta, we're playing the Falcons, and it was very hot. Pic took himself out of the game, and he would never do that on his own. He just couldn't breathe. They took him back to Chicago and found out he had cancer.

We all went to visit him in the hospital. He had an operation and then got out. We had a basketball team in the off-season but Pic couldn't play anymore, so we made him our coach. Then, after one game, Pic told me he thought he felt a lump or something in his chest. So back to the hospital he went.

When we would talk about it, Gale Sayers, who was so close to Pic, would always say, "Well, give him a holler; it'll pick him up."

And when we did, Pic would usually say, "Yeah, everything's fine."

But it wasn't. I was in the National Guard on bivouac in June of 1970 and I called Pic the night before he died. I was in a tent and they hooked up this phone for me and I got a call in to him. But this time it was very different. Pic could hardly talk.

I said, "Hang in there, Pic." But, of course, he didn't have a choice in the matter.

At the PROFESSIONAL FOOTBALL WRITERS OF AMERICA dinner in New York in May 1970, Gale Sayers, after a remarkable comeback the previous season from a knee injury, was given the George Halas

THE BRIAN PICCOLO AWARD

After his death, the Chicago Bears instituted THE BRIAN PICCOLO AWARD.
Based on the voting of Bear veteran players, the award is given to the
Bear rookie who best exemplifies the courage, loyalty, teamwork,
dedication and sense of humor of the late Brian Piccolo.

1970	**Glen Holloway** G		1983	**Jim Covert** T
1971	**Jerry Moore** S		1984	**Shaun Gayle** S
1972	**Jim Osborne** DT		1985	**Kevin Butler** K
1973	**Wally Chambers** DT		1986	**Neal Anderson** RB
1974	**Fred Pagac** TE		1987	**Ron Morris** WR
1975	**Roland Harper** RB		1988	**James Thornton** TE **Mickey Pruitt** LB
1976	**Brian Baschnagel** WR		1989	**Trace Armstrong** DE
1977	**Ted Albrecht** T		1990	**Mark Carrier** S
1978	**John Skibinski** RB		1991	**Chris Zorich** DT
1979	**Dan Hampton** DE		1992*	**Troy Auzenne** T *rookie* **Mike Singletary** LB *veteran*
1980	**Bob Fischer** TE		1993*	**Myron Baker** LB *rookie* **Todd Perry** G *rookie* **Tom Waddle** WR *veteran*
1981	**Mike Singletary** LB			
1982	**Jim McMahon** QB			

*Following the 1992 season, the Bears chose to honor both a rookie and a veteran for the Brian Piccolo Award.

award for the Most Courageous Athlete of the Year.

When George Halas handed him the trophy, Sayers looked out at the large gathering of people there to honor him. He told them a mistake had been made that night, this fine award should have been given to his friend and former roommate Brian Piccolo.

"Think of Brian and his courage and fortitude," Sayers said, "shown every day in the months since last November, in and out of hospitals, hoping to play football again but not too sure at any time what the score was or might be. Brian Piccolo has never given up.

"He has the heart of a giant and that rare form of courage that allows him to kid himself and his opponent: cancer. He has the mental attitude that makes me proud to have a friend who spells out the word courage 24 hours a day, every day of his life.

"You flatter me by giving me this award, but I tell you here and now that I accept it for Brian Piccolo.

"Brian Piccolo is the man of courage who should receive the award. It is mine tonight. It is Brian Piccolo's tomorrow.

"I love Brian Piccolo and I'd like all of you to love him. When you hit your knees to pray tonight, please ask God to love him, too."

"He doesn't look any different coming at you;
but when he gets there, he's gone."
—George Donnelly, 49er defensive back

SEVEN

THE COMET: GALE SAYERS

The name came from his days as a halfback at the University of Kansas.

The "Kansas Comet" they called him.

In 1965, when he joined the Bears, Gale Sayers quickly became the "Chicago Comet." George Halas said in training camp, before the Comet had carried the ball in a single NFL regular season game, "I haven't seen a running back like that since Grange or McAfee."

Comet? Well, on the football field he did resemble that fiery heavenly body, a dazzling streak of light and extraordinary speed. But unlike a comet, he had moves . . . a sudden spurt with the ability to turn a corner on a dime and cut back across the grain with grace.

George Donnelly, a defensive back for the San Francisco 49ers described it best when he said, "He doesn't look any different coming at you; but when he gets there, he's gone."

Rosey Grier, a great defensive tackle for the Los Angeles Rams, remembered another side to him. "It was on an 80-yard run on a screen pass he made against us. I hit him so hard near the line of scrimmage I thought my shoulder must have busted him in two. I heard a roar from the crowd and figured he must have fumbled. I was on the ground and when I looked up he was 15 yards down the field and going for the score."

Born in Wichita, Kansas in 1943, his family moved to Omaha which is where Gale Sayers first started playing football. At Omaha Central High School, he won all-state honors in football as well as several state track medals. Many colleges tried to recruit him, but everybody thought he would go to Nebraska and join its prized football program. But he didn't. He chose Kansas. "I knew that was the place where I would play," he said later, "and that's all I wanted, just the chance to be out there and play."

Play he did.

Sayers came out of Kansas a two-time All-American. He set Big Eight records for rushing, kick returns and pass reception yardage and was coveted by the Kansas City Chiefs of the AFL in those pre-merger years of war between the two leagues. He was drafted in the first round in each league, but chose the Bears and the NFL. "It was simple," he said later. "I always wanted to play in the National Football League. It was established with a lot of really great players who were just playing better football at the time."

Sayers made the NFL look even better his rookie year.

In a pre-season game against the Rams he gave a hint of what was to come. He returned a punt 77 yards for a touchdown, followed that a little later with a 93-yard kickoff return for a touchdown, and then astounded everyone with a left-handed, 25-yard touchdown pass.

Sayers did not start in the first two regular season games of 1965, but in the second, against the Rams, he scored on an 18-yard option play. It was the first of 56 touchdowns he would score for the Bears. The next week he started.

In his first start, at Green Bay against Vince Lombardi's mighty Packers and despite such premier defenders as Ray Nitschke, Willie Davis, Herb Adderley, and Willie Wood, Sayers ran for two touchdowns and picked up 80 yards rushing on 17 carries.

In Chicago the following week, the Comet broke that tackle against the Rams which Rosey Grier thought had left Sayers in two pieces.

It was the beginning of the most spectacular rookie season ever posted by an NFL running back.

The next week, at Minnesota, with the Bears down 37-31 and just over two minutes remaining, Sayers took a kickoff at the four, headed up the middle, made a move to the left then cut back to the right and headed for the sideline. Once he reached it there were only Vikings in his wake. The Bears went ahead, 38-37. Then fellow Bear rookie, linebacker Dick Butkus, picked off a Fran Tarkenton pass, and Sayers, on the next play, burst through for his fourth touchdown of the afternoon, tying the club record set by Rick Casares.

He topped that effort in December with an historic performance against the 49ers in Wrigley Field. The 49ers watched Sayers tie the NFL record of six touchdowns in a game and average 12.6 yards-per-carry on nine rushes. His combined yardage for the day was 336 yards, with 134 yards on five punt returns and 89 on two pass receptions. His last touchdown that day, and 21st of the season, broke the NFL record held jointly by Lenny Moore of the Colts and Jim Brown of Cleveland. Sayers upped it to 22 the following week in the last game of the season against Minnesota.

Sayers gained 867 yards rushing as a rookie by averaging 5.2 yards per carry. He averaged 31.4 yards on 21 kickoff returns which included scoring plays of 96

and 86 yards. His 16 punt returns averaged 14.9 yards and an an 85-yard TD; and he added 29 pass receptions for 507 yards. In all, Sayers gained 2,272 yards and scored 132 points.

Gale was a private person, sometimes uncomfortable with his celebrity status. To the media, Sayers was an "enigma". . ."shy". . ."affable but reserved". . ."cooperative but cautious". . ."arrogant". . ."withdrawn". . ."a brooding young man" . . ."one who takes interviews to be sparring sessions". . .depending on who you read or listened to in those days. But the one word that could not be used to describe him was "ungrateful."

His typical post-game interview always led to talking about somebody other than himself. Asked about a spectacular 61-yard run against the Colts in Baltimore in 1965, he responded, "Bob Wetoska (the Bear right tackle) did the whole thing. He made the big block when he took out (Colt defensive end) Lou Michaels. It was such a great block all I had to do was get rid of (Colt defensive back) Bobby Boyd when he came up to take me."

The next year, 1966, Sayers rushed for 1,231 yards, a new Bear record and, at that time, only the third time a Bear back broke the 1,000-yard mark (Beattie Feathers gained 1,004 in 1934 and Casares had 1,126 in 1956). In the last game of that year, he rushed for 197 yards against the Vikings, another club record at the time. Sayers would break his own record in 1968 when he became the first Bear to rush for more than 200 yards in a game, gaining 205 against the Packers in Green Bay.

The first knee injury came in the next game against the 49ers at Wrigley Field. A tackle by San Francisco safety Kermit Alexander left Sayers with massive ligament damage to his right knee. It was the ninth and final game

Sayers with Coach Halas.

of the 1968 season for Sayers.

He returned the following year and rushed for 1,032 yards on a Bear team that won only one of 14 games—their worst season in history. Sayers, however, received every Comeback Player of the Year award for the 1969 season.

In a 1970 game against St. Louis, he went down with an injury to his left knee. He tried a comeback in 1971, but it did not work, and he retired.

Gale Sayers gets a textbook block from wide receiver Dick Gordon (45).

and an unequalled NFL rookie record.

He returned a kickoff 103 yards for a touchdown in a game against the Steelers in 1967, the longest in club history. His career kickoff return average of 30.6 is not only a Bear record but an NFL one as well. The six touchdowns he scored on those kickoff returns is also an NFL record which he shares with Ollie Matson and Travis Williams. His single season KOR average of 37.7 is by far the highest in club history.

Like a comet he came—but didn't stay very long—lighting up the sky spectacularly as he passed through. In his brief career he brought all professional football fans to their feet with his dazzling plays.

Sayers still holds many Chicago Bear records. No one has ever bested the 36 points, or the 6 touch-downs that he left on the scoreboard against the 49ers in 1965. Only two other NFL players have ever scored six touchdowns in a single game, Ernie Nevers and Dub Jones. His 22 touchdowns in a season remain a Bear standard

Two other records he shares are four rushing touch-downs in a game, with Rick Casares and Bobby Douglass, and seven consecutive games scoring a rushing touchdown, with Walter Payton.

Sayers was inducted into the Pro Football Hall of Fame in 1977, presented by the man who both drafted and coached him, George Halas, who said, "I did so with love and joy. I loved to watch him and he brought joy to so many fans." At 34, Gale Sayers was the youngest person ever to be enshrined in the Hall at Canton.

Hall of Famers Gale Sayers (1965–1971)
and Mike Ditka (1961–1966).

83

EIGHT

MY NOMINEE FOR BEAR FAN HALL OF FAME

by Tony Hillerman

Last year in the Dallas American Airlines terminal I spotted a tall, bald, square-chinned fellow who rang a bell in the depth of my memory. He reminded me of someone I had known a long, long time ago. But who? And when? And where? By the time I came up with any answers he had disappeared.

I finally remembered the when and where, but not the name. The when was 1942 and the where was Fort Benning. The Army was training thousands of teenagers to be infantrymen. I happened to be one of those kids in a platoon run by a Tech Sergeant we called "Grizzly," and thus I knew how I could have identified the tall, bald fellow even without his name.

I would walk up behind him and shout FEDEROVICH! If he didn't shout "TACKLE" in response, I would know he wasn't one of the kids who survived training in Grizzly's platoon.

Grizzly was a true-blue Chicago Bears' fan. He had come to the training cadre from the Illinois National Guard. While his body was now in South Georgia his heart remained always in Wrigley Field. If the Army had been smart enough to put George Halas in charge of the war effort, he'd tell us, the Japanese would never have won any of those victories in the Pacific. (The Redskins had just beaten the Bears 14-6 for the National Football League title, which would never have happened, Grizzly assured

us, had Halas stuck to coaching instead of joining the Navy.)

I became a favorite of Grizzly by default. I came off an Oklahoma farm, with no NFL connections. Much of the platoon had been drafted out of New York, and a good many of the others from a reception area in Washington. Grizzly took for granted the latter were Redskins fans, and while our sergeant delighted in reminding us of Chicago's 73 to zip humiliation of the Redskins in 1940, the fact remained that the Bears had just lost the 1942 title to the same team. That was bad. But if Grizzly looked on his Washington trainees with suspicion, he looked on the big New York delegation with contempt. New Yorkers had committed the most outrageous violation of human decency in history—the 30-13 defeat of his heroes in 1934 in the infamous Sneakers Game. As we often heard, the Polo Grounds turf was sheet ice that day, and, at midpoint, the Bears led 13−3. But the Giants came out of the locker room for the second half wearing sissy tennis shoes. They scored 27 points in the fourth quarter while the Bears skated around on their cleats.

Whether or not we were Bear fans, Grizzly took for granted that any male American would know NFL football. And that meant knowing the Bears. So when time came for the "night war games," the Super Bowl of our training period, Grizzly installed his own password system.

Gary Famiglietti carries the ball for the Bears against the Redskins in 1943.

We couldn't trust the passwords assigned by battalion headquarters because the competing units could get them by buying a beer for the right guy in headquarters. Grizzly was sure of this because he did it himself. Therefore we would use a system he had worked out himself, which was foolproof.

The man on guard would challenge with "Federovich" and the man sneaking home from patrol would respond with "Tackle." Or the man on guard would yell "Maniaci" and the response would be, of course, "Line Backer."

I still remember the scene—Technical Sergeant Grizzly sitting on the top step of our tarpapered barracks and the platoon gathered around him. He gave us a terror-provoking account of the damage done to facial features when one is shot at close range by the blank ammunition we'd be using in the night maneuvers. This was followed by an even more chilling description of what he would do to those of us who screwed up on the passwords.

"Don't have to learn anything," Grizzly assured us. "It's foolproof. But maybe you better stay away from Luckman and Bussey and McAfee. Even the Germans know about them."

This produced a strained silence among the troops.

"Well," Grizzly said. "In case some of you guys from New York or Washington forgot, I'm going to stick the team roster on the bulletin board."

And thus it is a half century later and a lot of elderly former riflemen and machine gunners from THE WAR can still tell you what positions Bob Nowaskey, Hamp Pool, Gary Famiglietti, and Bob Swisher played with the Chicago Bears.

Tony Hillerman is an award-winning novelist and a longtime Bear fan.

85

"Hold them down Chicago,
Hold them down,
Is the cry of everybody in our town."
—from the Bears first fight song, 1922

NINE

DECADE BY DECADE

The 1920s

The National Football League was founded and the Bears were one of the 14 charter members. They also gained the distinction of becoming one of only two of the original franchises destined to survive (the other is the Chicago Cardinals).

The biggest names to wear the navy blue and orange during those years were end George Halas, halfback Ed "Dutch" Sternaman and his younger brother quarterback Joey, tailback Paddy Driscoll, tackle Ed Healey, center George Trafton, and, of course, the legendary halfback Red Grange. Through the first decade, the Bears compiled a record of 84-31-19 (.730), winning one NFL title and experiencing only one losing season.

· 1920 ·

A. E. Staley, owner of a corn products company in Decatur, Illinois, hires George Halas and Dutch Sternaman to organize a professional football team.

The team, named the Decatur Staleys, joins the newly formed American Professional Football Association, which would be renamed the National Football League in 1922.

· 1921 ·

Halas and Sternaman take over ownership of the ballclub and move it to Chicago where they play as the Chicago Staleys at Wrigley Field.

Chicago wins its first NFL title with a record of 9-1-1, barely beating out the 9-1-2 Buffalo All-Americans. The Bears only loss was to Buffalo, 7-6.

· 1922 ·

The team's name is changed to the Chicago Bears.

The Bears consummate their first player deal, acquiring tackle Ed Healey from the Rock Island Independents for $100. Healey

---

George Halas commissioned the Bears' first fight song in 1922. The lyrics:

From the East and from the West,
They send their very best
To play against the pride of old Chicago.
There is none of them compare with our Chicago Bears.
Through the line they go,
Hold them down Chicago,
Hold them down,
Is the cry of everybody in our town.
Just watch the way they meet and tumble their foe,
Out to win Chicago Bears, they will always go.
Cross that line, Chicago, cross that line,
That's the way to play, you're doing fine,
And when the season's o'er
And you have to play no more,
Chicago Bears will stand out fore.

At Wrigley Field. Joey Sternaman is the quarterback, appearing to be barking out an audible . . . but it seems there are 16 Bears on the field... and no opposition.

both Red Grange and Paddy Driscoll in their backfield.

Season	Win/Loss	Percentage
1920	10-1-2	(.909)
1921	9-1-1	(.900)
1922	9-3-0	(.750)
1923	9-2-1	(.818)
1924	6-1-4	(.857)
1925	9-5-3	(.643)
1926	12-1-3	(.923)
1927	9-3-2	(.750)
1928	7-5-1	(.636)
1929	4-9-2	(.308)

would go on to earn his way into the Pro Football Hall Of Fame.

·1923·

Record: George Halas returns a Jim Thorpe fumble 98 yards for a touchdown against the Oorang Indians at Wrigley Field, an NFL record until 1972.

·1924·

Quarterback Joey Sternaman of the Bears leads the league in scoring with 75 points (6 touchdowns, 9 field goals, 12 PATs).

·1925·

The Bears sign All-American halfback Harold "Red" Grange and he plays his first game for the team on Thanksgiving Day, five days after playing his last college game for Illinois.

·1925–1926·

The team, featuring Grange, goes on two historic barnstorming tours across the country.

·1926·

Records: Triple-threat back Paddy Driscoll, wooed to the Bears from the Chicago Cardinals that year, sets an NFL standard in scoring with 86 points (6 touchdowns, 12 field goals, 14 PATs) which will not be broken until Don Hutson scores 95 for the Green Bay Packers in 1941. Driscoll's record of 12 field goals that year will stand until Cleveland Browns' Lou Groza kicks 13 in 1950.

·1929·

The Bears post their first losing season despite having

The 1930s

Despite the Great Depression, it was one of the Bears' golden eras. The team became one of the most potent forces in the league during the decade because of such stars as halfback Red Grange, fullback Bronko Nagurski, end Bill Hewitt, guard Danny Fortmann and tackles George Musso and Link Lyman, all of whom eventually made it to the Pro Football Hall of Fame.

Chicago won two NFL championships, and when the league broke into two divisions in 1933 and matched the top teams from each in a title game after

Bear halfback Beattie Feathers, the first player ever to rush for more than 1,000 yards in a season (1,004 in 1934) and still holder of the NFL record with an 8.44 yard average gain rushing that season.

88

the season the Bears were in three of the first seven. During the ten years of the '30s, the Bears never had a losing season and posted the first undefeated regular season record in NFL history (13-0 in 1934). The Bears were 84-28-11 (.750) during the regular seasons of the 1930s, with a record of 2-2 in post-season games.

·1930·

George Halas turns over the head coaching reins to Ralph Jones.

The Bears play the NFL's first indoor football game, a post-season exhibition at Chicago Stadium to benefit unemployment relief. The Bears defeat the Chicago Cardinals 9-6 on an 80-yard field.

·1931·

Record: Joe Lintzenich booms the longest punt in Bear history, 94 yards in a game against the New York Giants.

·1932·

The Bears play an unofficial, yet still deciding, NFL championship game, again indoors at the Chicago Stadium, against the Portsmouth Spartans, on a field

A Bear uniform of the 1930's.

80 yards long. Chicago wins it 9-0.

Records: The Bears set an NFL record which has never been broken when they allow only 44 points in 14 games, an average of only 3.1 points per game. Their eight shutouts that season is another NFL mark unlikely to be broken.

After the season Dutch Sternaman sells his half-interest in the Bear franchise to George Halas.

·1933·

George Halas returns as head coach.

The Bears' then-NFL record of 16 consecutive games without a loss ends with a 10-0 defeat at the hands of the Boston Redskins.

Chicago plays in the first official NFL championship game and defeats the New York Giants 23-21 behind the toe of "Automatic Jack" Manders who kicks three field goals and two extra points. Each Bear player receives a title game bonus of $210.34.

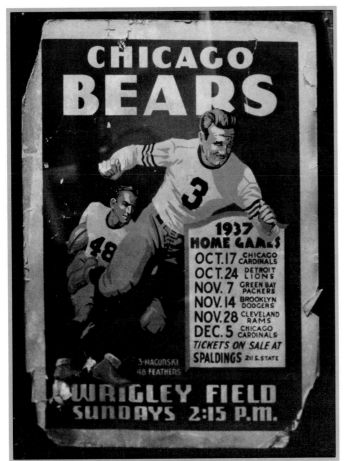

In the championship season of 1932, fullback Bronko Nagurski led the NFL in rushing touchdowns. He scored four. Red Grange was second with three. Grange, however, was second in the league in points scored with 42, catching four touchdown passes, behind Portsmouth Spartan tailback Dutch Clark who scored 55 points.

From inside the huddle, 1933.

A memento from the 1933 championship Bears, a hideskin at the Pro Football Hall of Fame.

·1934·

The Bears play in the first College All-Star football game before 79,432 fans in what would become an NFL pre-season tradition. The game, pitting the previous year's NFL titleholders against the nation's top college football players, was sponsored by the Chicago Tribune Charities. Final score: Bears 0, Collegians 0.

Records: Rookie halfback Beattie Feathers, running behind the blocking of Bronko Nagurski, becomes the first NFL rusher ever to exceed 1,000 yards in a single season (1,004 on 119 carries). His average gain of

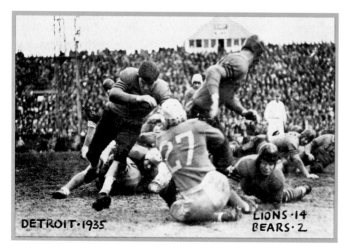

Bill Hewitt, notorious for playing without a helmet, 1935.

8.44 yards per carry remains the all-time NFL best. Feathers also becomes the first Bear to rush for 100 yards in a game, a feat he accomplished four times in 1934.

The undefeated Bears, 13-0-0, meet the Giants for the NFL crown in New York and lose 30-13 in the famous "Sneakers Championship" on a frozen field at the Polo Grounds.

·1935·

Chicago's NFL record of 17 consecutive regular season victories, which began November 26, 1933, is ended on opening day with a 7-0 loss to the Packers at Green Bay. The streak is still the longest in NFL annals.

·1936·

Tackle Joe Stydahar from West Virginia becomes the Bears' first first-round draft pick in the NFL's newly installed college football draft.

·1937·

Chicago wins the Western Division title with a record of 9-1-1 but loses in the NFL title game to the Washington Redskins with their sensational rookie tailback Sammy Baugh, 28-21.

·1939·

Record: Fullback Bill Osmanski records the longest

90

run from scrimmage in Bear history when he races 86 yards for a touchdown against the Chicago Cardinals.

Season	Win/Loss	Percentage
1930	9-4-1	(.692)
1931	8-5-0	(.615)
1932	6-1-6	(.857)
1933	10-2-1	(.833)
1934	13-0-0	(1.000)
1935	6-4-2	(.600)
1936	9-3-0	(.750)
1937	9-1-1	(.900)
1938	6-5-0	(.545)
1939	8-3-0	(.727)

Fullback Bill Osmanski follows a block by Hall of Fame guard Danny Fortmann against the Lions in 1940.

The 1940s

The Bears were a dynasty during the first seven years of the decade, winning four world championships. With the innovation of the T-formation with a man in motion and the conversion of Sid Luckman from a single wing tailback to a T quarterback, George Halas revolutionized the offensive scheme of play in the NFL.

Piloted on the field by Luckman and supported by such other future Hall of Famers as halfback George McAfee, center/linebacker Clyde "Bulldog" Turner, and tackle Joe Stydahar, the Bears rewrote entire sections of the NFL record book during nine winning seasons. Their regular season record for the 1940s was 81-26-5 (.757). In 1940s playoff games they were 5-1.

·1940·

The Bears win the NFL championship by defeating the Washington Redskins 73-0, the most points and largest margin of victory in any regular season or post-season game in NFL history. Ten different Bears score touchdowns, and each player receives a share of $873 for the victory.

Records: Bobby Swisher becomes the first Bear receiver to gain 100 yards in a game when he picks up 106 on two catches against the Packers.

Rookie tackle Lee Artoe sets an NFL record when he kicks a 52-yard field goal against the New York Giants.

·1941·

Chicago introduces its new fight song "Bear Down, Chicago Bears."

Record: The Bears set NFL records by scoring 396 points and averaging 36 points per game, both of which will stand throughout the decade. They also become the first team to pass for more than 2,000 yards in a season (2,002).

To decide the Western Division title, the Bears and Packers meet in the league's first divisional playoff game. Bears triumph 33-14, and then defeat the New York Giants 37-9 for the NFL crown.

Record: Halfback George McAfee sets a club playoff record when he rushes for 119 yards against the Packers, a mark that has not yet been equaled.

·1942·

Bears win their division for the third year in a row, but lose to the Washington Redskins in the title game, 14-6.

The undefeated regular season is

The Bears introduced their new fight song, "Bear Down, Chicago Bears" in 1941. It has become a Chicago tradition. The words and music were composed by songwriter Al Hoffman, who also can lay claim to the Hit Parade song he wrote entitled "If I Knew You Were Coming, I'd Have Baked a Cake."

CHICAGO BEARS FOOTBALL CLUB
—INCORPORATED—
37 S. WABASH AVE., CHICAGO, ILL.

91

Ken Kavanaugh, a fingertip touchdown catch against the crosstown rival Cardinals in 1948 at Wrigley Field.

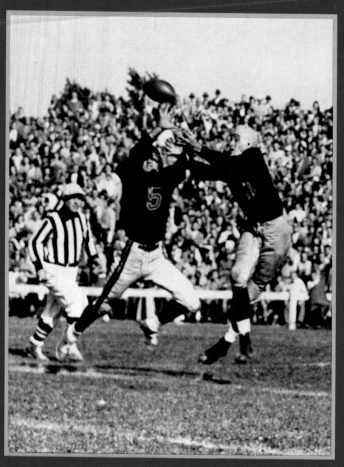

George McAfee (5), a Hall of Fame Bear, battles a Packer for a pass in the late 1940s.

Defensive back Johnny Lujack bats the ball out of the hands of Ram quarterback Jim Hardy as Bulldog Turner (66) moves in.

Clyde "Bulldog" Turner, Hall of Fame center and linebacker, played for the Bears from 1940 through 1952.

the second in club history and gives the Bears the distinction of being the only team in NFL history to have gone undefeated and untied in two regular seasons.

·1943·

With George Halas having left for service in the U.S. Navy, Hunk Anderson and Luke Johnsos take over as co-head coaches.

Records: Sid Luckman sets two NFL game records by passing for seven touchdowns and 433 yards against the New York Giants. His seven TDs passing has since been equaled in the NFL but never surpassed.

Luckman also logs single-season NFL records by throwing for 28 touchdowns and 2,194 yards. His 28 TD passes are still the most in Bear history, and he also gains the distinction of being the first Bear to pass for more than 2,000 yards in a season.

Bob Snyder sets a club record by kicking eight extra points in a game, as the Bears beat the Giants 56-7.

Chicago wins its fourth consecutive conference title, an accomplishment that has only been repeated twice in NFL history (Cleveland Browns in the 1950s and Buffalo Bills in the 1990s).

The Bears win their third NFL championship of the 1940s by defeating the Washington Redskins 41-21.

·1946·

George Halas returns to take over command of the Bears and Chicago wins its fourth championship in seven years, beating the New York Giants by a score

Packer great Don Hutson hauls in a pass at Wrigley Field in 1944 despite the efforts of Sid Luckman in the days of the 60-minute players. Other Bears in the picture are Jim Fordham (3), Gary Famiglietti (23), George Wilson (30), Bulldog Turner (66), Jake Sweeney (13), and George Zorich (14).

of 24-14 before an NFL record title-game crowd of 58,346 at the Polo Grounds.

·1947·

Records: End Jim Keane sets three Bear records when he catches 64 passes for 910 yards and 10 touchdowns (the previous standards were 28 receptions by George Wilson, 535 yards from Harry Clark and eight TDs for Scooter McLean).

Sid Luckman becomes the first Bear to pass for more than 300 yards in a game when he totals 314 against the Philadelphia Eagles.

The team also sets a league record for first downs in one season with 263.

·1948·

The Bears showcase one of the best rookie crops ever when they add quarterbacks Johnny Lujack of Notre Dame and Bobby Layne from Texas, and tackle George Connor from Notre Dame.

·1949·

Records: End Jim Keane sets a club mark that still stands today when he catches 14 passes in a game against the New York Giants at the Polo Grounds.

Quarterback Johnny Lujack sets an NFL mark by passing for 468 yards in a game against the Chicago Cardinals which the Bears won 52-21. His feat, too, still stands as the Bear all-time record.

Season	Win/Loss	Percentage
1940	8-3-0	(.727)
1941	10-1-0	(.909)
1942	11-0-0	(1.000)
1943	8-1-1	(.889)
1944	6-3-1	(.667)
1945	3-7-0	(.300)
1946	8-2-1	(.800)
1947	8-4-0	(.667)
1948	10-2-0	(.833)
1949	9-3-0	(.750)

The 1950s

It was an era most fans thought of as a roller coaster ride. Only twice did the Bears play beyond the regular season, but they did post seven winning seasons against three sub .500 years. There were a variety of greats, such Hall of Famers as tackle/linebacker

The "Three B's,"
(l to r) Rudy Bukich, Zeke Bratkowski, and Ed Brown

George Connor, linebacker Bill George, guard Stan Jones, and defensive end Doug Atkins.

The Bears ended the decade with 70 wins, 48 losses, 2 ties (.593). They were 0-2 in post-season appearances.

·1950·

The Bears and the Los Angeles Rams share the National Conference title with records of 9-3-0 (Chicago beat the Rams in their two regular season meetings). The Bears, however, fall 24-14 in the playoff game at the L. A. Coliseum before a crowd of 83,501. The Rams, coached by former Bear Joe Stydahar, feature Bob Waterfield, Norm Van Brocklin, Elroy Hirsch, Tom Fears and Glenn Davis.

Record: Johnny Lujack becomes the first Bear to account for more than 100 points in a season on 11 touchdowns, three field

goals, and 34 PATs for a total of 109 points.

·1951·

The Bears have a chance to once again tie the Rams for the conference title and force a playoff but are upset by their crosstown rivals, the Chicago Cardinals, 24-14, in the last game of the regular season.

·1954·

Records: End Harlon Hill sets a Bear single-game record when he gains 214 yards on seven catches in a game against the San Francisco 49ers, a record that still stands today.

Hill also sets club season records with 12 touchdowns and 1,124 yards on pass receptions.

·1955·

After the season, George Halas steps down as head coach for the third time, naming former Bear great Paddy Driscoll to replace him.

·1956·

Chicago, 9-2-1, makes it to the NFL championship game for the first time since 1946 after edging out the 9-3-0 Detroit Lions for the Western Conference crown. The Bears fall 47-7 to the New York Giants, with a lineup that included Frank Gifford, Charlie Conerly, Sam Huff, Kyle Rote, Andy Robustelli, Roosevelt Brown, and Emlen Tunnell.

Records: Fullback Rick Casares becomes only the second Bear to rush for 1,000 yards in a season, gaining 1,126 on 234 carries. He also sets two team touchdown records for a season, 14 overall and 12 rushing, and a single game mark with four against the San Francisco 49ers.

Salaries

The following pay-scale list was prepared by the National Football League and submitted to the Anti-Trust Subcommittee of the U.S. House of Representatives in July 1957.

Team	Total Salaries	Individual Salary Range
Cleveland Browns	$368,031	$6,000–19,000
Los Angeles Rams	$352,958	$5,500–20,000
Chicago Bears	$342,525	$6,500–14,200
San Francisco 49ers	$332,614	$5,600–20,100
Detroit Lions	$330,375	$5,500–20,000
New York Giants	$324,258	$5,200–16,000
Chicago Cardinals	$318,441	$5,500–20,000
Baltimore Colts	$294,392	$6,000–17,500
Philadelphia Eagles	$283,483	$5,750–13,500
Green Bay Packers	$277,642	$5,000–18,500
Pittsburgh Steelers	$276,875	$5,250–12,250
Washington Redskins	$275,942	$5,000–14,000

The highest paid player, garnering that $20,100, was 49er quarterback Y. A. Tittle.

Eddie Macon, the first black to wear a Bear uniform,
gains some yardage in a game against the Lions in 1953.

One of the Bears' greatest receivers, Harlon Hill (87) holds onto
an Ed Brown pass despite a hoard of Ram defenders in 1958.

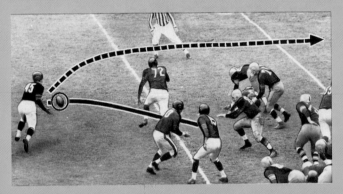

Ed Brown pitches out to Bobby Watkins (45) who runs it in for a
touchdown against the Packers in 1955. Other Bears are Chick
Jagade, looking as if he is to take a handoff, Bill Wightkin (72),
and Bill McColl (83).

Johnny Lujack (32) to Julie Rykovich (11)
in a game against the Rams in 1950.

Johnny Morris takes off around left end in a 1959 game
against the Cardinals.

Bear receiver Jim Dooley has one hand on the ball against the Packers at Green Bay in 1952.

·1958·

George Halas once again takes over as head coach.

The Bears and Rams meet at the Coliseum and draw an NFL record crowd of 90,833 paid attendance in a 41-35 Chicago loss.

Season	Win/Loss	Percentage
1950	9-3-0	(.750)
1951	7-5-0	(.583)
1952	5-7-0	(.416)
1953	3-8-1	(.273)
1954	8-4-0	(.667)
1955	8-4-0	(.667)
1956	9-2-1	(.818)
1957	5-7-0	(.417)
1958	8-4-0	(.667)
1959	8-4-0	(.667)

The 1960s

The decade was highlighted by a world championship, 1963, and lowlighted by the worst season in Bear history, 1969. The Bears could, however, claim more winning than losing seasons, five against four with one .500 year.

There were some dazzling stars, the two most famous coming by way of the 1965 draft in running back Gale Sayers and linebacker Dick Butkus. Tight end Mike Ditka, drafted in 1961, would also reach the Hall of Fame.

And, for the fifth consecutive decade, the Bears posted a winning record, 67-65-6 (.508).

·1961·

Records: Quarterback Bill Wade throws a 98-yard touchdown pass to end Bo Farrington in a game against the Detroit Lions, the longest Bear pass play ever.

Roger Leclerc kicks the most field goals by a Bear in a single game when he connects on five against the Detroit Lions. The feat is tied later in the decade by Mac Percival.

The Bears were known for their defense in 1963, the best in the NFL that year. But they also had an offense and the top scorer on the team that year was tight end Mike Ditka with 48 points, the result of eight touchdown receptions.

It was not Ditka's first slot at the top; he was the team's top scorer in 1961 as well when he scored 72 points on 12 touchdown catches.

On Being Wrong and Admitting It.

The prize of the 1961 Bears draft was a tight end from the University of Pittsburgh named Mike Ditka. Down the line that year the Bears also selected a squatty-built fullback from Illinois named Bill Brown.

Brown played his rookie season in Chicago, but in 1962 the Bears drafted Joe Marconi. They already had Rick Casares, so George Halas decided to trade Brown to the young Minnesota Vikings, who were in only their second year of play.

Ditka, a pal of Brown's, went to Halas. "I told him I knew it wasn't any of my business, but he was going to make one hell of a mistake if he got rid of Brown."

"Halas looked up at me and said, 'You're right, it isn't any of your business.'"

The trade was made and for the next dozen years Brown went on to become a Pro Bowl fullback at Minnesota. Some of his best games came against Chicago.

After one Bear-Viking game in Minnesota, after Halas had retired as coach, he shared an elevator with Kay Brown, wife of the Viking fullback. When someone introduced them Halas doffed his hat, took her hand, and said, "Young lady, I want you to know that sending your husband here was the worst trade I ever made."

·1962·

Records: Quarterback Bill Wade becomes the first Bear to pass for more than 3,000 yards in a season and complete more than 200 passes (3,172 on 225 completions). The yardage record has yet to be equaled in club history.

·1963·

George "Mugs" Halas, Jr., son of owner and founder George Halas, is named president of the Bears.

The Pro Football Hall of Fame opens in Canton, Ohio with 17 charter inductees. Three are Chicago Bears: George Halas, Red Grange, and Bronko Nagurski.

The Bears win their first NFL championship since 1946 by defeating the New York Giants 14-10 at Wrigley Field. The Bears' winning share is $5,899 each.

Brian Piccolo takes a handoff from Jack Concannon.

·1964·

Records: Bill Wade completes the most passes in a single game in Bear annals when he connects on 33 against the Washington Redskins.

Flanker Johnny Morris sets an NFL record when he catches 93 passes in a single season. That, and the 1,200 yards he gained on pass receptions remain the single-season highs in Bear history.

·1965·

The Bears have a spectacular year at the NFL draft, selecting two future Hall of Famers, running back Gale Sayers and linebacker Dick Butkus, in the first round.

Records: Rookie running back Gale Sayers ties the all-time NFL mark by scoring six touchdowns in one game during a 61-20 Bear

Continued on page 100

97

The way it was at Wrigley Field from 1921 through 1970. The Bears take on the Packers in a crucial 1963 game which Chicago won 26-7.

Hall of Fame meeting: Doug Atkins (81) brings down Jim Taylor of Green Bay in 1962. Other Bears are Rosey Taylor (24), Bill George (61), Richie Petitbon (17), and Larry Morris (33).

Ronnie Bull carries for the Bears against the Vikings, 1962.

A fake to Gale Sayers (40) and Virgil Carter (15) bootlegs it around left end behind George Seals (67) against Green Bay in 1968.

Touchdown at Wrigley Field . . . scored by Willie Galimore (28).

Jim Dooley (left) and Abe Gibron on the sideline. Both would become head coaches of the Bears.

Papa Bear gives a thumbs-up to his depiction to Mayor Richard J. Daley before the 1963 championship game against the Giants. Looking over his shoulder is quarterback Bill Wade.

Joe Marconi (34) has some running room after taking a handoff from Bill Wade (9) in a game against the Rams in 1962. On the ground is Mike Ditka (89), and the Ram at the left is Jack Pardee (32), destined to one day coach the Bears.

Soldier Field

Neill Armstrong, head coach, 1978-81. His regular season record was 30-34. He took the Bears to the playoffs in 1979 with a record of 10-6, his best season.

The coach and CEO watching . . .

Bob Avellini, 1975–1984.

Season	Win/Loss	Percentage
1970	6-8-0	(.428)
1971	6-8-0	(.428)
1972	4-9-1	(.307)
1973	3-11-0	(.214)
1974	4-10-0	(.286)
1975	4-10-0	(.286)
1976	7-7-0	(.500)
1977	9-5-0	(.643)
1978	7-9-0	(.438)
1979	10-6-0	(.625)

The 1980s

The decade began and ended on losing notes, but had as its centerpiece one of the most successful and exciting eras in Chicago football history, capped by the Bears' monumental victory in Super Bowl XX.

The Bears set many new club records during the decade as Mike Ditka became the second most successful coach in team history, following George Halas.

During the '80s, the Bears were 92-60-0 (.605), and in the five winning years between 1984-88 they were 62-17-0 (.785). The 62 victories in five straight seasons is the most by any team in NFL history over a similar

period of time. The Bears were 5-4-0 in the five years they appeared in post-season play.

·1980·

Record: The Bears tie the club record for most points in a regular season game when they annihilate the Green Bay Packers 61-7 at Soldier Field. In the process, they also set a team record for first downs (33).

·1982·

Former Bear tight end and assistant offensive coach of the Dallas Cowboys, Mike Ditka, is appointed head coach by George Halas.

·1983·

Jim Finks resigns as executive vice president and general manager of the Bears.

Founder, owner, former coach and player, George Halas dies on October 31, 1983 at age 88.

Mike McCaskey is named president of the Bears, only the third in franchise history after George Halas and his son George "Mugs" Halas.

·1984·

Chicago wins the NFC Central Division title, defeats the Washington Redskins 23-19 in the divi-

Vince Evans, 1977–1983.

103

sional playoff but loses in the NFC championship game 23-0 to the San Francisco 49ers.

Records: Walter Payton breaks Jim Brown's all-time National Football League rushing record of 12,312 yards.

Defensive end Richard Dent establishes the Bears standard for sacks in one season, credited with 17.5.

·1985·

The Bears repeat as division champs, winning 15 of their 16 games and tying the NFL record for the most regular season wins in a single season.

With back-to-back shut-outs in the playoffs, 21-0 over the New York Giants and 24-0 over the Los Angeles Rams, the Bears advance to Super Bowl XX. The Bears rout the New England Patriots 46-10 at the Superdome in New Orleans, setting seven Super Bowl records including most points scored by one team and the largest margin of victory.

Record: Kevin Butler scores more points in one season than any other Bear in history, 144 on 31 field goals and 51 PATs.

·1986·

A third consecutive division title is won by the Bears

The Bears set an unprecedented number of single-season team records in the Super Bowl year of 1985. The most noteworthy new marks:	
Most points	456
Most extra points	51
Most field goals	31
Most safeties	3
Most first downs	343
Most first downs, rushing	176
Most first downs, passing	145
Most yards gained	5,837
Fewest passing yards allowed, game	-22
Most opponent kickoff returns*	78
*which means the Bears scored a lot.	

with 14 regular season victories, the second most in club history.

Record: The Bear defense sets an NFL 16-game mark by allowing only 187 points, an average of only 11.7 per contest.

Chicago loses 27-13 in the playoffs to the Washington Redskins.

·1987·

Bears win their fourth straight NFC Central crown.

Chicago falls again in the playoffs to the Redskins, this time 21-17.

·1988·

For the first time since 1951, the Bears post five consecutive winning seasons, and for the fifth year in a row they win their division.

In what would become known as the "Fog Bowl," at Soldier Field, the Bears defeat the Philadelphia Eagles, 20-12. They then lose to the San Francisco 49ers in the NFC championship game, 28-3.

Season	Win/Loss	Percentage
1980	7-9-0	(.438)
1981	6-10-0	(.375)
1982	3-6-0	(.333)
1983	8-8-0	(.500)
1984	10-6-0	(.625)
1985	15-1-0	(.938)
1986	14-2-0	(.875)
1987	11-4-0	(.733)
1988	12-4-0	(.750)
1989	6-10-0	(.375)

The 1990s

The full story of this decade remains to be told. There is the pledge of innovation, change and improvement, and efforts continue towards a new stadium and new training facilities. Like all NFL clubs, the Bears face the formidable task of adapting operations to a dramatically changed league structure.

The fill-in Bears play during the players' strike of 1987 in an unfilled stadium.

Tom Waddle, wide receiver, 1989-94.

Through the first four years of the decade, the Bears have maintained a winning record, 34-30-0 (.531), making the playoffs twice. Their post-season record thus far is 1-2-0.

·1990·

Andrew McKenna and Patrick Ryan, two Chicago businessmen, purchase approximately 20 percent of the team.

The Bears once again prevail in the NFC Central, winning their sixth division title in seven years.

Records: Johnny Bailey adds a new record when he returns a punt 95 yards for a touchdown in a game against the Kansas City Chiefs.

Rookie Mark Carrier sets a new club mark with 10 interceptions, the most in one season since Rosey Taylor snatched nine in 1963.

Chicago defeats the New Orleans Saints in the playoffs 16-6, but then loses to the New York Giants 31-3.

·1991·

Mike Ditka records his 100th victory as head coach of the Bears.

The Bears gain a wild card entry into the playoffs, but lose in the first round to the Dallas Cowboys, 17-13 at Soldier Field.

·1992·

Records: Place kicker Kevin Butler becomes the Bears' all-time leading scorer when he moves ahead of the 750 points scored by Walter Payton.

In the post-season, linebacker Mike Singletary is voted to the Pro Bowl for the tenth time, most by any Bear.

·1993·

Dave Wannstedt, defensive coordinator of the Dallas Cowboys, is hired to replace Mike Ditka as the Bears' 11th head coach.

The Bears play their 1,000th NFL game, the first team in league history to reach that landmark. Just as they did in their first game against the Moline Tractors in Decatur back in 1920, the Bears win it, defeating the Atlanta Falcons 6-0 at Soldier Field.

Records: Kevin Butler kicks two 55-yard field goals, which equal the longest in Bear history.

Quarterback Jim Harbaugh becomes the Bears' all-time leader in pass completions (1,023) and pass attempts (1,759), records held by Sid Luckman since his retirement in 1951.

Defensive tackle Steve McMichael takes two records from Walter Payton: consecutive regular season games played, 187, and total games played, 191.

·1994·

The Bears, along with the National Football League, celebrate the 75th anniversary of their existence.

Season	Win/Loss	Percentage
1990	11-5-0	(.688)
1991	11-5-0	(.688)
1992	5-11-0	(.313)
1993	7-9-0	(.438)

William Perry (72) and Mike Singletary taking a breather.

Richard Dent with a takeaway.

Jim Covert (74) prepares to take on Colt defenders as Jim McMahon drops back to pass and Emery Moorehead (87) moves out.

Walter Payton in the rain, Matt Suhey watches from the ground after throwing a block.

Dan Hampton, Tyrone Keys and Richard Dent attempt to block a Buffalo field goal.

Al Harris moves upfield.

Mike Hartenstine, defensive end, 1975–1986.

Otis Wilson (55), William Perry (72), Jim McMahon,(9) and Ron Rivera (59).

The "Fog Bowl," the 1988 playoff game against the Eagles.

(right) Mike Tomczak tosses one into the haze as Jay Hilgenberg shunts off All-Pro Reggie White's pass rush.

(below) Jim McMahon hands off to Neal Anderson as Jim Covert pulls out to block.

The eyes... Mike Singletary.

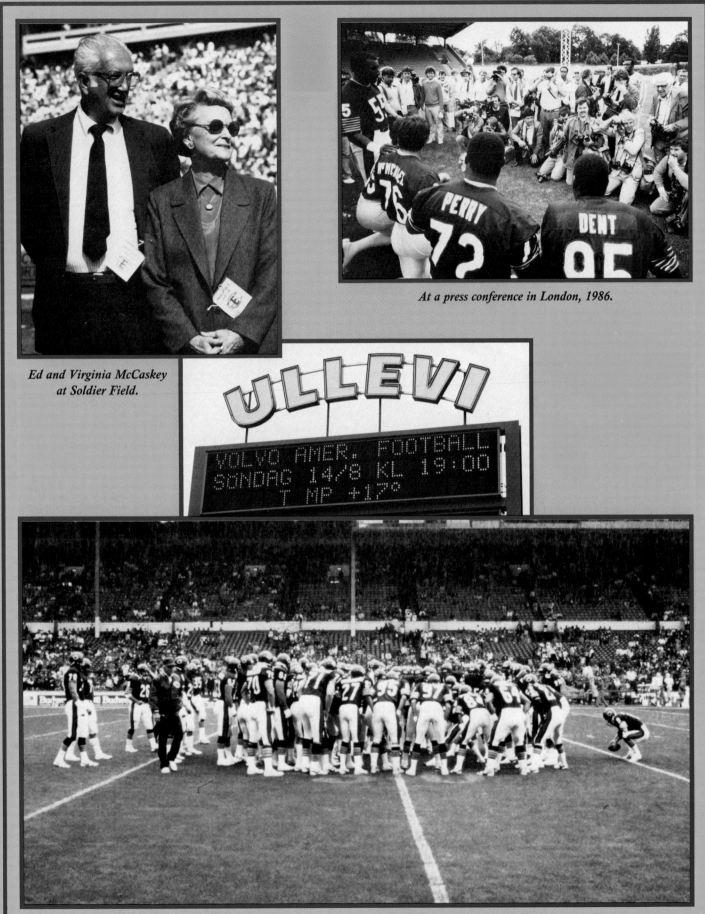

*Ed and Virginia McCaskey
at Soldier Field.*

At a press conference in London, 1986.

The Bears huddle before an exhibition game at Ullevi Stadium in Gothenburg, Sweden, 1988.

and George Allen guiding the defense for him, had one of the most complicated defensive programs in pro football. It was an enormous adjustment from college football, Butkus later admitted. But as Allen later described him in his book on the greatest football players he had ever seen or coached, "If one had to construct a model for a pro football middle linebacker, he might start with Dick Butkus' dimensions (6'3", 245 pounds) and playing disposition (unfriendly)."

Butkus had some major shoes to fill when he arrived. Bill George, a 14-year Bear veteran, was one of the most widely admired linebackers the game had yet seen. George was a calculating, shrewd defender. His ability to read offenses and be in the right place at the right time redefined the middle linebacker position, something that Butkus would have to absorb and combine with his natural ferocity.

He did.

In his first start in the NFL, Butkus registered 11 unassisted tackles against the San Francisco 49ers, a game the Bears, despite his efforts, lost 52-24. "I made a bunch of rookie mistakes," he said after the game. "But don't worry, I'm gonna do much better."

He did.

There is a wonderful picture of him that appeared in LIFE magazine that rookie year. Butkus is rising from the ground, the number 51 glaring from the front of his jersey, wearing only his flattop crewcut because his helmet had been stripped off his head. But he has the ball in his hand, which he had stripped. There is such an enraged look on his face that, you

Dick Butkus, about to do what he liked best.

could only hope whoever ended up with his helmet fled to a country that had no extradition treaty with the United States. He said early in his career, "I wouldn't ever set out to hurt anybody deliberately unless it was, you know, important—like in a league game or something."

He handled the middle linebacking chores from that rookie year through 1973. His philosophy: "Find the enemy, make contact, let them know you were there." He was honored as an All-Pro seven of his nine seasons with the Bears, and he played in every Pro Bowl game except the last when his knee injuries had finally got to him. He recovered 25 opponents' fumbles which was an NFL record when he retired, and intercepted 22 passes. His 47 takeaways was a Bear record until Gary Fencik broke it. He also caught two passes for extra points. And he scared the hell out of every offense that ever went up against him.

Butkus played with injury and pain. First, his right knee went out in 1970. The other one went not too long afterwards. Finally, in 1973, he took himself out of a game, the first and last time he ever did that. He limped to the sideline, but strode into the Pro Football Hall of Fame.

When it was all over, he said, "Few people get to earn a living at what they like to do, and there are hazards in any profession. Football is something I was made for. I gave the game all I could for as long as I could. I guess my only regret was that my career was too short."

It wasn't.

Dick Butkus (51) in action, destroying a 49er and springing Gale Sayers (40) free for a 97-yard touchdown return of the opening kickoff in a 1967 game. Number 59 on the Bears is Rudy Kuechenberg.

REMEMBERING BUTKUS

Brian Piccolo: "Scrimmaging against Butkus isn't exactly tranquilizing. When Dick is on the other side of the scrimmage line glaring at you with those boiling eyes, it makes you wish you could change places with the equipment boy."

MacArthur Lane, running back for the Packers in the 1960s: "If I had a choice, I'd sooner go one on one with a grizzly bear. I pray that I can get up after every time Butkus hits me."

Bob DeMarco, center with the Cardinals and other teams: "He had some cute tricks. He'd back up five yards and time it just right and really tee off on me. . . . Once we were in a pileup and I looked and there was Butkus staring, close as could be. He said, 'I'm gonna knock that mustache right off your face!'. . . . He was the type of guy who, if you got in a fight with him, you'd have to kill him 'cause he wouldn't quit."

Face to face, Butkus and a Packer.

Making a point.

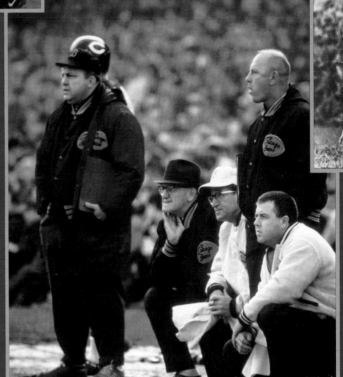

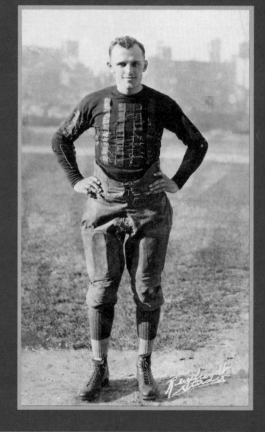

WARNING

BEAR COUNTRY

■ Bears are large, powerful and unpredictable.
■ Bears defend their territory fiercely.
■ Bears never back down from a challenge.
■ Be alert. Bears can be everywhere.
■ Bear tracks are a sure sign that Bears are near.
■ Keep your distance. Even at 100 yards, a Bear may feel crowded.
■ If you encounter a Bear, never run. You cannot outrun a Bear.
■ If a Bear approaches, remain calm and back away.
■ Avoid confrontation with a Bear.
      The Bear will always win.

Removal of this sign is illegal and may result in injury to others.

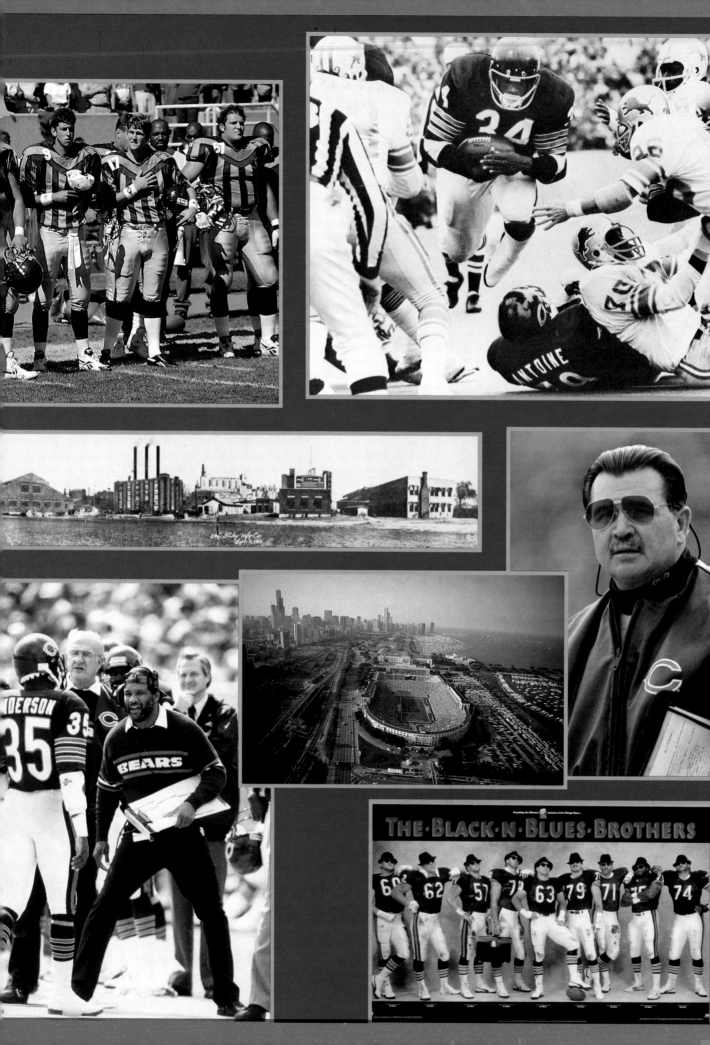

THE·BLACK·N·BLUES·BROTHERS

Attempts to restrain a raging Butkus were usually futile.

BEAR WEATHER

by Jim Belshaw

RAF Station Woodbridge, England
—1545 hrs., 29 Dec. 63

"Ten-hut!"

Guardmount begins.

The swing shift, four to midnight, eight hours walking the concrete around U.S. Air Force fighter-bombers, each with a red-tipped tactical nuclear weapon snug against the fighter's belly.

Eight hours "humpin' the ramp," eight hours of numbing boredom.

But tonight the Bears play.

A tech sergeant quickly walks the ranks. His troops are barely escaped from high school.

I have just turned nineteen, a son of the South Side, born in Little Company of Mary Hospital in Evergreen Park, taught by nuns at St. Kilian's, a Sox fan.

It is winter and we crammed ourselves into insulated long johns, insulated flight pants, and heavy parkas with thick fur ringing the hood. A lucky few wear surplus World War II "bunny boots," the bomber crew footwear of our fathers and uncles.

The sergeant's inspection is perfunctory. We wear too many clothes to concern ourselves with spit shines or razor-sharp creases.

"At ease!" the sergeant barks.

He quickly falls into the monotone reserved for reading briefing notes from his clipboard, departing from it only once to slip into the cadence of the military threat, a strange vocal pattern requiring every third word to be hit hard—"You will NOT act in

ANY way strictly PROHIBITED by regulations. . . "

I carry two radios—one a Motorola two-way for communication while on post, the other of a much more critical nature, especially tonight.

In the right pocket of my parka I can feel the comfortable weight of the second radio, a transistor small enough to fit into the palm of my hand, entirely illegal, and set for AFN, the Armed Forces Network.

Tonight the Bears play the Giants for the National Football League championship.

Nick, a Bear fan, pulls motorized patrol. He swears he will name his first kid after Bill Wade if the Bears win tonight. (He does, too.)

We wear our game faces. We are ready for the New York Giants. We have received a sign from God—well, in truth, it was a Christmas card from George Halas.

Weeks before, the Bear fans in the barracks had sent a Christmas card to Papa Bear and wished him luck.

The day before the championship game, his Christmas card to us—more likely his public relations director's Christmas card—arrived.

All of which was irrelevant to us. The card had his name and something purporting to be his signature. It was enough for us.

We relieve the day shift. JD (another Bear fan) and I take the rear of the area, while two others go to the front.

Three hours into the shift, the North Sea begins rolling in the evening's billowing mounds of fog. Voices carry in the black stillness. A dog barks somewhere. A laugh carries across the silent flight line.

Four hours into the swing shift. Game time. I switch on the radio.

Already, JD and I are optimistic. It's eight degrees in Chicago. Bear weather. Perfect conditions for the historic Bear defense that has allowed an average of only ten points a game in the 1963 regular season.

If they just wait for Tittle to make a mistake. . .

But the Bears make the first mistake. Wade fumbles on the Giant 17-yard line.

The radio—the one issued with the rifle, not the transistor—crackles to life with a quick, unauthorized transmission. It comes from a nameless Giant fan somewhere in the fog of the fighter base.

"Fumble! Fumble!" he screams.

The Giants march 83 yards and score first. The English night becomes colder, the fog heavier. I begin pacing the worn trail behind the hangar.

Willie Galimore fumbles on the Bear 31. The Giants recover. I'm tempted to turn off the radio. I can't take much more of this.

But I don't. The AFN signal weakens suddenly and I press the radio closer to my ear. On the next play, Tittle throws a perfect touchdown pass to Del Shofner—and Shofner drops it!

From the next post, I hear JD, trying to holler quietly, but his excited whisper carries clear as a bell through the mist.

"All right! All right!"

Larry Morris picks off a Tittle pass and runs the ball to the Giant 5. Wade takes in a quarterback sneak for the tying touchdown.

The Motorolas crackle with unauthorized transmissions.

"Touchdown!"

"Score!"

"Touchdown!"

An angry sergeant cuts in: "Knock it off!"

"Touchdown!" somebody radios in reply.

The Giants add three points to make it 10-7 Giants at the half. JD

and I meet at the blast pads.

"We got 'em," he says. "Ten points. The Bear average. Ten points is all you get against the Bears."

He doesn't mention that the Bears have only 7 at the time. I don't either.

The second half starts and the titanic defensive battle continues. Then late in the third quarter, Tittle is intercepted again. This time by Ed O'Bradovich.

Three plays later, Wade sneaks in and the Motorolas come to life again.

"Bears! Bears!"

"Touchdown!"

"Knock it off!"

"Go Bears!"

"I said knock it off! Now!"

"Bears! Bears!"

The fourth quarter is about to begin when I hear a voice from the front of the alert area.

"Go up front. Nick's at the gate," the voice says. "I'll swap posts with you."

Nick, the Bear fan on mobile duty tonight, has parked his truck near the aircraft gates. We make no pretense of hiding our transistors now. They're in the open, his on the truck hood, mine in my hand, volume cranked up.

Tittle throws pass after pass. One is intercepted! Then another interception!

We did it! The Bears won the whole thing!

There is much whooping and hollering and the Motorolas snap cryptic messages back and forth concerning the payoff of bets.

Then the familiar silence returns to the flight line. Nick drives off into the black mist. I go back to my post behind the hangar. The temperature has dropped, the fog thickened, moistening everything it touches. It is the worst combination—cold and wet, chilling every living thing to the bone.

Bear weather.

Jim Belshaw, writer, veteran, and longtime Bear fan.

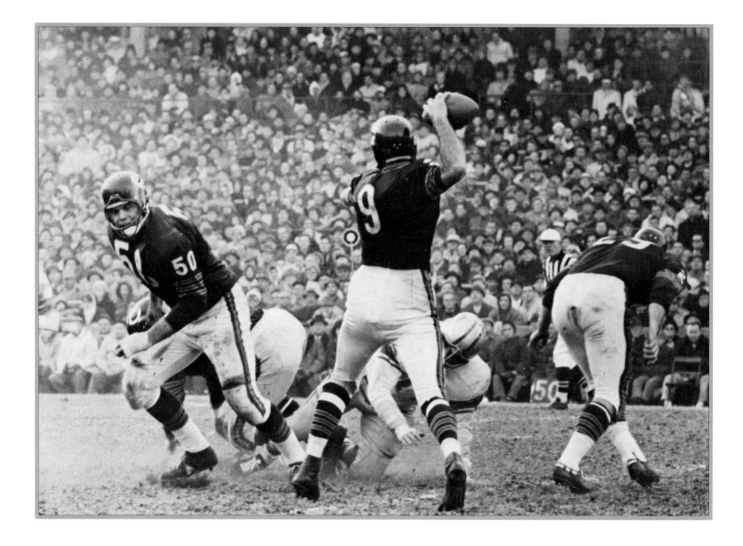

"All I could think was, 'My God, if he catches it, we win!'
And he did catch it, and we did win."
—Bob Wetoska, 1963

TWELVE

TRUE CHAMPIONS

Super Bowl XX, that pageant down in New Orleans; 1963, that bone-chilling afternoon at Wrigley Field; 1940, the unparalleled massacre in Washington. In 1934, the game a few pair of basketball sneakers decided; 1932, amid the scents of the circus they followed in the first indoor championship game. The Bears participated in some of the most colorful NFL championships ever.

The Bears have won nine NFL championships and have played in 13 championships since the season-end classic first began back in 1933.

These were the illustrious years, the Bears brought home the trophy.

·1921·

It was the team's first year in Chicago, still playing under the name Staleys, and it was the league's second year of existence. The Staleys had come in a close second the year before with a record of 10-1-2.

Co-owners George Halas and Dutch Sternaman, an end and halfback respectively, were determined not to let that happen again. They went out and got All-American halfback Chick Harley from the University of Michigan. To sign him, they were forced to offer a partnership in the team. The partnership never came to be, but Harley did play the season for Chicago.

The Staleys played nine straight games at their new home field, Cubs Park. They lost only one game during that streak, a squeaker to the Buffalo All-Americans, 7-6. Two weeks later, the Staleys got revenge by defeating Buffalo, 10-7. A win over the Canton Bulldogs, who no longer had the services of the great Jim Thorpe, and a scoreless tie with the Cardinals left the Staleys with a record of 9-1-1. Buffalo had the same won-lost figure but had two ties.

1921 Chicago Staleys

1921 Champion Chicago Bears

Position	Player	Height	Weight
LE	Guy Chamberlin	6'0"	190
LT	Ralph Scott	6'2"	234
LG	Tarzan Taylor	5'11"	170
C	George Trafton	6'1"	230
RG	Russ Smith	5'10"	220
RT	Hugh Blacklock	6'0"	220
RE	George Halas	6'0"	175
QB	Pete Stinchcomb	5'8"	152
LH	Dutch Sternaman	5'7"	170
RH	Chick Harley	5'8"	165
FB	Ken Huffine	6'0"	208

Newly appointed commissioner Joe Carr proclaimed Chicago the 1921 league champion.

Besides being such a fine debut year in Chicago, it also marked the first meeting in what would become one of the game's most intense rivalries when the

The 1921 Final Standings	Won	Lost	Tied
Chicago Staleys	9	1	1
Buffalo All-Americans	9	1	2
Akron Pros	8	3	1
Canton Bulldogs	5	2	3
Rock Island Independents	4	2	1
Evansville Crimson Giants	3	2	0
Green Bay Packers	3	2	1
Dayton Triangles	4	4	1
Chicago Cardinals	3	3	2
Rochester Jeffersons	2	3	0
Cleveland Indians	3	5	0
Washington Senators	1	2	0
Cincinnati Celts	1	3	0
Hammond Pros	1	3	1
Minneapolis Marines	1	3	1
Detroit Heralds	1	5	1
Columbus Panhandles	1	8	0
Tonawanda Kardex	0	1	0
Muncie Flyers	0	2	0
Louisville Brecks	0	2	0
New York Giants*	0	2	0

*The franchise is in no way related to the present-day New York Giants which were founded in 1925. The 1921 Giants went out of business after the season ended.

Green Bay Packers, under coach/tailback Curly Lambeau, came down to Chicago and were beaten by the Staleys 20-0.

George Halas announced that not only had they brought Chicago its first pro football championship, "Wonder of wonders, we paid all our bills and still had $7 in the bank." Records found later showed they actually had $7.70 in the bank, and that was after he and Dutch Sternaman divided profits of more than $21,000.

·1932·

Ralph Jones was the head coach, George Halas having reliquinshed that role after the 1929 season. The Bears had a backfield which included legends Red Grange and Bronko Nagurski.

With the Great Depression in full swing, there were only eight teams in the NFL in 1932, the fewest since the league began back in 1920. Rosters were limited to 20 players, but Halas, despite the lean times, talked commissioner Joe Carr into extending that to 22. The season was a three-way race between the Bears, the Packers and the Portsmouth (Ohio) Spartans (who would later become the Detroit Lions).

The Packers had a dynasty in the making. They had three future Hall of Famers in their backfield—quarterback Arnie Herber, halfback Johnny Blood McNally, and fullback Clarke Hinkle—as well as two on the line, tackle Cal Hubbard and guard Iron Mike Michalske. Portsmouth had tailback Dutch Clark, a triple-threat, who was the league's leading scorer and another star bound for the Hall of Fame.

The Bears played three consecutive scoreless ties to

1932 Champion Chicago Bears

Position	Player
LE	Bill Hewitt
LT	Lloyd Burdick
LG	Zuck Carlson
C	Ookie Miller
RG	Joe Kopcha
RT	Tiny Engebretsen
RE	Luke Johnsos
QB	Keith Molesworth
LH	Red Grange
RH	Dick Nesbitt
FB	Bronko Nagurski

1932 World Champions

open the season, then lost 2-0 to the Packers at Wrigley Field. After that, however, Chicago got its offense in gear and did not lose again, outscoring their opponents by a total of 151-44.

When the wintry winds of December rolled in, the Bears had a record of 4-1-6, the Packers were 10-1-1, and the Spartans were 5-1-4 (there was not a lot of uniformity in the schedules back then). The Packers, however, fell apart, losing in two successive weeks to the Spartans and the Bears.

The last game was essential for Chicago—against the hated Packers—and Chicago provided a typical winter day for the game—snow, a frozen field and winds whipping icy darts everywhere.

A brave crowd of 5,000 stayed into the fourth quarter to see Tiny Engebretsen kick a field goal to break the scoreless tie. Then Nagurski somehow thundered across the frozen turf 56 yards for a touchdown.

With ties not a factor in the standings then, the Bears and the Spartans with records of 6-1-6 and 6-1-4 were at the top of the heap at season's end. The Packers, at 10-3-1, were relegated to third place.

With the stalemate, the league, at the urging of Halas and Potsy Clark, the Portsmouth coach, decided on a special playoff game to determine that year's champion. Chicago was chosen as the site, but during the week the weather grew even worse than it had been for the Green Bay game.

So they decided to play indoors.

It was agreed the game would be played in the Chicago Stadium . . . with certain necessary modifications. The field was to be 80 yards long, all the Stadium could accommodate. To somehow rectify this situation, it was agreed that each time a team crossed midfield it would be penalized 20 yards. There

The 1932 Final Standings	Won	Lost	Tied
Chicago Bears	6	1	6
Portsmouth Spartans	6	1	4
Green Bay Packers	10	3	1
Boston Braves	4	4	2
New York Giants	4	6	2
Brooklyn Dodgers	3	9	0
Chicago Cardinals	2	6	2
Staten Island Stapletons	2	7	3

NFL Championship Playoff Game

	1st	2nd	3rd	4th	Final
Bears	0	0	0	9	9
Spartans	0	0	0	0	0

was also only one goal post, which would be shared, and it was moved from the end line to the goal line to save the 10 yards. Hash marks were introduced for the first time, 10 yards in from the sidelines because the sidelines were so close to the stadium retaining walls.

Portsmouth had a distinct problem, however. Their star Dutch Clark had left the team after the last regular season game to go out to Colorado College where he was the basketball coach in the off-season. When the championship playoff game was announced, he

The indoor championship game at Chicago stadium, 1932. Bears 9, Portsmouth Spartans 0.

was already on a train for Colorado Springs.

The teams and the fans also had a problem. The week before the game, the Chicago Stadium had played host to a circus. The sod that covered the concrete floor, as a result, was in the words of George Halas, "a very swell brand of dirt," which meant it was laced with the dung of elephants, horses and other assorted four-footed circus creatures. As one sportswriter put it the next day, "It was warm inside, but a little too aromatic." A crowd of nearly 12,000 showed up, which produced gate receipts of about $15,000, according to Halas.

Despite the loss of team-leader Clark, Portsmouth hung through three quarters, and the game was scoreless heading into the final period. But then Ace Gutowsky, filling in at tailback for Clark, threw a pass in Portsmouth territory which Bear defensive back Dick Nesbitt picked off. The Bears had a first down at the Spartan 7-yard line.

They gave the ball to the bull, Nagurski. He burst through for two. They gave it to him again, but Portsmouth stopped him. On third down the Spartans did not let him get beyond the line of scrimmage. Fourth down, and again the handoff was to Nagurski . . . but let the Bronk tell the story.

"I lined up as usual, four yards back. Red (Grange)

went in motion. The ball was handed to me by our quarterback, Carl Brumbaugh, and I took a step or two forward as though to begin the plunge everyone expected. The defenders were doubled up on the line to stop me. There was no way through. I stopped. I moved back a couple of steps. Grange had gone around end and was in the end zone, all by himself. I threw him a short pass. He was falling down but he caught it."

Protestations erupted. Potsy Clark was on the field, his players were screaming. The rule in those days was that any passer had to be five yards behind the line of scrimmage in order to throw a pass. Nagurski was not, the Spartans claimed. The referee did not agree, and the touchdown stood.

Tiny Engebretsen kicked the extra point and a few minutes later Portsmouth fullback, Mule Wilson, fumbled in the end zone and the ball bounced out for a safety. And so, in the aromatic confines of Chicago Stadium, the Bears won their second world championship by the score of 9-0.

·1933·

This was the first "official" NFL title game. At the urging of George Halas and the owner of the Boston Redskins, George Preston Marshall, the league was divided into two divisions in 1933 with the winner of each slated to meet at the end of the season to determine the NFL championship.

The Bears, now owned solely by Halas after he bought out Dutch Sternaman's half-interest, glided through the NFL West with a record of 10-2-1. The New York Giants did the same in the East division, winning 11 and losing just three. The Giants had five future Hall of Famers in their starting lineup—halfback

1933 World Champions

122

1933 Champion Chicago Bears

Position	Player
LE	Bill Hewitt
LT	Link Lyman
LG	Zuck Carlson
C	Ookie Miller
RG	Joe Kopcha
RT	George Musso
RE	Bill Karr
QB	Carl Brumbaugh
LH	Keith Molesworth
RH	Gene Ronzani
FB	Bronko Nagurski

Ken Strong, tackle Steve Owen (also their coach), center Mel Hein, and ends Ray Flaherty and Red Badgro. The Bears had Grange, Nagurski, end Bill Hewitt, and tackles George Musso and Link Lyman. The two teams had met twice during the regular season, the Bears winning the first, 14-10 at Wrigley Field, and the Giants triumphing 3-0 at the Polo Grounds. The tone was set for, in the words of one New York sportswriter, "The Title Tilt of the Titans."

The site was Wrigley Field, a week before Christmas, and about 26,000 came out to watch the titanic tilt on a foggy day that would turn to rain before the game was over. What they saw was a wildly innovative and entertaining game that was not decided until the final play.

It began with a trick play. Hein, the Giant center, explained it: "We put all the linemen on my right except the left end. Then he shifted back a yard, making me end man on the line while the wingback moved up on the line on the right. Harry Newman came right up under me like a T formation quarterback. I handed the ball to him between my legs and he immediately put it right back in my hands—the shortest forward pass on record." Newman faded back as if to pass and the Bears swarmed after him. Hein tucked the ball under his jersey, looking a little pregnant, and started to walk down the field. "After a few yards," he later explained, "I got excited and started to run, and the Bear safety, Keith Molesworth, saw me and knocked me down. I got about 30 yards but we didn't score."

"Automatic" Jack Manders got the Bears out to an early lead with two field goals, but before the half the

Giants went ahead 7-6 after a touchdown pass from Newman to Badgro.

Manders gave the Bears the lead in the third quarter with his third field goal of the day. The Giants came right back and scored a touchdown to take a 14-9 lead, but then the Bears scored on an 8-yard jump pass from Nagurski to Bill Karr—Bears 16, Giants 14.

The Giants followed with their second wild play of the day. Harry Newman described it. "It was a handoff by me to Strong, who would then buck the line. The hole was plugged up, so Ken spun out. He saw me there in the backfield and just lateralled the ball back to me. I was surprised and suddenly all the Bears were coming after me. They chased me all over back there. Then, in a flash, I saw Strong in the end zone with nobody near him. I threw it back to him and we had a touchdown." Giants 21, Bears 16.

The Bears marched back, reaching the Giant 33. Then it was Chicago's turn for a trick play. Nagurski got the ball, started to run with it and then pulled up and threw a jump pass to Bill Hewitt who raced for the sideline. About 15 yards downfield he was about to be tackled by Ken Strong and whirled and lateralled the ball back to Bill Karr who was trailing him. Bear halfback Gene Ronzani appeared as if from out of nowhere and threw a block that took out Strong and

The 1933 Final Standings	Won	Lost	Tied
Eastern Division			
New York Giants	11	3	0
Brooklyn Dodgers	5	4	1
Boston Redskins	5	5	2
Philadelphia Eagles	3	5	1
Pittsburgh Pirates	3	6	2
Western Division			
Chicago Bears	10	2	1
Portsmouth Spartans	6	5	0
Green Bay Packers	5	7	1
Cincinnati Reds	3	6	1
Chicago Cardinals	1	9	1

NFL Championship Game

Giants	0	7	7	7	21
Bears	3	3	10	7	23

another Giant defender, the only two who had a shot at Karr, who carried it the remaining 19 yards for a touchdown and a 23-21 Bear lead.

The Giants came back and with only seconds remaining they were threatening. On the last play of the game, Newman threw a pass to Badgro who could see the end zone and only one player, Red Grange, between him and a touchdown. As Badgro told it, "I planned to lateral to Hein as soon as Grange went for the tackle. But instead of going low for a conventional tackle he grabbed me around the arms and the upper body, pinning the ball to me so I couldn't lateral. Had I been able to get the ball to Hein we would have won the championship." As George Halas said later, "That play Grange made was the greatest defensive play I ever saw."

In that first official NFL title game, each winning Bear share was $210.34, each Giant took back to New York $140.22

·1940·

The Bears went to Washington, D. C., to face the Redskins in the NFL championship game still smarting from a controversial 7-3 loss to the Skins a few weeks earlier. The Bears had a chance to win that one but Bill Osmanski, about to catch the winning touchdown, was clearly interfered with and could not hold onto the ball. The referee did not see it that way, however, and that was the game. Afterwards,

1940 Champion Chicago Bears	
Position	Player
LE	Bob Nowaskey
LT	Joe Stydahar
LG	Danny Fortmann
C	Bulldog Turner
RG	George Musso
RT	Lee Artoe
RE	George Wilson
QB	Sid Luckman
LH	Ray Nolting
RH	George McAfee
FB	Bill Osmanski

Washington owner George Preston Marshall, made the monumental mistake of stating to the press, "They're quitters . . . just a bunch of crybabies. They fold up when the going gets tough."

Marshall's remarks did not sit well in the Chicago camp, and now the Bears had an opportunity to avenge themselves. Future Hall of Fame halfback George McAfee described the atmosphere as the Bears embarked for the title match-up. "It was real quiet on the train going down to Washington. We were all very intense, remembering the loss three weeks earlier and all of Marshall's remarks. We all had our playbooks out on the train, studying the

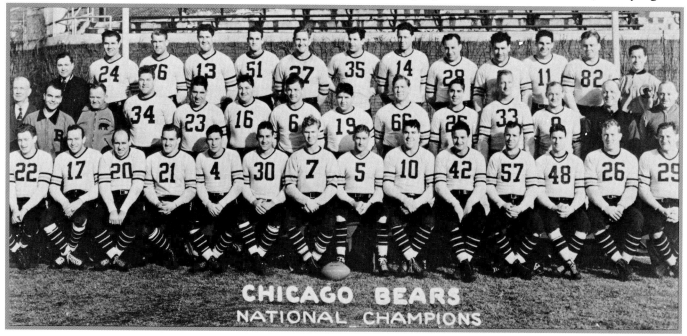

1940 World Champions

124

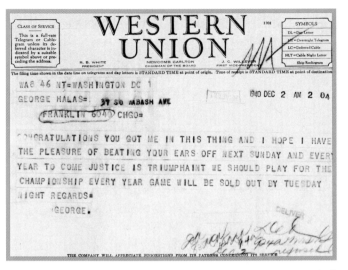

The telegram Washington Redskin owner George Preston Marshall sent to George Halas just before the 1940 NFL championship game.

plays and talking to each other about what we could do. We didn't talk about anything else. We were just getting ourselves ready for them mentally."

Both teams were very good. The Redskins had tailback Sammy Baugh running their single wing, the Bears and their T formation were led by Sid Luckman. Both teams were, as they were wont to say back then "star-studded."

Despite the earlier loss, the oddsmakers put the Bears down as a 7-5 favorite (point-spreads were not the norm in 1940), which prompted these responses. Marshall: "That's ridiculous . . . We already beat them . . . The bookmakers must be crazy." Halas: "Those guys (the bookmakers) must be crazy. This is an even-money game or nothing at all."

The first Bear to arrive at Griffith Stadium that championship game morning was George Halas. He spent the first few minutes in the locker room tacking up copies of the clippings of Marshall's remarks after their previous encounter with the Redskins. Coach and psychologist.

Fullback Bill Osmanski remembered it vividly. "When we came into the dressing room, we saw the pages on the wall. When we were ready to go out, he pointed to them. 'Gentlemen, that's what George Preston Marshall thinks of you. That's what the people in Washington are saying about you. I know you are a great football team, probably the greatest ever assembled. Go out there on the field now and show them, show the world.' We almost broke down the door."

Well, they did show the world and it took only 55

The Morning After

The events of the day offered the opportunity for many memorable quotes. After the carnage was over, here are a few that are worth remembering.

Sammy Baugh, when asked if the outcome might have been different had end Charley Malone not muffed what appeared to be a touchdown pass in the first quarter with the score a mere 7-0, Bears: "Hell, yes, the score would have been 73-6."

Bob Considine, noted New York newspaper columnist: "The Chicago Bears massacred the Washington Redskins 73-0 yesterday. . . . The unluckiest guy in the crowd was the five-buck bettor who took the Redskins and 70 points."

Bill Stern, the most famous sports radio broadcaster of the day: "It got so bad that, toward the end, the Bears had to give up placekicking the extra points and try passes instead because all the footballs booted into the stands were being kept by the spectators as souvenirs, and they were down to their last ball."

Red Smith, in his column "Sports of the Times" for the New York Times: "George Preston Marshall, the mettlesome laundryman who owned the Redskins, looked on from the stands—except when he turned his back to charge up the aisle and throw a punch at a dissatisfied customer—and when his ordeal was over, every hair in his raccoon coat had turned white."

And a wag in the pressbox, when the final gun signaled a merciful end to the slaughter, with a look of horror on his face, turned to the reporter sitting next to him and said, "My God, Marshall just shot himself!"

seconds to implant the idea. Halas tested the Washington defense with a few plays and quickly ascertained it was the same one the Redskins had used so effectively three weeks earlier. Only this time, the Bears had prepared to cope with it. Halas countered with a fake to McAfee, who the Redskins

1941 World Champions

McAfee and a 42-yard fumble return by end Ken Kavanaugh along with an inspired defense resulted in a final score of 37-9.

The Bears had become the first team in NFL history to win back-to-back championships since the title game was instituted in 1933.

·1943·

The war was in full swing and NFL rosters had been depleted considerably with players going off to serve in the military. The effect on the Eagles and the Steelers was so great that they were forced to combine into one team which took the name Phil-Pitt Steagles. And the Bears lured 34-year-old Bronko Nagurski down from Minnesota to rejoin the team after he had retired in 1937.

George Halas was serving in the Navy and had turned the head coaching duties over to former Bears Hunk Anderson, who handled the defense, and Luke Johnsos, the offense. The Bears were favored to win

1943 Champion Chicago Bears

Position	Player
LE	Jim Benton
LT	Dominic Sigillo
LG	Danny Fortmann
C	Bulldog Turner
RG	George Musso
RT	Al Hoptowit
RE	George Wilson
QB	Sid Luckman
LH	Harry Clark
RH	Dante Magnani
FB	Bob Masters

The 1943 Final Standings	Won	Lost	Tied
Eastern Division			
Washington Redskins	6	3	1
New York Giants	6	3	1
Phil-Pitt Steagles	5	4	1
Brooklyn Dodgers	2	8	0
Western Division			
Chicago Bears	8	1	0
Green Bay Packers	7	2	1
Detroit Lions	3	6	1
Chicago Cardinals	0	10	0

NFL Championship Game

Redskins	0	7	7	7	21
Bears	0	14	13	14	41

128

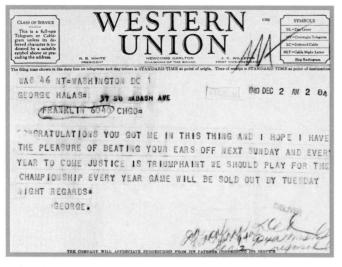

The telegram Washington Redskin owner George Preston Marshall sent to George Halas just before the 1940 NFL championship game.

plays and talking to each other about what we could do. We didn't talk about anything else. We were just getting ourselves ready for them mentally."

Both teams were very good. The Redskins had tailback Sammy Baugh running their single wing, the Bears and their T formation were led by Sid Luckman. Both teams were, as they were wont to say back then "star-studded."

Despite the earlier loss, the oddsmakers put the Bears down as a 7-5 favorite (point-spreads were not the norm in 1940), which prompted these responses. Marshall: "That's ridiculous . . . We already beat them . . . The bookmakers must be crazy." Halas: "Those guys (the bookmakers) must be crazy. This is an even-money game or nothing at all."

The first Bear to arrive at Griffith Stadium that championship game morning was George Halas. He spent the first few minutes in the locker room tacking up copies of the clippings of Marshall's remarks after their previous encounter with the Redskins. Coach and psychologist.

Fullback Bill Osmanski remembered it vividly. "When we came into the dressing room, we saw the pages on the wall. When we were ready to go out, he pointed to them. 'Gentlemen, that's what George Preston Marshall thinks of you. That's what the people in Washington are saying about you. I know you are a great football team, probably the greatest ever assembled. Go out there on the field now and show them, show the world.' We almost broke down the door."

Well, they did show the world and it took only 55

The Morning After

The events of the day offered the opportunity for many memorable quotes. After the carnage was over, here are a few that are worth remembering.

Sammy Baugh, when asked if the outcome might have been different had end Charley Malone not muffed what appeared to be a touchdown pass in the first quarter with the score a mere 7-0, Bears: "Hell, yes, the score would have been 73-6."

Bob Considine, noted New York newspaper columnist: "The Chicago Bears massacred the Washington Redskins 73-0 yesterday. . . . The unluckiest guy in the crowd was the five-buck bettor who took the Redskins and 70 points."

Bill Stern, the most famous sports radio broadcaster of the day: "It got so bad that, toward the end, the Bears had to give up place-kicking the extra points and try passes instead because all the footballs booted into the stands were being kept by the spectators as souvenirs, and they were down to their last ball."

Red Smith, in his column "Sports of the Times" for the New York Times: "George Preston Marshall, the mettlesome laundryman who owned the Redskins, looked on from the stands—except when he turned his back to charge up the aisle and throw a punch at a dissatisfied customer—and when his ordeal was over, every hair in his raccoon coat had turned white."

And a wag in the pressbox, when the final gun signaled a merciful end to the slaughter, with a look of horror on his face, turned to the reporter sitting next to him and said, "My God, Marshall just shot himself!"

seconds to implant the idea. Halas tested the Washington defense with a few plays and quickly ascertained it was the same one the Redskins had used so effectively three weeks earlier. Only this time, the Bears had prepared to cope with it. Halas countered with a fake to McAfee, who the Redskins

The 1940 Final Standings	Won	Lost	Tied
Eastern Division			
Washington Redskins	9	2	0
Brooklyn Dodgers	8	3	0
New York Giants	6	4	1
Pittsburgh Pirates	2	7	2
Philadelphia Eagles	1	10	1
Western Division			
Chicago Bears	8	3	0
Green Bay Packers	6	4	1
Detroit Lions	5	5	1
Cleveland Rams	4	6	1
Chicago Cardinals	2	7	2

NFL Championship Game

Bears	21	7	26	19	—	73
Redskins	0	0	0	0	—	0

1941 Champion Chicago Bears

Position	Player
LE	Dick Plasman
LT	Ed Kolman
LG	Danny Fortmann
C	Bulldog Turner
RG	Ray Bray
RT	Lee Artoe
RE	John Siegal
QB	Sid Luckman
LH	Ray Nolting
RH	Hugh Gallarneau
FB	Norm Standlee

were keyed on, and had Luckman pitch out to Bill Osmanski going the other way. Osmanski broke away and, with a great block from end George Wilson, ran 68 yards for a touchdown, 7-0 Bears.

The "crybabies" followed with 66 more unanswered points. The result was the most devastating defeat of any team in any game in NFL history, 73-0 when the final gun echoed through Griffith Stadium. Halas met the press after the game and, with a wry smile and, surely, thoughts of a stewing, mortified George Preston Marshall, said, "It was just one of those days. Everything we did, we did right. Everything they did, they did wrong."

·1941·

The Bears, after what they did to the Redskins in the 1940 title game, came into the season with a reputation. Bert Bell, new owner of the Pittsburgh Steelers, said, "Nobody's going to beat the Bears. They're simply the greatest football team ever assembled."

It was at the start of the 1941 season that the Bears acquired the nickname "Monsters of the Midway," laid on them by a New York writer who somehow thought they played their games or at least practiced out on the Midway Plaisance of the University of Chicago. Whatever the origin, the nickname was a good one, Halas loved it, and Chicago kept it forever.

The Bears lived up to their new nickname. They surged through the season, averaging 36 points a game and outscoring their opponents 396 to 147. They lost only one game during the regular season, a 16-14 setback against the Packers, but they ran up scores against other NFL teams that were embarrassing. They ended

The 1941 Final Standings	Won	Lost	Tied
Eastern Division			
New York Giants	8	3	0
Brooklyn Dodgers	7	4	0
Washington Redskins	6	5	0
Philadelphia Eagles	2	8	1
Pittsburgh Steelers	1	9	1
Western Division			
Chicago Bears	10	1	0
Green Bay Packers	10	1	0
Detroit Lions	4	6	1
Chicago Cardinals	3	7	1
Cleveland Rams	2	9	0

Western Division Playoff game

Packers	7	0	7	0	—	14
Bears	6	24	0	3	—	33

NFL Championship Game

Giants	6	0	3	0	–	9
Bears	3	6	14	14	–	37

the regular season with a record of 10-1.

The last game of the season was played on the day the Japanese bombed Pearl Harbor, and it was crucial to the Bears because the ever-painful Packers had lost only one game during the season. The Bears had to win and they were facing the Cardinals who, even though they were awful that year, were always a problem because of the intra-city rivalry. Despite the fact the Bears had destroyed them earlier, 53-7, Halas was worried about the south-siders, but the Bears won easily, 34-24.

It left them in a tie with the Packers for the NFL East divisional title. Green Bay had the best end in the business, Don Hutson, and other future Hall of Famers like Clarke Hinkle and Tony Canadeo in their back-field as well as the game's leading passer that year, Cecil Isbell.

The showdown was at Wrigley Field, a special playoff game to determine the victor in the NFL West. Rabid football fans along with the rest of the nation were wrapped up in the fact that the United States was now officially at war, but still more than 43,000 showed up at Wrigley Field on a frigid

---

Scoring, Scoring

In the 73-0 annihilation of the Redskins on December 8, 1940, 10 different Bears scored the 11 touchdowns, and, counting extra points, a total of 15 Bears put points on the scoreboard that afternoon. Here is how it went.

First Half:

Bill Osmanski runs 68 yards for a touchdown. Jack Manders kicks extra point

Sid Luckman scores on quarterback sneak. Bob Snyder kicks extra point.

Joe Maniaci runs 42 yards for a touchdown. Phil Martinovich kicks extra point.

Ken Kavanaugh catches a 30-yard TD pass from Luckman. Snyder kicks extra point.

Second Half:

Hampton Pool returns an interception 15 yards for a touchdown. Dick Plasman kicks extra point.

Ray Nolting runs 23 yards for a touchdown. Plasman misses extra point.

George McAfee intercepts and runs 35 yards for a touchdown. Joe Stydahar kicks extra point.

Bulldog Turner returns an interception 20 yards for a touchdown. Joe Maniaci's extra point is blocked.

Harry Clark, on a double reverse, runs 44 yards for a touchdown. Gary Famiglietti misses the extra point.

Famiglietti carries it in from the two for a touchdown. Maniaci catches a pass from Solly Sherman for the extra point.

Harry Clark plunges in from the one for the final touchdown. A Bob Snyder to Maniaci pass for the extra point is incomplete.

Later, after looking at the day's stats, George Halas remarked, *"A number of missed extra points. And looking over the movies, I can see where we should have scored another touchdown."*

December 14 afternoon to see who would win the NFL title game.

The Packers got on the scoreboard quickly, but the issue was just as quickly decided after that. Hugh Gallarneau returned a punt 81 yards for a Bear touchdown. Three more scores in swift succession gave Chicago a 30-7 halftime lead, and the Packers were never in the game again. The final, Bears 33, Packers 14.

So, the New York Giants, winners of the NFL East with a record of 8-3, came to Chicago to determine who would wear the NFL crown for 1941.

A crowd of only 13,341 attended, the smallest ever in the history of the NFL championship game, despite the fact the temperature was an unseasonably warm 47 degrees, Maybe it was because it was just a few days before Christmas or that the worries of the new war were overriding.

At any rate, it was a much better contest than the play-off game a week earlier, at least through the first half. The Giants hung in and scored six points while Bear field goal kicker Bob Snyder put nine points on the board for Chicago. In the second half, however, the newly-nicknamed Monsters of the Midway awoke from hibernation. Two touchdowns by fullback Norm Standlee, another by halfback George

127

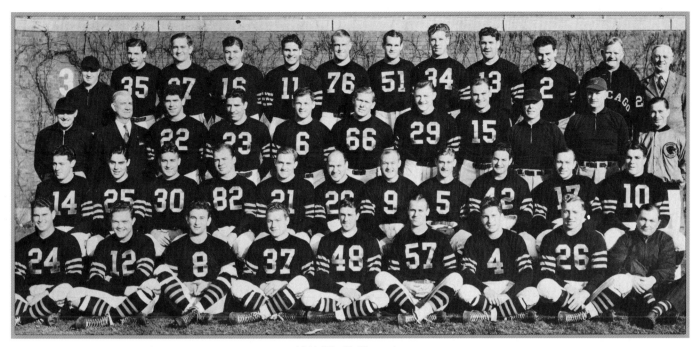

1941 World Champions

McAfee and a 42-yard fumble return by end Ken Kavanaugh along with an inspired defense resulted in a final score of 37-9.

The Bears had become the first team in NFL history to win back-to-back championships since the title game was instituted in 1933.

·1943·

The war was in full swing and NFL rosters had been depleted considerably with players going off to serve in the military. The effect on the Eagles and the Steelers was so great that they were forced to combine into one team which took the name Phil-Pitt Steagles. And the Bears lured 34-year-old Bronko Nagurski down from Minnesota to rejoin the team after he had retired in 1937.

George Halas was serving in the Navy and had turned the head coaching duties over to former Bears Hunk Anderson, who handled the defense, and Luke Johnsos, the offense. The Bears were favored to win

1943 Champion Chicago Bears

Position	Player
LE	Jim Benton
LT	Dominic Sigillo
LG	Danny Fortmann
C	Bulldog Turner
RG	George Musso
RT	Al Hoptowit
RE	George Wilson
QB	Sid Luckman
LH	Harry Clark
RH	Dante Magnani
FB	Bob Masters

The 1943 Final Standings	Won	Lost	Tied
Eastern Division			
Washington Redskins	6	3	1
New York Giants	6	3	1
Phil-Pitt Steagles	5	4	1
Brooklyn Dodgers	2	8	0
Western Division			
Chicago Bears	8	1	0
Green Bay Packers	7	2	1
Detroit Lions	3	6	1
Chicago Cardinals	0	10	0

NFL Championship Game

Redskins	0	7	7	7	21
Bears	0	14	13	14	41

The Bronk Came Back

Fourth quarter . . . Bears losing by 10 in the last game of the season . . . a game they needed to clinch the division title. Bronko Nagurski, 34, in the lineup as a tackle after having been out of the game since 1937. The Bears, in desperation put him at his old fullback position.

William Goldman, author and screenwriter, summed it up better than anyone in his novel *Magic*.

He's comin' in, the Bronko. The Bronko. And I sat there thinking omijesus, what a great spot for a legend to be in, coming back after so many years, one quarter to play, the title on the line, and ten points behind. . . .

And then the crowd started screaming like nothin' you ever heard because on the bench he stood up. Nagurski. And he reached for his helmet. . .

Well, everybody knew they were going to give the ball to Bronko . . . and if you're smart and everybody knows what you're going to do, well, you don't do it, you fake it and do something else and when they came out of the huddle and when they lined up with Nagurski at fullback and Luckman at quarterback well it had to be a decoy thing. . . . Only it wasn't no decoy. . . . they gave it to him and he put it under his arm and just kind of ran slow, straight into the Cardinal line. They were all waiting for him. And Nagurski tried, you could see that, but they just picked him up, the Cardinals did, and for one second they just held him on their shoulders. . . .

He kind of got up and shook himself off and went back into the huddle and out the Bears come again and this Luckman, he hands the ball to Nagurski and he lumbers up and they're waiting, only this time he falls forward for eight . . . . First down.

But it was starting to get a little eerie on the field. You could see the Cardinal linemen slapping each other on the asses and the Bears come out again and this time they did fake and the pass was good for another first down and the next play was Nagurski kind of slipping down for six. He was like an ax hitting a tree. It doesn't matter how big the tree is, when the ax starts coming, you better look out.

Now the Bears were inside the twenty. And there wasn't any doubt about what was gonna happen. It was gonna be the Bronko up the middle, and all these Cards, they bunched, waiting, and sure enough, here he comes, and they hit him and he hits them and for a second they did what they could but then he bursts through and he's doing five, six, eight, and then they knock him down and he's crawling—crawling for the goal, and everybody's screaming and there's a Cardinal on his back, trying to make him stop but he can't, he can't, and finally about six guys jumped him at the one and stop him short of the TD.

But they were scared now. They knew he was coming and they knew there wasn't anything they could do about it, and they waved their fists and tried to get steamed up but old Bronko, he just lined up behind the quarterback and the quarterback give him the ball and they're all waiting . . . and this old man starts forward and they're braced and he jumps sideways at them, the old man flies at them and they parted like water and he was through and the rest of the game was nothing, the Bears slaughter them behind the Bronko. . . .

the NFL East, but the Green Bay Packers gave them a run for it until the last game of the season.

It was a game that seemed like such a simple thing. The Bears merely had to beat their crosstown rivals, the Cardinals, who were winless at 0-9. But at the end of the third quarter, the Bears were losing 24-14. On came Nagurski, who had been playing tackle. He moved now to fullback and put on a remarkable per-

formance, destroying the Cardinal defense as he ran on aged legs. In the fourth quarter he carried the ball 16 times and gained 84 yards. The Bears rebounded to win 35-24 and clinch the division title.

If the game to get them to the championship was Nagurski's, the title game belonged to Sid Luckman. The Washington Redskins came to Chicago to face the Bears for the crown for the third time in four

Championship game, 1943; Bears 41, Redskins 21.

years—another classic Sid Luckman-Sammy Baugh encounter. In this one, however, Baugh went to the bench with a concussion after the first play of the game, and Luckman shone.

The Redskins managed to score the first touchdown of the day, but after that it was all Chicago—Luckman threw five touchdown passes and was 15 of 26 for 286 yards. Again, Nagurski moved to fullback when he was needed and scored a touchdown, his last in the NFL, a three-yard plunge in the second quarter.

The Bears turned a 14-7 halftime score into a 41-21 rout. And they could claim three world championships in four years.

·1946·

The war was over. George Halas was back after more than three years in the Navy and comfortably resettled in place as head coach. The Bears were coming off a disappointing season, 3-7, the worst in the team's then 26-year history. Halas shrugged that off and predicted not just a turnaround, but a winner.

Many great players were coming back from military service but the brand-new All-America Football

1943 World Champions

1946 Champion Chicago Bears

Position	Player
LE	Ken Kavanaugh
LT	Fred Davis
LG	Rudy Mucha
C	Bulldog Turner
RG	Ray Bray
RT	Mike Jarmoluk
RE	George Wilson
QB	Sid Luckman
LH	Dante Magnani
RH	Hugh Gallarneau
FB	Bill Osmanski

Conference (AAFC) founded by Chicago Tribune sports columnist Arch Ward was trying to capture many of them along with a lot of pro football fans. Chicago, the only city that had maintained two NFL teams, now had another to contend with, the Rockets in the AAFC. There were offers to Sid Luckman, George McAfee and Bulldog Turner—the Bears' three most famous players—to defect to the new league. All three turned the AAFC down and a confident George Halas went into the season determined to carry out his pledge.

They had little trouble conquering the NFL

The 1946 Final Standings	Won	Lost	Tied		
Eastern Division					
New York Giants	7	3	1		
Philadelphia Eagles	6	5	0		
Washington Redskins	5	5	1		
Pittsburgh Steelers	5	5	1		
Boston Yanks	2	8	1		
Western Division					
Chicago Bears	8	2	1		
Los Angeles Rams	6	4	1		
Green Bay Packers	6	5	0		
Chicago Cardinals	6	5	0		
Detroit Lions	1	10	0		
NFL Championship Game					
Bears	14	0	0	10	—	24
Giants	7	0	7	0	—	14

West, winning eight of 11 games, losing two and tying one. The Giants were a little more pressed in the East but managed to take it with a record of 7-3-1. One of the Bears' two losses, however, had been a 14-0 embarrassment at the hands of the Giants, a shutout in a year the team had otherwise averaged almost 30 points a game.

Then, on the eve of the championship match at the Polo Grounds in New York, a scandal broke. Frank Filchock, New York's tailback, and fullback Merle Hapes were accused of being involved with gamblers in

BINGO-KEEP-IT

The play in the fourth quarter that decided the 1946 NFL championship game was a little piece of razzle-dazzle that was not in the ordinary Bear game plan. Sid Luckman later described it.

We had a play called Bingo-Keep-It, where I ran with the ball. Halas didn't like me to run with the ball too often. We had practiced it during the regular season although we never used it. But this was the championship game.

Bingo worked like this. We had George McAfee at halfback and he was such a tremendous threat as a runner, the best breakaway back in the game. He had been running well off left end all day in that championship game, and the Giants were constantly looking for him. So, in the middle of the fourth quarter, with the score tied and a crucial play coming up, I took a time-out and went over to talk to Coach Halas on the sideline. I said, "Now?" He knew the play I meant. We'd actually talked it over before the game.

He nodded, "Now."

So I went back out and called Bingo-Keep-It. When I got the snap, I faked to McAfee and he headed off around left end with the Giants in wild pursuit. I just tucked the ball against my leg and danced around right end. I got two great blocks from (Bulldog) Turner and (Ray) Bray and went the 19 yards for a touchdown. It was one of the few times in my life I ran for a touchdown, and it's one of my greatest memories.

Halas said later, "It was a great play, perfectly executed. As a reward, I let Sid play defense for a while after it, and darned if he didn't intercept a pass."

1946 World Champions

a bribery plot to throw the game. Both players had declined to take part but made the mistake of not reporting the offer to the league or their coach. Hapes was suspended, but Filchock was allowed to play.

Filchock tried his best. As his coach, Steve Owen, later wrote, "It was not for lack of effort by Filchcock. The boy's nose was broken early in the game, but he kept on fighting through every play with blood and mud coating his face and uniform. In his heart he hoped the past would be forgotten."

The Bears, however, were equally dedicated that afternoon. Luckman threw a touchdown pass to Ken Kavanaugh and Dante Magnani picked off a Filchock pass and ran it back for a touchdown in the first quarter. The Giants fought back and by the fourth quarter the score was tied at 14-14. Then the Bears pulled one out of the small print of their playbook, a perfect bootleg and Luckman carried it in for what was the winning score. A field goal from Frank Maznicki added the bow to the gift-wrapped package. The Bears triumphed, 24-14, and had their seventh NFL championship.

· 1963 ·

The football year began with a simple statement from George Halas at training camp, "If we're going to win this thing, we have to beat Green Bay twice." No easy feat. The Packers, under Vince Lombardi, had won the NFL title the year before and had a team which boasted such future Hall of Famers as Bart Starr, Jim Taylor, Ray Nitschke, Willie Davis, Forrest Gregg, Herb Adderley and Willie Wood. The one star they did not have however, was Paul Hornung, suspended for the year because of gambling.

The Pack was a heavy favorite to repeat in the NFL West, but what the oddsmakers failed to take into consideration was the Bear defense—and defense, according to many football scholars, is what prevails in the final analysis.

The Bears had their first shot at the Packers on opening day in hostile Green Bay. The defense held the Pack to a field goal that afternoon and the offense provided 10 points. It was the first time the Bears had defeated Green Bay since opening day 1960. One down, one to go, according to Halas.

The Bears won their first five games in a row that season, allowing their opponents an average of less than 10 points in each. An upset loss to the 49ers in San Francisco interrupted three more successive wins before they faced the Packers again, but this time it was in the friendlier confines of Wrigley Field.

132

When the two teams met on November 17, both had identical records of 8-1. Even though there were four games remaining, this was the one. Again it was the defense . . . which held the Packers scoreless through three quarters while the offense responded with 26 points. The final: Bears 26, Packers 7.

The Bears were then held to two 17-17 ties and won their last two games to round out the season with a record of 11-1-2. The Packers finished 11-2-1. George Halas had proven a true soothsayer back in training camp.

So the Bears earned the way to their first NFL championship game since 1956, and it was against the same team they had faced then, the New York Giants, who had rung up a record of 11-3 in the NFL East.

The Giants, behind the passing of Y. A. Tittle and the running of Frank Gifford, were a 10-point favorite when they came to Chicago. It was bitterly cold when New York—the best offense in the NFL—took the field against Chicago—the best defense in football.

It was a classic confrontation, and it was defense that prevailed that frigid afternoon.

Interceptions by end Ed O'Bradovich and linebacker Larry Morris set up two touchdowns for the Bears, both scored on quarterback sneaks by Bill Wade. True to regular season form, the Bear defense allowed only 10 points. The final: Bears 14, Giants 10.

The game ball was awarded to defensive coordinator George Allen.

Packer coach Vince Lombardi, who was in the stands, said, "They beat up the Giants. I'm happy for Papa George, he's a helluva guy."

Papa George told the players in the locker room, they were a helluva team.

The 1963 Final Standings	Won	Lost	Tied
Eastern Conference			
New York Giants	11	3	0
Cleveland Browns	10	4	0
St. Louis Cardinals	9	5	0
Pittsburgh Steelers	7	4	3
Dallas Cowboys	4	10	0
Washington Redskins	3	11	0
Philadelphia Eagles	2	10	2
Western Conference			
Chicago Bears	11	1	2
Green Bay Packers	11	2	1
Baltimore Colts	8	6	0
Detroit Lions	5	8	1
Minnesota Vikings	5	8	1
Los Angeles Rams	5	9	0
San Francisco 49ers	2	12	0

NFL Championship Game

Giants	7	3	0	0	10
Bears	7	0	7	0	14

1963 Champion Chicago Bears

Offense Position	Player	Defense Position	Player
WR	Bo Farrington	LDE	Ed O'Bradovich
LT	Herman Lee	LDT	Stan Jones
LG	Ted Karras	RDT	Fred Williams
C	Mike Pyle	RDE	Doug Atkins
RG	Roger Davis	LLB	Joe Fortunato
RT	Bob Wetoska	MLB	Bill George
TE	Mike Ditka	RLB	Larry Morris
FL	Johnny Morris	LCB	Bennie McRae
QB	Bill Wade	RCB	Dave Whitsell
RB	Willie Galimore	S	Richie Petitbon
RB	Joe Marconi	S	Roosevelt Taylor

1963 World Champions

When I think of "The Game," many different thoughts go racing through my mind: the red, white and blue bunting hanging from the Wrigley Field facade, the intense cold, seeing the Giants face-to-face in the pre-game warm-ups, the terrible nauseating feeling of anxiety in the pit of my stomach just before the kickoff.

But then, the moment that so clearly stands out, Y. A. Tittle's long, high pass into the end zone with just seconds left to play in the game. I can still see my old roommate Richie Petitbon jumping for the ball with outstretched arms. All I could think was, "My God, if he catches it, we win!" And he did catch it, and we did win.

—Tackle Bob Wetoska

Almost . . .

The Bears played in four NFL championship games they did not win besides the six official and one unofficial title contests in which they were triumphant.

· 1934 NFL Championship Game ·

Bears	0	10	3	0	13
Giants	3	0	0	27	30

This was the year the Bears went undefeated in the regular season, 13-0, the first team ever to accomplish that feat. They had faced the New York Giants the year before and defeated them for the title. But this time they were not prepared for an additional opponent, the frozen field of the Polo Grounds.

Both teams slipped and slid all over during the first three quarters and the Bears had built a 13-3 lead on a Bronko Nagurski one-yard touchdown run and two field goals from Jack Manders. In the fourth quarter, however, the Giants wore basketball sneakers, which made a world of difference. They no longer slipped and slid on the ice-covered turf and scored 27 unanswered points.

The final: Giants 30, Bears 13, which ever since has been known as the "Sneakers Championship."

· 1937 NFL Championship Game ·

Redskins	7	0	21	0	28
Bears	14	0	7	0	21

Sammy Baugh was a rookie and the Redskins were playing their first season in Washington after having moved down from Boston. The Bears had gone 9-1-1 in the regular season in the NFL West while the Skins were 8-3 in the East.

The Bears were considered the favorite and they jumped out to a 14-7 lead in the first quarter on two touchdowns scored by halfback Jack Manders, but Baugh came to life in the third quarter and threw three touchdown passes.

With the score 28-21 in the fourth quarter, the Bears twice had drives into Washington territory, but both times the Redskins stopped them, and the game ended with neither team scoring in the final period.

· 1942 NFL Championship Game ·

Bears	0	6	0	0	6
Redskins	0	7	7	0	14

The Bears had won the NFL title two years in a row coming into this championship game. They had demolished the Redskins 73-0 in 1940 and the Giants 37-9 in 1941. The Bears were a 22-point favorite.

Chicago had once again gone undefeated in the regular season, 11-0, to breeze through the NFL West, while the Redskins won easily in the East with a 10-1-1 record. George Halas had left in mid-season for military duty in the U. S. Navy and the team was coached by Hunk Anderson and Luke Johnsos. Still, they had Sid Luckman, Bulldog Turner and Danny Fortmann on the field as well as quite a few other stars.

Chicago took the lead in the second quarter when tackle Lee Artoe returned a fumble 50 yards for a touchdown. Sammy Baugh countered with a touchdown pass but the Bears had missed the extra point and therefore trailed 7-6 at the half. Both teams scored a touchdown in the second half, but only one counted, Washington's. Hugh Gallarneau's touchdown run for the Bears was nullified by a penalty.

The Skins pulled off the biggest upset up to that point in NFL championship game history.

· 1956 NFL Championship Game ·

Bears	0	7	0	0	7
Giants	13	21	6	7	47

The Bears had not been to an NFL championship game in a decade. They had fought their way through the division and ended up on top with a 9-2-1 record just ahead of the 9-3 Detroit Lions. In the NFL East, the Giants, with a record of 8-3-1, had nosed out the Chicago Cardinals.

The game was considered a toss-up. At Yankee Stadium, the day was reminiscent of the one when the Bears lost the "Sneakers Championship" in 1934. The ground was frozen. This time, however, both teams wore rubber-soled shoes instead of cleats.

They did not help the Bears, however. The Giants scored on their first possession and ran up a 34-7 half-time lead. The touchdown run by Rick Casares was the only score the Bears could put on the board that frigid day in New York.

ALL-DECADE TEAMS

For the 75th anniversary of the Chicago Bears, we conducted a poll of
pro football historians, sportswriters and broadcasters, and other authorities
on the history of the team to determine All-Decade team honors.
The following are the Bear honorees.
An asterisk (*) indicates there was a tie in the voting.

1920s

Position	Player	Bears Career
End	George Halas	1920–1929
End	Duke Hanny	1922–1927
Tackle	Ed Healey	1922–1927
Tackle	Link Lyman	1926–1928, 1930–1931, 1933–1934
Guard	Hunk Anderson	1922–1927
Guard	Jim McMillen	1924–1929
Center	George Trafton	1920–1932
Quarterback	Joey Sternaman	1922–1925, 1927–1930
Halfback	Paddy Driscoll	1920, 1926–1929
Halfback	Red Grange	1925, 1929–1934
Fullback	Buck White	1923–1925, 1927–1929
Kicker	Paddy Driscoll	1920, 1926–1929

LYMAN

1930s

Position	Player	Bears Career
End	Luke Johnsos	1929–1936, 1938
End	Bill Hewitt	1932–1936
Tackle	George Musso	1933–1944
Tackle	Joe Stydahar	1936–1942, 1945–1946
Guard	Joe Kopcha	1929, 1932–1935
Guard	Danny Fortmann	1936–1943
Center	Ookie Miller	1932–1936
Quarterback	Carl Brumbaugh	1930–1934, 1936, 1938
Halfback	Red Grange	1925, 1929–1934
Halfback	Beattie Feathers	1934–1937
Fullback	Bronko Nagurski	1930–1937, 1943
Kicker	Jack Manders	1933–1940

MANDERS

1940s

Position	Player	Bears Career
End	Ken Kavanaugh	1940–1941, 1945–1950
End	Ed Sprinkle	1944–1955
Tackle	Joe Stydahar	1936–1942, 1945–1946
Tackle	Fred Davis	1946–1951
Guard	Danny Fortmann	1936–1943
Guard	Ray Bray	1939–1942, 1946–1951
Center	Bulldog Turner	1940–1952
Quarterback	Sid Luckman	1939–1950
Halfback	George McAfee	1940–1941, 1945–1950
Halfback	Hugh Gallarneau	1941–1942, 1945–1947
Fullback	Bill Osmanski	1939–1943, 1946–1947
Place Kicker	Johnny Lujack	1948–1951
Punter*	Sid Luckman	1939–1950
Punter*	George Gulyanics	1947–1952

GALLARNEAU

1950s OFFENSE

Position	Player	Bears Career
End	Bill McColl	1952–1959
End	Harlon Hill	1954–1961
Tackle	George Connor	1948–1955
Tackle	Bill Wightkin	1950–1957
Guard	Herman Clark	1952, 1954–1957
Guard	Stan Jones	1954–1965
Center	Larry Strickland	1954–1959
Quarterback	Ed Brown	1954–1961
Halfback	Bobby Watkins	1955–1957
Halfback	Willie Galimore	1957–1963
Fullback	Rick Casares	1954–1964
Place Kicker	George Blanda	1949–1958

HILL

1950s DEFENSE

Position	Player	Bears Career
Defensive End	Ed Sprinkle	1944–1955
Defensive End	Doug Atkins	1955–1966
Defensive Tackle	Fred Williams	1952–1963
Defensive Tackle	Bill Bishop	1952–1960
Linebacker	George Connor	1948–1955
Linebacker	Bill George	1952–1965
Linebacker	Joe Fortunato	1955–1966
Defensive Back	Don Kindt	1947–1955
Defensive Back	Johnny Lujack	1948–1951
Defensive Back	J. C. Caroline	1956–1965
Defensive Back	Erich Barnes	1958–1960
Punter	Ed Brown	1954–1961

CAROLINE

137

1960s OFFENSE

Position	Player	Bears Career
Wide Receiver	Johnny Morris	1958–1967
Wide Receiver	Dick Gordon	1965–1971
Tight End	Mike Ditka	1961–1966
Tackle	Herm Lee	1958–1966
Tackle	Bob Wetoska	1960–1969
Guard	Stan Jones	1954–1965
Guard	Jim Cadile	1962–1972
Center	Mike Pyle	1961–1969
Quarterback	Bill Wade	1961–1966
Running Back	Gale Sayers	1965–1971
Running Back	Ronnie Bull	1962–1970
Place Kicker	Roger Leclerc	1960–1966

CADILE

1960s DEFENSE

Position	Player	Bears Career
Defensive End	Doug Atkins	1955–1966
Defensive End	Ed O'Bradovich	1961–1972
Defensive Tackle	Earl Leggett	1957–1960, 1962–1965
Defensive Tackle	Stan Jones	1954–1965
Linebacker	Bill George	1952–1965
Linebacker*	Joe Fortunato	1955–1966
Linebacker*	Larry Morris	1959–1965
Linebacker	Dick Butkus	1965–1973
Defensive Back	Richie Petitbon	1959–1968
Defensive Back	Rosey Taylor	1961–1969
Defensive Back	Dave Whitsell	1961–1966
Defensive Back	Bennie McRae	1962–1970
Punter	Bobby Joe Green	1963–1973

WHITSELL

1970s OFFENSE

Position	Player	Bears Career
Wide Receiver	James Scott	1976–1980, 1982–1983
Wide Receiver	Brian Baschnagel	1976–1984
Tight End	Greg Latta	1975–1980
Tackle	Dennis Lick	1976–1981
Tackle	Ted Albrecht	1977–1981
Guard	Revie Sorey	1975–1981, 1983
Guard	Noah Jackson	1975–1983
Center	Dan Neal	1975–1983
Quarterback	Bob Avellini	1975–1984
Running Back	Walter Payton	1975–1987
Running Back	Roland Harper	1975–1978, 1980–1982
Place Kicker	Bob Thomas	1975–1984

JACKSON

138

1970s DEFENSE

Position	Player	Bears Career
Defensive End	Willie Holman	1968–1973
Defensive End	Mike Hartenstine	1975–1985
Defensive Tackle	Jim Osborne	1972–1984
Defensive Tackle	Wally Chambers	1973–1977
Linebacker	Dick Butkus	1965–1973
Linebacker	Doug Buffone	1966–1979
Linebacker	Waymond Bryant	1974–1977
Defensive Back	Allan Ellis	1973–1977, 1979–1980
Defensive Back	Virgil Livers	1975–1979
Defensive Back	Doug Plank	1975–1982
Defensive Back	Gary Fencik	1976–1985
Punter	Bob Parsons	1972–1983

LIVERS

1980s OFFENSE

Position	Player	Bears Career
Wide Receiver	Willie Gault	1983–1987
Wide Receiver	Dennis McKinnon	1983–1988
Tight End	Emery Moorehead	1981–1988
Tackle	Keith Van Horne	1981–1993
Tackle	Jim Covert	1983–1990
Guard	Mark Bortz	1983–1993
Guard	Tom Thayer	1985–1992
Center	Jay Hilgenberg	1981–1991
Quarterback	Jim McMahon	1982–1988
Running Back	Walter Payton	1975–1987
Running Back	Neal Anderson	1986–1993
Place Kicker	Kevin Butler	1985–1993

THAYER

1980s DEFENSE

Position	Player	Bears Career
Defensive End	Al Harris	1979–1987
Defensive End	Richard Dent	1983–1993
Defensive Tackle	Dan Hampton	1979–1990
Defensive Tackle	Steve McMichael	1981–1993
Linebacker	Otis Wilson	1980–1987
Linebacker	Mike Singletary	1981–1992
Linebacker	Wilber Marshall	1984–1987
Defensive Back	Gary Fencik	1976–1987
Defensive Back	Todd Bell	1981–1986
Defensive Back	Dave Duerson	1983–1988
Defensive Back	Shaun Gayle	1984–1993
Punter	Maury Buford	1985–1989

DUERSON

"My boy, my pride in you has no bounds.
You were the consummate player."
—George Halas

FOURTEEN

SID LUCKMAN

The scene: a flat in Brooklyn, the kitchen. The year, early 1939. The characters: a young All-American football player; his wife, a beauty named Estelle; and a jut-jawed older man who had a deal to offer.

Sid Luckman was the young man. He had just completed his college career, playing tailback for Columbia under the widely respected coach Lou Little. The other man in the kitchen was George Halas, who was planning on changing the offense of the Chicago Bears from the single wing to the T formation with a man in motion. He needed a quarterback who could lead the team in this new and more complex scheme, a ballhandler who could pass, run, make instant on-field decisions, read defenses . . . all the prerequisites for the much more wide-open offense he wanted to employ. Halas felt the young Luckman was the player who could handle it.

Luckman, however,

told Halas that he had no intention of playing pro football. He said he had been offered a good job after graduation and, besides, he added, as an Ivy League player, he probably was not good enough to play in the pros. Luckman thought the discussion was over.

But Halas was insistent. In Luckman's words: "He was the salesman, and the buyer. He came back several times. The last time we met was in our little apartment in New York. Estelle made dinner for the three of us. He gave me his spiel, he told me what just might happen if we did it together, the championships, the competition, all that kind of stuff. He got me to rethink my future.

"After dinner, he made me a fair and equitable offer. He had the contract with him, already made out, and handed it to me. I signed it. Then he walked around the table and kissed Estelle on the cheek. He sat back down and lifted up a glass of

Sid Luckman signing his contract with George Halas in 1939.

wine and said, 'You and Jesus Christ are the only two people I'd ever pay that much money to.' I think it was $6,000."

The drama that then unfolded would change the course of professional football. Luckman apprenticed as a halfback on offense and defense in 1939, his first year with the Bears. Then came the transformation.

"It was very difficult," Luckman explains. "We worked very hard during the day, Coach Halas and Carl Brumbaugh (the Bears' aging former quarterback) and me. We would spend about two hours after each practice. There was all the spinning for handoffs or fakes, and new signal-calling. All the fundamentals were different from what I had played as a tailback. I'd go home and study the playbook with Estelle. I'd tell her I had to know what the guards and tackles were doing on each play, or what they were supposed to do. Coach Halas would call me up in the night and we would talk."

It all worked. Luckman became a T formation quarterback and proved over the next decade to be not only the first but one of the very best ever at the position. He proved immediately he could pass the football and, more importantly, run the offense, just what Halas had felt assured of a year earlier.

In 1940, the Bears came out with the Halas version of the T. They won the NFL championship that year by an unbelievable score of 73-0 over the Redskins in the title game. It was not really the T that won that game by such an astronomical score, but it was that year, that innovation, which changed the game forever. Other teams began picking it up because they knew it opened up the offense. At Washington, Sammy Baugh was converted from a tailback to a T quarterback. "It was the most difficult thing I ever had to do in my football career," Baugh said later. "Hell, I remember talking to Sid Luckman one time and he told me when he switched over to the T he darn near cried it was so frustrating. But he sure learned it, and we all just followed along."

Luckman played for the Bears through the 1950 season. During those 12 years he set record after

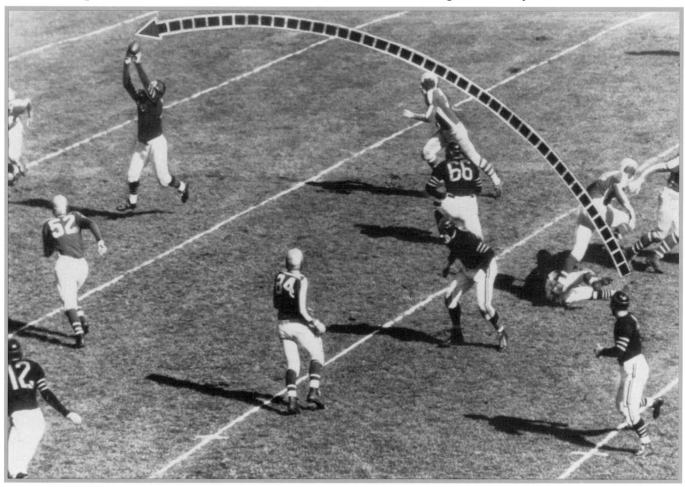

Sid Luckman connects with one of his many favorite receivers, Hampton Pool, against the Eagles in 1943.

142

record in the NFL. The teams he quarterbacked won four NFL championships and played in five title games. No one has ever thrown more touchdown passes in an NFL game than the seven he tossed against the Giants in 1943. He still holds many Bear passing records despite the increased emphasis on passing in the modern era and the fact that teams now play 16 games a season. When Luckman retired after the 1950 season he had completed 904 of 1,744 passes for 14,686 yards and 137 touchdowns. Luckman won All-Pro honors five times in an age of great quarterbacks like Baugh, Bob Waterfield and many others who had taken to the T. He was inducted into the Pro Football Hall of Fame in 1965 with the third class of enshrinees.

Luckman remained close to Halas and the Bears. He served as an assistant coach from 1954 through 1970.

In the last days of the life, Halas wrote Luckman a letter in which he said:

"My boy, my pride in you has no bounds. You were the consummate player. Remember our word, 'Now?' (referring to the Bingo-Keep-It play that won the 1946 NFL championship game). Every time I said it to you, you brought me another championship. You added a luster to my life that can never tarnish."

That meeting at that apartment in Brooklyn in 1939 was indeed an important one in the history of the Bears as well as the National Football League, and a deeply meaningful one for two men who today share space in the honored Hall in Canton, Ohio.

GREAT MOMENTS

There have been many great moments in the Bears' 75-year history—glittering performances, unforgettable games. Halas storming the sideline. A Butkus tackle, its impact echoing through Soldier Field. A dazzling, deer-like Sayers run, darting through defenders. A Payton catapult into the end zone over blockers and would-be tacklers. Singletary's eyes in deadly focus just before an enemy snap. The 73-0 avalanche in Washington in 1940. The 14-10 survival in the bitter cold of Wrigley Field for the '63 title. Super Bowl XX.

Here are a few of those great moments . . .

LUCKMAN'S DAY

It was almost not Sid Luckman's Day. On the train going out to New York in November 1943, the Bear quarterback was nursing a shoulder he injured the week before in a game against the Packers.

There was a lot of talk on the train about not playing him, it was not a game the 6-0-1 Bears really needed. "But I really wanted to play," Luckman said. "It was back in New York, my hometown, and it was supposed to be a special day."

It was.

Sunday, November 14, 1943, was designated "Sid Luckman Day" at the Polo Grounds. The New York football fans had not forgotten the young man who grew up in Brooklyn and played tailback so memorably for Columbia, even though he had changed his allegiance to Chicago after turning pro.

Before the game, the borough of Brooklyn presented him with a $1,000 U.S. war bond. His teammates had pitched in and presented him with another. His mother was in the stands. She rarely attended a game to watch Sid play—in high school, at Columbia, or in the NFL—because she was uneasy with the violence of the game of football and cringed every time he had his hands on the ball. "You can get hurt out there," she said.

His wife Estelle was there. So were many of his friends and old school chums from Brooklyn.

There was no way he was going to miss this game.

"The day of the game the shoulder was still sore as could be." Luckman said, "but our trainer, Andy Lotshaw, put some hot liniment on it and gave me a little shot to dull the pain. And so I said, 'Let's give it a try.'"

And that's when it truly became Sid Luckman's day, or, in his words, "It was like a miracle out there." He threw a touchdown pass to end Jim Benton . . . then one to Connie Mack Berry . . . then one to Hampton Pool . . . another to Harry Clark . . . one to Dante Magnani. Five touchdown passes, and he was brought back to the bench to rest his shoulder. Co-coach Luke Johnsos telephoned down from the press box. He told co-coach Hunk Anderson that Luckman was only one touchdown pass away from the NFL record set by the Redskins' Sammy Baugh two weeks earlier.

So Luckman went back out on the field and tossed one to end George Wilson. Somehow, word of the accomplishment spread through the stands at the Polo

Grounds. And a chant went up: "Break it, Break it." And this was New York, home of the Giants, not Chicago.

With the game drawing to a close, Luckman dropped back, rolled out of the pocket and let fly with a 40-yarder to Pool, his seventh touchdown pass of the day.

The Bears won that day 56-7. Luckman set the NFL record of seven TD passes in a game, a record that has been matched but not surpassed. He set another NFL record by passing for 433 yards, 100 more than the previous record held by Cecil Isbell of the Packers.

When a reporter asked Luckman's mother about her son and his record performance, her reply was, "Oh, it's been a nice day, but I just wish they didn't give the ball to Sid so much."

HILL'S DAY

Wide receivers on the Bears, at least in the old days, were like pawns on a chessboard. The big pieces were the running backs, guys like Grange, Nagurski, Casares, Galimore . . . and the monstrous defenders like Turner, Connor, Atkins.

But there was one day when a wide receiver turned that all around. Harlon Hill was one of those serendipitous finds, an end who had played for tiny Florence State Teachers College in Alabama and was acquired by the Bears in 1954. He could catch the ball and run with it. George Halas said , "When I first saw him at training camp he reminded me of Don Hutson (the Green Bay Packer legendary end)."

In his rookie year, Hill led the NFL in touchdown pass receptions, 12, and became the first Bear pass receiver to gain over 1,000 yards—1,124. Hill broke the single season record of 910 yards Jim Keane had set back in 1947.

On one afternoon in 1954, Hill caught seven passes for a total of 214 yards. No Bear had ever come close to amassing that much yardage on pass receptions. In club history, the 200-yard milestone has only been broached one other time, when Johnny Morris gained 201 on ten catches in 1962.

Hill's day, however, was one of the great ones, and one of the most exciting games in team history, a storybook ending for both Hill and the Bears.

The Bears were 3-2 when they met the 49ers out at Kezar Stadium in San Francisco in 1954. The 49ers, with players like Y. A. Tittle, Hugh McElhenny, and Leo Nomellini, were 4-0-1. Both teams felt they had a shot at the reigning Western Conference champion

Detroit Lions, and this game was a crucial one.

The Bears had shifted to a passing attack that day, and in the first three quarters, George Blanda kept finding Hill, three times for touchdowns. With less than a minute to go in the game, the sky dark and a typical San Francisco wind whipping around the field, the score was tied at 24, but the 49ers had gotten into field goal position. Gordie Soltau booted it through the uprights and the fans began to head for the exits.

Nobody paid much attention to the ensuing kickoff, a short one that Bear end Ed Sprinkle fielded and carried out of bounds to stop the clock with 35 seconds left. For the 49ers and the few fans who still remained in their seats, it was obvious the Bears would pass, their only hope.

Blanda took the snap, but he didn't fade back. The guards did not set to pass block but pulled out and Blanda pitched to his halfback who headed around right end. Only the halfback on this play was back-up quarterback Ed Brown. Just as he was about to cut upfield, Brown stopped and let fly with a pass that sailed about 40 yards in the air. And there was Harlon Hill, the ball coming to him out of the darkness. He grabbed it without losing a step and raced down the sidelines for the game-winning touchdown.

It gave the Bears a 31-27 victory, and Hill 214 yards and four touchdowns on pass receptions for the day, both Bear records which still stand (Mike Ditka tied the four TD mark in 1961).

IN THE MUD. . .

It was an awful day in Chicago. The rain had come down hard in the early morning hours on December 12, 1965, turning Wrigley Field into what sports announcers like to call a quagmire.

Rookie Gale Sayers, known as the "Kansas Comet," looked at the field before the game and shook his head. "I was very concerned about the weather conditions. It was a rainy, muddy day and I actually didn't like playing in that kind of weather. So many things can happen; you can slip, pull a muscle, tear a hamstring."

He also had some other thoughts: "We were on a roll of sorts, and we wanted revenge. The 49ers had killed us in the first game of the season (52-24) and we had something to prove."

The first memorable play was a screen pass from Rudy Bukich. Sayers took it 80 yards through the slop for a touchdown. The next was a 21-yard run

from scrimmage, his second TD of the day. Then a simpler one, seven yards for a score; then a 50-yard whirling-dervish run that left mud in the faces of most 49er defenders. A one-yard plunge made it five for the day. Finally, he was back in the muck when a rain-soaked, punted ball fell into his hands at the Bear 15. Sayers started one way, then made his move, cutting back against the grain and was gone. Eighty-five yards later he had his sixth and last touchdown of the day.

He had tied the NFL record for the most touchdowns in a single game. It

A PIECE OF TRIVIA

When Gale Sayers scored six touchdowns in one game in 1965, he equaled a feat accomplished only two other times in NFL history.

Both of them were, ironically enough, in games against the Bears. In 1929, Chicago Cardinal fullback Ernie Nevers set the standard when the Cards beat the Bears, 40-6, at Comiskey Park. More than two decades later, at a game with the Browns in Cleveland in 1951, halfback Dub Jones ran for six TDs again in a 42-21 defeat of the Bears.

REMEMBERING THE DAY. . .

George Halas: "I never saw such a thing in my life! It was the greatest performance ever by one man on a football field."

San Francisco 49er assistant coach and Hall of Fame quarterback, Y. A. Tittle, "I just wonder how many that Sayers would have scored if we hadn't set our defense to stop him."

was also the 21st he had scored that season, breaking an NFL record that had been shared by Lenny Moore and Jim Brown.

Sayers summed it up, "Everything went just right for us that day, and we got our vengeance. We beat them 61-20.

"The way things were going I probably could have scored eight touchdowns that day. But back then no one cared about records. I didn't even know I'd tied the six-touchdown record until after the ball game. We won, and that was the most important thing at the time."

Gale Sayers sweeps left as George Halas, hands on hips, watches.

THE LONGEST RUN,
SORT OF. . .

It was a game played on the Sunday in 1963 after President John F. Kennedy was assassinated in Dallas. The NFL decreed that the season would go on despite the national tragedy. And so the Bears traveled to Pittsburgh to take on the Steelers.

It was a very important game for the Bears. They could not afford to lose it, not with Vince Lombardi's Packers growling at their heels in the race for the NFC title. The Bears were a favorite going in, but Halas was worried about it. "Buddy Parker (the Steeler head coach) really wants this one," he said before the game. We cannot let him have it."

But they almost did. It was the fourth quarter and the Bears were down 17-14, and things in general were just not working right for the favored Chicagoans.

It was becoming desperate midway through the fourth quarter. The Bears were on their own 22 yard line and it was second down and 36 yards to go for a first down.

"I remember I was dead tired," Bear tight end Mike Ditka said later. "I came into the huddle and (quarterback Bill) Wade asked me if I could run a deep pattern and I said no. Maybe I can hook up ten yards, see what we can get out of it. But that's it."

Wade took the snap and dropped back, looked deep and found nobody open . . . then spotted Ditka, only

about five yards from the line of scrimmage, and unloaded it to him.

Maybe it was Ditka's extraordinary sense of competition, or possibly Halas' words, "We cannot let them have it," but he began moving upfield on a mission. A defensive back hit him and bounced off, and Ditka kept going. A linebacker had as much luck. Just beyond the 50-yard line a trio of Steelers hit him and all that was left was a jumble of bodies and flailing arms . . . and out of it came Ditka, still making his way down the field.

Steeler defensive back Clendon Thomas finally caught up to him at the Pittsburgh 15-yard line and brought him down. Thomas, incidentally, was the Steeler who Ditka had first run over far back down the field. Some reporters in the press box said ten different Steelers had their hands on Ditka as he made his way down the field. Ditka said, "I lost my legs. They were completely dead. I just plain ran out of gas."

Still, by himself, Ditka got the first down, got them 63 yards in fact and in field goal range. Roger Leclerc came on and booted an 18-yard field goal that tied the game. Had the Bears lost that game, they would not have been able to go on to win the NFL championship for 1963.

275 YARDS,
A LONG WAY TO GO. . .

Even General George S. Patton would have been impressed. He used his tanks and infantrymen to gouge out yard after yard on his way to Bastogne and,

ON DITKA'S RUN. . .

Flanker Johnny Morris: "I was on the field, trying to block somebody, but I saw him going down the field and it was incredible. He knocked down everybody who touched him. I remember feeling terribly disappointed when the last guy tackled him. If anybody deserved to go all the way, Mike did.

Bill Wade: "It was some fantastic effort. I mean inhuman almost."

Ditka on Ditka's run: "It was just a series of bouncing off people . . . it wasn't so much the running, more the lousy tackling. I don't really think it was that special. If it'd been the best play I ever made, I would have scored a touchdown. I would have outrun that last guy."

Walter Payton picks up a few of the 275 yards he rushed for on that record-setting day against Minnesota in 1977.

ultimately, Berlin in World War II. Had he been around on November 20, 1977, he would have made Walter Payton his lead tank commander.

Carrying the ball for 275 yards in one game was a phenomenal feat. Payton set the NFL single-game rushing record that Sunday afternoon in 1977 at Soldier Field against the Vikings.

Payton had tied the club record three weeks earlier, equaling Gale Sayers' mark of 205 yards rushing in a game. Now he took the NFL record from Buffalo's O. J. Simpson when he carried the ball 40 times for the Bears, an average of almost seven yards a carry. His record still stands.

He did it for a team that was just beginning to come into its own. The Bears were 4-10 the year Walter joined them in 1975, 7-7 the next year. Jack Pardee was the coach in 1977 and the Bears were building. There was also an intensity growing that had not been there in some time. Going into the game against Minnesota, there was not a lot of talk about the playoffs; the Bears had not made it to post-season play since they won the title back in 1963.

It was a damp, cold day, typical of Chicago in late November. "I was feeling weak," Payton later recalled. "I had a flu bug coming on. I didn't even think I was going to play." But it was an important game. The Bears were 4-5, but things were beginning to click. Earlier in the year they had lost to the Vikes, who were now 6-3, in an overtime game at Minnesota. If there was a chance at all for the Bears of 1977, it was this particular afternoon.

After the opening kickoff, Payton forgot his flu bug. He took a handoff from Bob Avellini and picked up a few yards . . . a pitchout and a few more . . . and a few more. He carried it in from the one for a touchdown in the second quarter. At halftime the Bears had a 10-0 lead, and Minnesota knew its only hope was to stop Payton.

They didn't, obviously. Nine of his carries from scrimmage that day were for ten yards or more.

David Williams

Going into the fourth quarter, the score was 10-7, Bears. With Payton's dominant running and a fired-up defense, that score stood.

"I remember as the game was coming down," Payton said, "I had something like 271 or 273 yards and we were down on the 10-yard line. Coach Pardee, opposed to kicking the field goal and going for the points, called for a running play and I got the 275, the record (Simpson's NFL record was 273 at the time).

The Bears did not need the field goal that day, and Payton walked off the field having turned in the most productive game of his entire career, the best of any running back in the history of the NFL.

What effect did Payton's record run have on the Bears? They won their next four games to finish 9-5 and made it to the playoffs for the first time since 1963.

THE SHORTEST OT EVER

The best choice the Bears made on Thanksgiving Day in 1980 was to receive when they won the coin toss to start the overtime period against the Detroit Lions.

The Bears were 4-8 at the time and pretty much out of the running for a playoff berth. They had not given up, though, and were seeking an upset win at the Pontiac Silverdome over the Lions, who were in a hot race with the Vikings for the NFC title. With a last-minute drive led by quarterback Vince Evans, the Bears fought to a 17-17 tie at the end of regulation play.

Detroit kicked off, more a line drive than a boot with some hang-time. David Williams, a running back and the Bears chief kick returner that year, was averaging 21 yards a return. He took the ball at the five yard line and headed straight upfield and found, as they say, daylight.

Twenty-one seconds after the ball was kicked, Williams was in the Detroit end zone, a 95-yard touchdown return, and the Bears had the distinction of having won the shortest overtime game in NFL his-

Walter Payton catapaults into the New Orleans defense on the day in 1984 when he took the all-time rushing record from Jim Brown.

tory by the score of 23-17. Williams was mobbed by his teammates in the end zone with such enthusiasm that he suffered a broken nose, but the Lions had not laid a single hand on him.

It must have provided some kind of inspiration because the Bears in their next game annihilated the Green Bay Packers 61-7, matching the highest number of points the team had ever scored in a regular season game (the other when they beat the 49ers 61-20 in 1965).

ALL-TIME NFL RUSHER

Everybody was waiting for it that October afternoon at Soldier Field in 1984. They knew it was coming, but they didn't know when.

Walter Payton talks with President Ronald Reagan after the game in which he broke Jim Brown's all-time NFL rushing record in 1984. Looking on is Bear director of marketing and broadcasting Ken Valdiserri.

The game was an important one; the Bears were 3-2, but had lost two in a row. A win was the foremost thing on Walter Payton's mind. But the game was lost in the expectations of the moment. Then it came.

It was early in the second half. The New Orleans Saints' defense knew it was coming. So did the capacity crowd, that's why they were on their feet, stomping and shouting enough to make the venerable old Soldier Field concrete shudder.

The Bears broke the huddle. It was the third quarter. Dennis McKinnon went in motion, but nobody really paid any attention to him. Jim McMahon took the snap and tossed to Payton who went to the left, saw a a hole and burst through, bouncing off one would-be-tackler before being dragged

to the turf. The six yards he gained were all that was needed.

With that run, Walter Payton had gained more than 12,312 yards rushing in the 10th year of his career. He broke an NFL record held by Jim Brown since 1965, football's preeminent record.

In the broadcast booth, radio announcer Joe McConnell was shouting " . . . the equivalent of breaking Babe Ruth's all-time home run record."

In the stands, the roar from the crowd needed no announcement and could be heard miles away.

On the field, Payton worked his way through a sea of cameramen to the sideline where he handed the ball to his running back coach, Johnny Roland. Payton gave teammate Todd Bell a high-five, took a hug from linebacker Otis Wilson, shook a few hands, and then trotted back on the field to finish the game.

Later, he said, "It was great, sure, but remember we won that game (20-7), and we needed it. We'd lost the two before it, we had to have that one to get back on track, to make something of ourselves."

Payton, of course, went on to extend that National Football League record to 16,726 yards rushing in a career that did not end until 1987.

NEEDING 33 POINTS . . .
. . . AND A LITTLE HELP

It was the last game of the 1979 season and the Bears were entertaining the St. Louis Cardinals at Soldier Field. They were old rivals, these two, whose battles went back to when the Cards were in Chicago and their games were played in Wrigley Field and Comiskey Park. The series went all the way back to 1920, the first year of the league.

And this was a special meeting. The Bears had a slender chance at making the playoffs, something they had only done once in the previous 17 years. To earn a wild card berth the Bears had to achieve a 33-point season-scoring differential over the Washington Redskins. They had to first defeat the Cardinals big, and the Bears had averaged only 17.6 points a game through the first 15 games of that season, and the Redskins would have to lose to the Dallas Cowboys.

The day began on a tragic note with the stunning news that Bear president Mugs Halas had died of a heart attack. It was a tremendous blow to everyone in the Bears' organization.

But out of tragedy sometimes comes inspiration and, for the Bears, that happened that December day at Soldier Field. Despite the shock of Mugs' death, despite a snowy, icy day with a wind-chill factor of -12 at game time, the Bears' offense exploded. Two drives in the first quarter resulted in a one-yard touchdown run by Walter Payton and an 11-yard touchdown pass from Mike Phipps to David Williams. In the next period, Payton carried it five yards for another score. At the half, the Bears held a 21-0 lead . . . but still had a long way to go. The Cardinals reminded them of that by scoring a touchdown midway through the third quarter—making the 33-point differential look even more distant.

But not out of sight. Rickey Watts took the ensuing kickoff at the 17-yard line, got through the first line of Cardinals and headed for the sideline and with blinding speed made it all the way to the Cardinals' end zone to make up the lost points.

Hope was restored. The Bear defense was magnificent. The offense marched. Payton scored his third touchdown of the day in the fourth quarter on a four-yard run. Phipps threw his second TD pass of the day, this time a 35-yarder to Watts.

Final score: Bears 42, Cardinals 6, a 36-point victory.

Walter Payton had rushed for 157 yards on 33 carries, Phipps passed for 233 yards, Watts gained 103 yards catching some of those passes. The defense recorded nine sacks, three of them by linebacker Jerry Muckensturm. The Bears outgained St. Louis in net yards: 456 to 113.

It was truly one of the great games in Soldier Field history . . . but Washington, playing the late game that Sunday afternoon had to lose and, with just four minutes remaining in the game, they were leading the Cowboys 34-21.

The Bears gathered around their cars in a chilly Soldier Field parking lot under the north stands, listening to the Redskins-Cowboys game on their car radios. They were feeling a terrible queasiness and helplessness as they saw everything they had worked so hard for slipping away.

Perhaps his son Mugs up there had something to do with it. Or maybe it was just Roger Staubach's great quarterbacking. But the Cowboys came back with two touchdown passes to win, 35-34.

There was pandemonium in the parking lot as the Bears were going to the playoffs.

THURSDAY NIGHT, MINNESOTA, 1985

It was a nationally televised game, the third of the regular season in 1985. The Bears had come close the year before, losing the NFC title game to the 49ers. They had attracted attention throughout the country with Mike Ditka, Jim McMahon, Walter Payton, and the now-infamous 46-defense.

The Vikings did not seem all that big a threat—they had only won three games the year before. But they were a team on a mission that night and the Bears had not taken them seriously enough. In the third quarter, Minnesota had the lead 17-9, and the Bears seemed to be going nowhere. Steve Fuller had been filling in at quarterback for Jim McMahon who was suffering both back and leg injuries.

Let McMahon tell the rest of the story.

"I was in Mike Ditka's ear most of the time on the sideline about putting me in. Steve wasn't playing all that bad; it's just that the team wasn't getting anything done. We needed some kind of spark.

"Finally Ditka said, 'Get your ass in there and throw a screen pass.'

"So I called a screen pass. But as I was dropping back, I stumbled. They were blitzing and I saw the linebackers coming as I was regaining my balance. What I also saw was Willie Gault running free down the middle, so I just unloaded it to him, and it was a 70-yard touchdown.

"When I got back to the sideline, Ditka said, 'What did you call?' I told him I called a screen pass. And he said, 'Why did you throw it to Willie then?' Because

he was open, I said. We both kind of just looked at each other and shrugged."

BUFFONE REMEMBERS '79"

I'll never forget the one that got us into the playoffs in '79. We had to destroy the Cardinals that day. We did something that day, really something.

We're punting and, on the punting team, I was in the backfield, calling the signals. So I turned around to (Bear punter) Bob Parsons—I had the right to call an audible on the punting team for a fake. So I called, "Yellow" which meant "Everybody alert!" Yellow meant we were not going to punt the ball.

The ball was supposed to be snapped to me, but I saw suddenly a linebacker had moved in there and was sitting right where I'd run with it. So I looked back again at Parsons and gave him the word for a screen pass instead, Parsons to get the snap and throw the screen pass to me. The way it worked was I'd let the Cardinal guy come in, bump him and spin off.

The guy comes in and Parsons—he'd been a quarterback at Penn State—rolls out and I peel off. He hits me with the ball. All of a sudden I'm wide open and I ran down the field some 35 or 40 yards.

So next thing you know we're calling audibles all over the place, on field goals, punts, fourth downs. We were just wild, we just went for it. And our defense—the Cardinals had to wish they'd stayed in St. Louis. It was just one of those days when you knew just how emotional a football game can be.

On Minnesota's possession, the Bears quickly picked off a pass from Tommy Kramer and had the ball at the Vikings' 25 yard line. McMahon came back on the field, bringing with him a Ditka play. "It was a bootleg," McMahon explained. "But my first two receivers were covered. Usually on that play you know that you're going to have either the running back in the flat or the tight end crossing, but neither of those guys were open. Then I just caught sight of Dennis (McKinnon) getting behind somebody in the end zone and so I unloaded it to him."

The Bear defense held Minnesota on four downs. McMahon came back, threw a couple of completions to get the drive going and then found McKinnon again, this time on a 43-yard bomb for a third touchdown. Suddenly the Bears had gone from a 17-9 deficit to a 30-17 lead. They won the game 33-24, and took a major step toward the Super Bowl.

DEFENSE

The word "Defense" has always been essential to the Bears' vocabulary. It won the 1963 NFL championship for them. Its standard-bearers over the years have included names like Stydahar, Turner, Connor, George, Atkins, Butkus, Hampton, Singletary and Dent. But the word has had no more shattering impact than it did November 17, 1985, down in Dallas.

The Cowboys were in a tie with the Giants for the NFC East with records of 7-3. They had run up 30 points when they defeated the Giants earlier, and 44

when they demolished the Redskins, another close contender for the division title. The Bears were 10-0, the NFL's only undefeated team. Also, Dallas had gone to Chicago and beaten the Bears 23-14 a year earlier.

Besides playing in the unfriendly confines of Texas Stadium, the Bears were without Jim McMahon, leaving the quarterbacking chores to back-up Steve Fuller. Head coach Mike Ditka made it clear before the game that the defense would have to be at its very best.

Remember that defense? Dan Hampton, Steve McMichael, William Perry, and Richard Dent were up front. The linebackers were Otis Wilson, Mike Singletary, and Wilber Marshall. In the secondary were Mike Richardson, Dave Duerson, Gary Fencik, and Leslie Frazier. And they were ready.

Dent started it off with a one-yard interception return for a touchdown after Hampton batted a Danny White pass straight up into the air. The defense then forced a turnover and Kevin Butler kicked a 44-yard field goal for a 10-0 lead. Richardson picked off another Dallas pass and raced 44 yards for a touchdown. Dallas spent almost the entire first half in their own territory and trailed 24-0 at the intermission.

Nothing changed in the second half. The Bear defense stifled the Cowboys every time they had the ball. Leslie Frazier picked off one pass, Ken Taylor another. The Bears sacked Cowboy quarterbacks six times, and held them to 171 net yards and just 12 first downs. The final score of 44-0 was the worst defeat Dallas had ever suffered in its 26-year history. And it was the first time the Cowboys had been shutout in 218 consecutive games.

Bear owner Mike McCaskey was on the sideline as the game was winding down and the disenchanted Dallas fans were streaming toward the exits. His fondest memory of that day was Mike Singletary, who looked over from his middle linebacking position and, seeing the fleeing crowd, shouted, "Wait, I want witnesses!"

New Passer on the Block

In 1949, the Bears had three quarterbacks of note: Sid Luckman, who was winding down a Hall of Fame career; Johnny Lujack, whom George Halas opted to keep instead of Bobby Layne; and rookie George Blanda. Lujack, the All-American and Heisman Trophy winner from Notre Dame, was the heir apparent to Luckman who had guided the Bears since 1939.

"A tough act to follow," Lujack later said.

On December 11, 1949, he proved more than worthy. Rain sprinkled down on Wrigley Field and the ground was muddy and slippery. The crosstown rival Cardinals were the visitor that day. They had spoiled the Bears' title hopes the two previous years. There was not a lot of conviviality between the two teams going into this game, the last one of the season. More than 50,000 ardent Chicago football fans showed up despite the dismal weather.

Lujack set the tone of the game in the first five minutes. He began with a 52-yard touchdown pass to halfback George McAfee and followed with a 17-yarder to end Ken Kavanaugh. In the second quarter, he found Kavanaugh again for a 37-yard touchdown, and then another for 18 yards to halfback J. R. Boone . In the second half, Lujack pitched two more scores to fullback John Hoffman, the last a 65-yarder.

Meanwhile, all the Cardinals could do was wish that they had stayed on the south side. When the day was over the Bears had triumphed 52-21, the worst shellacking they had laid on the Cards since 1941.

And Lujack? Well, it was a great day. He passed for 468 yards, a new NFL record, surpassing the 446 of Redskin Sammy Baugh. It is a Chicago Bear record that still stands today. His six touchdown passes were only one shy of the league record held by the man he replaced, Sid Luckman. As Chicago Herald-American sportswriter Jim Enright put it, "Out there today, Lujack did everything but take tickets."

Back to the Playoffs

In 1977, the Bears were on their way to their first winning season in 10 years as they approached the last game of the season with a record of 8-5. There was talk of playoffs, an uncommon topic around Chicago, because the Bears had not gotten beyond regular season play since 1963.

To reach the playoffs, however, they had to get by the Giants out in New York, the last game of the season.

It was a wintry day reminiscent of the famous "Sneakers Championship" game back in 1934. Giants Stadium in the New Jersey Meadowlands was carpeted with a treacherous mix of slush and ice.

The Bears, having learned about sneakers four and a half decades earlier, had brought along rubber-soled shoes as well as regular turf shoes. But they learned shortly after taking the field before the game that nei-

ther of these were, in fact, an advantage on the snow-covered artificial turf. Public relations director Ted Haracz was dispatched to the telephone and frantically began making calls to sporting goods stores. He finally found one that could provide cleated football shoes, and one of the Bear ballboys hopped into a car and, with a police escort, rushed over and bought more than $1,000 worth of the shoes. He arrived back at the stadium with the shoes just before halftime.

With their new shoes, the Bears managed to turn a 6-3 deficit in the fourth quarter into a 9-6 lead, a drive that ended with fullback Robin Earl carrying it in from the five. The extra point, however, was blocked, a grave misfortune because the Giants then marched to kick a field goal to send the game into overtime.

Either a loss or a tie would eliminate the Bears from a berth in the playoffs. And Chicago, it appeared in the extra period, seemed determined to avoid winning. First, they got within field goal range, but Bob Thomas's kick was no good. Then the Bears came back and reached the New York 10-yard line. It looked like this would be it . . . but on a muffed center snap the Bears turned the ball over to the Giants.

Time was running out now. There was just over a minute left when the Bears finally got the ball back. Bob Avellini found tight end Greg Latta twice, once for two yards and the next for 18. With 42 seconds left, the Bears used their last time-out. One more pass, this one to Walter Payton; he sloshed his way down the sideline to the Giants' 10, but he didn't get out of bounds.

The field goal team raced frantically onto the field.

FIRSTS

In Bears history, these were single-game milestones:

First to rush for 100 yards
Beattie Feathers, 101 against the Steelers in 1934

First to rush for 200 yards:
Gale Sayers, 205 against the Packers in 1968

First to pass for 300 yards:
Sid Luckman, 314 against the Eagles in 1943

First to pass for 400 yards:
Sid Luckman, 433 against the Giants in 1943

First to gain 100 yards on pass receptions:
Bobby Swisher, 106 against the Packers in 1940

First to gain 200 yards on pass receptions:
Harlon Hill, 214 against the 49ers in 1954

First to intercept 3 passes:
Hank Margarita, against the Lions in 1945

First to return interceptions for 100 yards:
Richie Petitbon, 101 against the Rams in 1962

First to return punts for 100 yards:
George McAfee, 108 against the Rams in 1948

First to return kickoffs for 200 yards:
Ron Smith, 208 against the 49ers in 1972

There were 12 seconds on the clock, deep snow on the field, and a swirling wind. Avellini got the snap and the ball down and this time Bob Thomas was right on the mark, a 27-yard field goal, a 12-9 win, and a ticket to the playoffs. It was also the first overtime victory ever for the Bears.

THE VERY FIRST PLAYOFF GAME

It was the first postseason game in NFL history that wasn't for a championship. The date was December 14, 1941, one week after the Japanese attacked Pearl Harbor. The Bears, coming off a championship season, had ended the season with a 10-1 record in 1941, their only loss to the Green Bay Packers, 16-14. Excluding the loss to the Pack, the Bears had averaged 38.2 points with the most prolific offense in NFL history.

That special playoff foe would be those same Packers whose only loss in their 11 games was a 25-17 defeat at the hands of the Bears.

The NFL decreed a playoff to see which team would face the NFL East champion New York Giants.

Chicago had the home-field advantage and despite a game-time temperature of 16 degrees, a crowd of about 43,500 showed up at Wrigley Field. As good a team as the Bears had—four future Hall of Famers in Sid Luckman, George McAfee, Bulldog Turner and Danny Fortmann—Green Bay also had an awesome lineup with the passing combination of Cecil Isbell to Don Hutson and the running of backs Clarke Hinkle and Tony Canadeo.

The Packers leaped to a seven point lead; but the Bears answered in the first quarter when rookie half-

back Hugh Gallarneau fielded a punt at the Bear 19 and zig-zagged his way 81 yards to tie the game. From that point on it was all Chicago. They scored 24 points in the second quarter, two touchdowns coming from fullback Norm Standlee, another rookie who had, ironically enough, been Gallarneau's running mate at Stanford the year before.

The score at the half was 30-7, Bears. The final was 33-14.

Lost within the scoring was the fact that halfback George McAfee had in many ways controlled the game with his running. McAfee, who one writer described as "combining a deer's speed with a rabbit's moves," gained 119 yards on 14 carries, still a Bear record for most yards gained rushing in a playoff game. McAfee was also the Bears' leading receiver that day, adding another 27 yards on two catches.

The win in that first divisional playoff game gave the Bears the opportunity to become the first team to win back-to-back NFL championship games when they defeated the Giants 37-9 a week later.

Defense scores. Wilber Marshall lofts the ball in triumph after scoring on a 52-yard fumble recovery return in the NFC title game against the Rams. Also celebrating are Otis Wilson (55) and William Perry (72).

SACKS

Defensive statistics rarely make it out of the log books of coaches. But there are some great moments that should not be forgotten.

One in particular is that September day in 1973 when the Bears went up against the division championship-bound Vikings and defensive tackle Jim Osborne broke through four times to sack the Minnesota quarterback, Fran Tarkenton, a club record that would stand for more than a decade.

Only defensive end Richard Dent has recorded more sacks in a single game, something he accom-

plished twice with 4.5 each in games against the Rams in 1984 and against the Raiders in 1987.

CYRIL PINDER'S RUN . . .

But everyone remembers the extra point.

It was November 14, 1971, as Pinder tells the story:

"We were playing the Washington Redskins, our first year in Soldier Field, and it looked as if we had a sure loss on our hands. Late in the fourth quarter Bobby Douglass handed the ball to me on a quick-trap, and I got free and took off for a 40-yard touchdown run. It was the biggest play in my career with the Bears.

"Everyone was screaming and cheering because it tied the score at 15. There was very little time left, and we needed the extra point.

"There was a mix-up on the snap. Douglass, who was the holder, could only jump up and bat it down. He managed to get control of the ball and run around. There were Redskins all over the place and no way for him to run it in.

"He lobbed it into the end zone where Dick Butkus was standing along with a couple of Redskins (Butkus had been in the backfield to block for the kick). They all jumped for it and when the bodies cleared there was Butkus with the ball and we had the extra point. We won 16-15.

"Now everybody remembers that extra point, and not many recall my run before it. But one person did. When I went to the White House the next year as the Bear representative in the Athletes Against Drug Abuse Program, President Nixon, known to have been a dedicated Redskin fan, greeted me and told me he had lost a wager on that game because of me. We had a big laugh over it."

155

THE BRONK

Bronko Nagurski was a legendary player. A fullback on offense and a tackle on defense for the Chicago Bears, he was feared and revered as the most battering, bruising ballplayer of the 1930s. Stories of his ferocious exploits abound . . . and they were justified.

He represented an era and had a physical prowess that did much to insure Doc Spears' great success as football coach at the University of Minnesota. "I saw a big lad pushing a plow," Spears later recalled. "No horse, just him. I asked directions of him and he picked up the plow and pointed with it. I decided he should go to Minnesota."

Nagurski grew up in International Falls, which probably contributed to his toughness. It's a tough place, hunkered down on the border that separates the United States from Canada.

Summers are short and bug-filled, winters are brutally cold. People from the Falls will tell you that if summer falls on a Sunday they sometimes have a picnic.

Bronko Nagurski was comfortable there. He left—

Bronko Nagurski, fullback/tackle, 1930–1937, 1943.

not for long, really—to become a giant in sport history. And a major part of that was in Chicago, as a Bear. Quite a few people remember that.

Clarke Hinkle, Hall of Famer from the Green Bay Packers:

"Bronko Nagurski was probably the greatest player I ever went up against. He had been at Minnesota while I was at Bucknell, but we never met in college. I remember in my first game, the Bears were up at Green Bay in 1932, I didn't know what to expect.

"From Nagurski, that, is.

"I had heard all those things about him, and I knew I was going to have play for my life.

"On the first series of downs, the Bears had the ball. It was handed off to Nagurski and he came through the line. I was backing up the line—we played both ways in those days—on the strong side and I waited for him to come to me.

"A terrible mistake! He darn near killed me. He knocked me on my back and

I ended up with four stitches on my face.

"I thought to myself, you either better start moving and go after him or just get the hell out of the way because otherwise you are going to get killed. So, from that day on, I figured, I'd either go at him or away from him."

Johnny Dell Isola, New York Giant linebacker:

"I had heard a lot about him, but I thought most of it was exaggerated. We were at the Polo Grounds when I first ran up against him. It was first and ten and they gave the ball to Nagurski up the middle.

Well, a huge hole opened and I saw him coming.

I put my head down and charged into the hole. We met at the line of scrimmage, and you could hear the thud all over the Polo Grounds.

I had my arms around his legs and my shoulder dug into him. It was the hardest tackle I ever made, but I made it, and I said to myself, "Well, I guess that will show you, Nagurski!"

Then, as I was getting up, I heard the referee shout, 'Second down and two!'"

Dick Richards, owner of the Detroit Lions in the 1930s: (And this story is as apocryphal as they come, although George Halas told it numerous times at banquets and over lunchtime conversations.)

"I once approached the Bronk before a game and said, 'Here's a check for $10,000, Nagurski. Not for playing with the Lions, because you belong to the Bears, but just to quit and get the hell out of the league. You're ruining my team.'"

A pair of Hall of Famers work out, end Bill Hewitt (left) and fullback Bronko Nagurski.

Bronko Nagurski, the most punishing runner of his time, heads upfield in a game in the 1930s.

George Halas:

"I always think about the incident in Bronko's rookie season during a game at Wrigley Field.

"Because it was designed as a baseball stadium, at one end of the field the outfield wall was not very far from the endline. The Bears were on about the two yard line. Nagurski got the handoff. With head down and legs churning, he plunged into the line.

"Nagurski blasted through two would-be tacklers as though they were a pair of old saloon doors, and kept on going right through the end zone.

"His head, still down, Nagurski ran full speed into the brick outfield wall there at Wrigley Field. He went down, then got up and trotted off the field.

"As he approached me on the sideline, he shook his head and said, 'That last guy really gave me a good lick, coach'."

What most people didn't know was that this big, bruising football player was a gentle man. He was much more comfortable living up there in the frigid Falls, out east of town on the Rainy River. He had a gas station and people would stop and talk to him about his sports exploits. The Bronk would smile and nod and check the oil and clump around. He never talked much about the past. And you needed a stick of dynamite to get him out of there to attend some big sports' function, like something at the Pro Football Hall of Fame of which he is a charter member.

Bronko Nagurski did not leave statistics like Walter Payton or Gale Sayers, but, without question, he left his mark on everyone who played against him or watched him perform for the Bears.

CORNER TURNERS:
George Halas, Jr. & Jim Finks

They were not a matched set, not on the surface, anyway—George Halas, Jr., Mugs as he was known from when he was a kid, and Jim Finks.

The two of them forced the Chicago Bears to turn a giant corner.

The Bears were dismal in the mid-Seventies. On the field, they were a National Conference foot-wipe. Off it, they were snickered at by the rest of the league and by those who watched it for a living. Before the 1974 season, Mugs Halas met with his father to talk about the Bears. Mugs was the club president. The conversation ended when Mugs hollered at a level all the secretaries could hear, and probably much of the pedestrian traffic along West Madison Street.

What he hollered was, "I am so sick of this!"

"This" was the state of the Bears. Mugs was referring to losing.

Nothing happened that day, except maybe Mugs was a little hoarse, but the Bears would not be the same again. Mugs Halas told his father . . . pro football's Columbus, when you think about it . . . that what the Bears needed was somebody better than either one of them, somebody to stop the bleeding. Somebody good. It was a huge statement to make, saying he couldn't do it and neither could his legendary father.

But Mugs knew somebody who could.

Jim Finks grew up downstate, in Salem. He was a schoolboy star in football, basketball and baseball. He even picked up tennis in the summer.

Finks played college football at Tulsa and pro for the Pittsburgh Steelers. His first few years with the Steelers he played pro baseball, too, as a catcher in the Reds farm system. Finks was a Steeler for seven years, a good quarterback on a team that wasn't very good. Playing out of the T formation, he gained the distinction of leading the NFL in passing in 1955 with 165 completions for a total of 2,270 yards.

He went from playing to a year as backfield coach for Terry Brennan at Notre Dame. From there he went to Calgary of the Canadian League. Finks thought he was going to scout for Calgary, however he started the season playing quarterback and ended it as general manager. He was fond of pointing out that he also sold program advertising. He was in Canada six years.

In 1964, the Minnesota Vikings hired Finks as their general manager. As had been the case at Calgary, he inherited a foundling franchise and left it robust and healthy. From 1967 until he resigned after the 1973 season, the Vikings dominated the NFC Central Division.

It was harder in Chicago, but it happened there, too, although after he had left. Finks joined the Bears in 1974 and left just before the 1983 season. The dominant team that would thrill Bear fans in 1985 was in place when Finks left . . . he put it there. Payton, Hampton, McMahon, Dent, Covert, Suhey, Gault, Hilgenberg, Wilson, McMichael, Singletary, Fencik, Van Horne. All acquired by Jim Finks.

The biggest reason it was harder in Chicago was that Mugs Halas died, depriving the Bears and the

National Football League of a valuable man. Many people didn't know that side of Mugs, he had lived in such an enormous shadow. But he was very bright. His grasp of complex league financial issues was sure and valued. He was courageous and loyal to the League.

The death of Mugs Halas deprived Finks even more deeply. Not only had he lost his key ally in the rebuilding of the Bears, Finks had lost a friend, too.

They were a strange pair. Mugs was intense, abrupt, a worry-wart. Finks loved to wisecrack, planned painstakingly and believed in himself. Mugs admired

Jim Finks, executive vice-president and general manager, 1975–1982.

162

Finks' coolness under fire, his ability to motivate others and his brass-bound practicality. Finks admired Mugs for his honesty, his loyalty and his courage.

They were the people who grabbed the franchise by the scruff of the neck and thrust it forward, into the Eighties. The Bears had missed the Seventies some-how. The two men had a relatively brief run together, but a lasting impact. They positioned the Bears so that the success of the Eighties might be within reach . . . way out there, beyond the foot-wipes and snickers.

Super Bowl XX came, and the Bears prevailed. The corner-turners certainly helped make it happen.

Mugs Halas, Bear president from 1963 to 1979.

163

*"You Chicago people are spoiled by Payton . . .
. . . he's a phenomenon."*
—Bud Grant

EIGHTEEN

SWEETNESS: WALTER PAYTON

They called him "Sweetness." The fans . . . not opposing linebackers and safeties, the ones who had to meet him head-on in the hole or, worse, in the open field. Not opposing coaches who stacked defenses against him for 13 years, defenses he always challenged and usually beat. They had great respect for him and for his abilities, but going up against him was anything but sweet.

In 1985 Ronnie Lott was the composite NFL safety and Walter Payton was king of the running backs. They met at Candlestick Park in San Francisco. The Bears led, but the going was still shaky in the fourth quarter. That was when Payton firmed things up; he carried 12 times on a 14-play drive, scoring a touchdown from 10 yards out. On the scoring play, he slipped the grasp of a linebacker, veered wide, and aimed for the corner of the end zone. Lott came up to challenge. Payton gathered himself on the fly and lowered his helmet. Lott did the same. It was like two mountain sheep clattering into one another. Payton drove Lott to his knees and flopped on top of him, just into the end zone. It was a total-effort play by both men.

He was the Bears' first-round draft choice in 1975

after a brilliant career at Jackson State in Mississippi. He was to have played in the College All-Star game, but an elbow infection kept him from being a factor. His first regular season game with the Bears was equally distressing—he carried eight times for a net of zero yards against the Baltimore Colts and departed Soldier Field with tears in his eyes.

At Tampa, in mid-career, he slanted left, found a hole plugged, and broke it outside. A lot of his holes were plugged at mid-career. He ran over a linebacker, then a safety. Someone caught him at the five . . . he never did have great speed . . . but the Tampa trainer had to come out and wake up the linebacker and the safety.

He wore #34 and wore it so well that no Bear will ever wear it again. He was inducted into the Pro Football Hall of Fame in 1993, the first year he was eligible. He was an automatic selection, in the same way Joe DiMaggio was in baseball, Oscar Robertson in basketball, and Ali in boxing. He set eight National Football League records and 26 Chicago Bear records.

Fans never saw him when he was at his best, out on the practice field. Football practice can be awfully bor-

ing, but it wasn't boring to him. He was perpetual motion. He skipped rope, led calisthenics, ran plays, punted, passed, kicked field goals, and made a pest of himself between plays. Gary Fencik, who played 12 years with him, said, "I don't think we ever had a quarterback who threw the ball more in practice than Walter did."

He has been the most durable running back . . . a position with a short-life. Bud Grant, who coached the Vikings, was asked once about the seemingly short career of Chuck Foreman, who starred at Minnesota. "His career was normal," said Grant. "You Chicago people are spoiled by Payton—he's a phenomenon."

Walter played 13 years and missed one game, in his rookie year. He played in a total of 190 games, 180 of them in a row. Everyone recognizes his greatness, but it's really hard to appreciate what he did. Opponents went to great lengths to set their defenses for him. What he accomplished, year after, year, was done against odds tilted cruelly against him.

He had a high voice, but a pleasant one because it was so melodic. Until he got right behind you and shouted . . . then you wondered if your tooth-fillings had cracked. He created "soxing"—a condition in which the one "soxed" was hit by a ball made of damp, dirty, tightly-rolled practice socks. It would

get your attention. He was a firecracker freak, he drove fast, and he sat in the same seat on team charter flights for 13 years . . . the first seats in coach behind first class, on the right as you face the rear of the plane. Roland Harper occupied another seat in that row, on that side, but after Harper retired, Walter sat alone. He'd put his feet in the tray cupboard, clamp on headphones, and close his eyes. Nobody joined him except by invitation.

Pro football's record books are loaded with testament to his accomplishments. Payton gained more yards rushing than any other player, in one game and for his career. He rushed for 275 yards against Minnesota in a 1977 game when he was sick with the flu. He broke Jim Brown's all-time career rushing record in 1984 in a game against New Orleans at Soldier Field. He broke Brown's mark early in the third quarter, a pitchout to the left and a five-yard gain. Play was stopped while photographers flooded the field. Eventually, Payton brought the record-setting football to the sideline, handed it to back-field coach Johnny Roland, and then started shooing people off the field.

The Bears were 6-10 in 1981 and the toughest loss was at Dallas, 10-9 on Thanksgiving Day. Dallas was good and the Bears weren't. Payton was almost demonic. He played that game with absolutely no regard for his well-being . . . he was Don Quixote, hurling himself like a lance at the windmill of the Dallas defense. When it was over he

had carried 38 times and gained 179 yards, and the Cowboy fans cheered his gallantry.

FINKS ON PAYTON

There were many statements and tributes offered when Walter Payton retired from professional football. The best came from the man who introduced him to Chicago and the NFL back in 1975, Jim Finks:

"He's rare in his whole approach to this business. He has answered the call every Sunday for thirteen years at a very demanding position. He's rare in that he never compromised his privacy or his family for extra dollars. He has handled notoriety as professionally as anybody I've ever known, by being himself. He let his work speak for itself."

Other fans started cheering him during road-game introductions late in his career, even in Green Bay, where they cherish the right to despise the Bears. It was recognition of the fact that he had risen above simply being the "enemy"—recognition of the fact that he was on a special course, heading out there to where no player had ever been before.

Unlike most great running backs, he was the complete package. He was a devastating blocker. In a game against the 49ers out in San Francisco, Roland Harper scored from in close on a play where Payton ran lead. Frank Nunley, a 49er linebacker, was in the hole and then he wasn't. Payton hit him so hard Nunley just flew through the air to the back line of the end zone.

He completed 11 of 34 passes for eight touchdowns. He punted once for 39 yards. He returned 17 kickoffs and averaged over 31 yards per return. In 1984, when the Bears were forced to use six people at quarterback because of injuries, he played quarterback in a game and threw a touchdown pass. And the most remarkable thing about his playing quarterback was that, at the time, it didn't seem all that remarkable. His secret ambition was to play defensive back.

Before a playoff game at Soldier Field in 1985 he was at the center of the team as it huddled before taking the field. Playoffs are different. It's great

Walter Payton, running back, 1975–1987

PAYTON'S NFL RECORDS

RUSHING

Most yards gained, career **16,726**

Most yards gained, game **275**

Most seasons, 1,000 yards **10**

Most 100-yard games, career **77**

Most touchdowns, career **110**

Most attempts, career **3,838**

NET YARDS
Rushing, Receptions, & Returns

Most yards, career **21,803**

Most attempts, career **4,368**

if you can bring passion to regular season games, but the playoffs demand it. That's what Payton was doing, down in the core of that circle of bodies. His eyes blazed and his voice was a war-cry. He was doling out purpose and fury, and it damned near made your hair stand on end.

Matt Suhey was his backfield mate after Harper, and was perfect in counterpoint to Payton. Where Suhey was droll and deliberate, trying to get Walter to sit still was like pinning a hair ribbon on a bolt of lightning.

They blocked for each

He even got along with the zebras.

other like demons. Suhey fumbled once, going in for a touchdown. "I was dying," he said. "We were trotting off the field after I fumbled and Walter gave me that sly grin. He asked me if I'd ever had a paper route. I said, 'What are you talking about? Paper routes?' Still with the grin he said, 'Well, you do that again and you better find yourself a paper route

because you sure won't be playing any more football'. It was crazy, but it was exactly what I needed. He got me back from being down on myself with his teasing."

It was not possible for him to simply stand there and engage in conversation with someone he knew. He had to touch you. To visit with Walter was to have your ribs counted, paunch patted, necktie straight-

170

PAIN . . . LESS

Fred Caito, the Bears trainer, talked about a side of Walter Payton that permitted him to climb to the top of "Mt. Rushmore."

"We were in Minnesota . . . it was when Neill Armstrong was coaching," Caito recalled. "Walter had a lot of fluid on his knee, but he never would let us take a needle to him so we couldn't drain it. The night before the game I told Coach Armstrong he'd better not plan on Walter for Sunday because that knee was so swollen.

"Sunday morning, real early, Walter and I went over to the stadium . . . the old Met. He went out and just jogged a little, but he didn't look good. I went in and called coach at the hotel and told him to forget about Payton.

"Walter came back in the locker room and said, 'I'll just dress and go out for warm-ups . . . at least let me do that'. So he did. He still was gimpy, but better. Then he told coach Armstrong, 'Just let me take the first series . . . see how it goes'.

"He played the whole game and gained 138 yards. Afterwards, I asked him how he did that, because I'd seen the knee. He said, 'I'm just kind of able to block out pain'.

"A couple days later the fluid was gone from the knee, but we didn't drain it."

ened, and pockets investigated. During a game, waiting for tacklers to unpile, he once reached out of the stack and untied an official's shoelaces.

He was humble, vain, bright, perceptive, fierce, unthinking, moody, and shy.

Which is to say, he was human.

There may have been better running backs, but not a better football player. Mike Ditka, his coach, said, "He's the best player I've ever seen and probably the best who's ever played the game."

A play that Walter recalled as a favorite

His signature, a catapault into the endzone. Here Walter does it against the Cowboys.

of Payton's shattering block on blitzer Joey Browner. The guy who ran for more yardage in the NFL than anyone, if you ask him, he remembers a block as his big play.

Payton played for 13 years, often over pain, often against long odds. He was a running back and more, he was a football player. He endured where others fell short. His style was to hack and slash and scrounge and gouge. Oh, he had the moves, and he could give you a burst, and when he'd hit the open field he'd put on that little

is very illuminating . . . it was at Minnesota and Jim McMahon threw a touchdown pass in the face of a big blitz. The reason he got the ball off was because

show-pony step he had, but his essence was to attack, raising welts on defenders throughout the league.

That's what he was like.

THE BEARS, FAMILY & FRIENDS

by John Coyne

When Mike McCaskey, president of the Chicago Bears, telephoned me in New York in January 1986 the team had already won the NFC championship and were bound for New Orleans. His call to me was every lifelong football fan's fantasy: "Want to fly on the Bears' charter and go to the Super Bowl?"

The first time Mike and I had spoken about seeing a Super Bowl together was not 1983, when his grandfather, George Halas, died and Mike's mother asked him to take over as president of the Bears. It was in 1966, in Ethiopia. We were both in the Peace Corps, and I had been ribbing him about how he would some day head the team his grandfather had founded. It seemed like a joke then and, as Mike pointed out, he had other brothers in his large family who were already more involved in the Bears. "Besides," he added, "I don't think my grandfather is planning on giving up the job."

Nevertheless, as we drove a Land Rover across the high plateau of Ethiopia, I made him promise that if the Bears ever got to a Super Bowl, he'd get me to the game. I had grown up in Chicago, grown up as a Bear fan and I always knew their time would come. When it did, Mike remembered his promise.

John Coyne, novelist and staunch Bear fan.

As we left Chicago on the chartered 747, the O'Hare tower gave our pilot runway instructions, then added, "Go, Bears, Go!"

Once in the air we were served hors d'oeuvres of sliced alligator meat. It was the Bears' good luck food that year, the flight attendant explained.

Shortly after checking into the hotel in New Orleans, I spotted Mike in the lobby. He had just finished an interview with *Sports Illustrated.* Now he was looking for a copy of the *Boston Globe,* but couldn't find one since the Hilton was, loyally, only stocking Chicago papers. I suggested that we walk over and check the New England Patriots' hotel for Boston papers.

"Unless," I added, "that's a violation of protocol."

"Oh, I don't think so. Let's go."

All the Boston papers were sold out, but the information desk suggested we try the Patriots' headquarters. Their security guard, a college-age football player wearing a slick yellow NFL jacket, didn't recognize Mike or his name, but others did and we were welcomed into the backroom by Chuck and Pat Sullivan of the Patriots.

Sitting around for 20 minutes, the Super Bowl team owners traded stories of what the week had been like,

how good the arrangements had been, and what they'd like to see done differently in future Super Bowls.

On Saturday afternoon I went to a small family party in the suite of Mike's parents, Ed and Virginia McCaskey. Mike explained that John, his baby son, had been to all the games that season except Miami, the only one they lost. "Nancy (Mike's wife) and I were on the team bus on Monday," Mike said, and (Bear defensive coordinator) Buddy Ryan looked around and asked, 'Where's John?' He said he had to be there in New Orleans. Here he's got the greatest defense in football history, but he's not taking any chances!"

Sunday, at 11 a.m. I attended the Bear mass in the hotel. The Chicago priest who says mass for the team before each game of the season asked God's blessing on the soul of George Halas, and then asked God to let the Bears "win by at least one point!"

After mass I told Mike, "You know, the Sullivans (owners of the New England Patriots) are having a mass, too, and I bet their priest is asking God for 20 points. You may have lost it at the altar."

When the Patriots scored first I had a sudden fear that I'd been right. I didn't have long to worry, though, because the Bears had no trouble and won by a lot more than one point.

Later on, at the victory party, I asked if the field goal in the first few minutes had frightened Mike.

"Why should it?" he laughed. "It made possible the greatest comeback in football history!"

The next morning, on the flight north, there was champagne, a victory cake, and a video of the game, but no alligator hors d'oeuvres. The long season was over. The Vince Lombardi Trophy was going to Chicago for the first time. Now it was time for the other teams in the NFL to look for good luck charms.

TWENTY

MIKE DITKA

Linebacker Bill George, who could play with the best of them himself, said, "He was the best rookie I ever saw."

The young man he was talking about had always liked playing football, even back in Aliquippa at St. Titus, in the fifth grade. He was born in Carnegie, born Dyzcko, but the name was too much of a mouthful so his folks had changed it by the time he started playing at St. Titus.

They changed it to Ditka.

He was the Bears first-round draft choice in 1961, coming out of the University of Pittsburgh. Houston of the AFL drafted him, too, but he wanted to play in the NFL. George Allen, then a Bears assistant coach, signed him to his first contract.

"He told me, 'You know, I'm paying you more money than the Bears have paid any rookie since Red Grange', or something like that. You knew he was lying, but still,

you had to laugh," Ditka said.

Dan Reeves, who coached with him at Dallas, said, "We were playing gin one night and he lost a couple hands. He picked up a chair and threw it at the wall. All four legs stuck in the wall, and I said, 'My Lord, this man does not like to lose.'"

Rookie tight end Mike Ditka flanked by quarterbacks Ed Brown (left) and Bill Wade, 1961.

Largely because of him, a position was forever changed.

Before Mike Ditka, tight ends were liberated tackles. Mostly, they had to be big and tough and block defensive linemen. Every so often they caught a little pass.

His rookie year, Ditka blocked like a scythe and caught 56 passes for 1,076 yards and 12 touchdowns. He was the NFL Rookie of the Year and played in the Pro Bowl. Over his 12 seasons as a player for Chicago. Philadelphia and Dallas, he caught 427 passes for 5,812 yards and 43 touchdowns, with a remarkable 13.6-yard average per catch.

"Do they always do that to the tight end?" Ditka asked.

"Not if you don't let them," Halas snapped.

He didn't.

He was the first tight end voted to the Pro Football Hall of Fame, and embarrassed by the honor . . . he said John Mackey and Jackie Smith and Ron Kramer should have been there, too.

He was an assistant coach at Dallas after his playing days. He coached like he played . . . fiercely. Tom Landry, his boss, was as flamboyant as a dish

"It was something," Ditka reflected, "to look back and realize I was a twenty-one-year old kid coming into the National Football League, and the head coach was sixty-five years old. Nobody ever assumed anything about his age, though . . . we all knew he was boss."

The easiest way to describe the player Ditka was to say he was tough . . . tough as the Pennsylvania mine

of prunes and every bit as dependable. He was the seeming opposite of Ditka, yet he secretly rejoiced in having such a firebrand on his staff.

Halas fired Neill Armstrong as coach of the Bears after the 1981 season. At a time before that event, Ditka had written a letter to Halas, saying he'd like

and mill country that spawned him. Talented, to be sure, but tough. He played over hideous pain. He hurt his knee as a rookie, then a shoulder. At Philadelphia, he had surgery on his foot and the foot never was right after that. He still played on it. Then he tore up a knee again. The old foot injury led to the crippling of his hip.

As a rookie, watching film, he saw Bear defender Joe Fortunato clothesline a Detroit tight end, then drive him right back into his own quarterback. Halas was in the room as Ditka watched the film.

Mike Ditka (89) in action against the 49ers in 1961.

to be considered someday for the job. Halas remembered the letter.

"We sat and talked at his kitchen table," said Ditka. "He asked me what my philosophy as coach was and I said it was like his—play football and teach sound fundamentals. He said 'Fine'.

"The only job I ever wanted was the Bear job," said Ditka.

"Anybody can think or write what they want, but it was just meant to be, that's all. You can call it fate or whatever you want, it was meant to be. I don't think if anybody ever wrote a script they would have written it with the sense of destiny I felt, beginning with my coming to Chicago in 1961 and my travels and my return twenty years later."

The first time he met with his Bear team, a team in tatters, he told them he was going to the Super Bowl and some of them would go with him.

"I'd never played on a team where the coach stated that as the goal," said Gary Fencik. "Everybody wants to go, but unless you publicly express it, it's kind of tough to be held accountable." Ditka looked at that 1982 team, Fencik recalled, and said half of them

wouldn't be there when the Bears reached the Super Bowl. "When we did get there," said Fencik, "I checked the two rosters, 1982 and 1985. There had been a 60 percent turnover in players."

Ditka, the coach, is more readily remembered for his fury than for his football. Understandable since some of his explosions were real classics. But his teams did win 112 games, six NFC Central division titles, played in three NFC championships, and won one Super Bowl. He was a bold, bright, excellent coach.

In the sixth week of the 1985 Super Bowl season, the Bears played at San Francisco, where they had been humiliated by the 49ers, 23-0, in the 1984 NFC championship game. In the closing moments of that 1984 game, 49er coach Bill Walsh had lined up Guy McIntyre, one of his offensive linemen, as a running back. The crowd loved it. Ditka didn't, but he remembered.

Back at Candlestick in '85, the Bears were within moments of taking the field for pre-game warm-ups. Ditka was in the coaches locker room, leaning back in a chair, puffing contently on a large cigar. He smiled through a cloud of smoke and his eyes were absolutely radiant.

With NFL commissioner Pete Rozelle before Super Bowl XX.

177

Head coach Mike Ditka demonstrates.

"We are ready," he said.

Payton rushed and tore up the San Francisco defense while the Bear defense stymied Montana and the vaunted 49er offense.

And in the final minutes . . . with the issue resolved and the crowd and Bill Walsh not loving it at all . . . William Perry chugged out onto the field and lined up in the backfield.

Ditka stared across the field at the silver-haired Walsh. The cigar was gone but the smile wasn't.

Meeting the press was not always his favorite thing.

A true Bear.

"I don't know about you guys, but second best
isn't good enough for me."
—Mike Ditka

TWENTY-ONE

SUPER YEAR

The Year the Bears Went to Super Bowl XX

The road to the Super Bowl for the Bears began iron-ically on a losing note . . . a year earlier.

Free safety Gary Fencik summed up the sentiments of just about all the Bears who would wear a Super Bowl ring after that wonderfully memorable season of 1985. "We really felt bad about losing in the 1984 playoffs (the 23-0 loss to the San Francisco 49ers in the NFC title game), and we were all in the locker room crying like little kids after that game."

The words of 49er All-Pro safety Ronnie Lott, heard by several Bears as they left the field in the gloom at Candlestick Park that day, did not set well either. "Next time, bring your offense," Lott suggest-ed.

"The next summer," Fencik remembered, "our first day in Platteville, Mike Ditka said at the team meeting, 'I don't know about you guys, but second best isn't good enough for me.' And that set the tone for the entire 1985 season."

Ditka was the NFL's Coach of the Year in 1985.

The Bear team that entered the 1985 season came in with a fine set of credentials. They were the NFC Central champions in 1984. They had gone to Washington to meet the Redskins in a playoff game and won 23-19 before losing to the 49ers.

They learned from the experience, and they regrouped after the setback in San Francisco. A few new faces were added. One of them was defensive tack-le William "Refrigerator" Perry, the club's first round draft pick that year. Another was placekicker Kevin Butler, selected in the fourth round. Other newcomers included tight end Tim Wrightman, run-ning back Thomas Sanders, cornerback Reggie Phillips, linebacker Jim Morrissey and free-agent quarterback Mike Tomczak. With those additions and the words of Ditka and Lott providing the background music, they were ready for the 1985 season.

The first game was not easy. On a sweltering

SUPER BOWL YEAR QUOTES

Dan Hampton, just before the start of the 1985 season:
"Last year we got a taste of the soup, this year we're going for the entree."

**Defensive coordinator Buddy Ryan early in the season
when asked how the "Refrigerator" Perry looked to him:**
"It depends on what speed you run the projector."

**William Perry, after the mammoth defensive tackle was caught from behind
at the Lions' 15 yard line after returning a Detroit fumble 59 yards:**
*"At first, I thought I was going to cruise on in.
If it had been the first quarter, it would have been no problem.
But when it's the fourth quarter . . . that's a long way to go."*

Mike Ditka, before the NFC title game with the Los Angeles Rams:
*"There are teams that are fair-haired and there are teams that aren't.
There are teams named Smith and teams named Grabowski.
The Rams are Smiths. We're Grabowskis."*

Otis Wilson, describing his teammates on the defense:
*"Mike Singletary is the quiet Christian type; I'm the wild one.
Fencik is the Ivy Leaguer. Dan Hampton is the politician.
Steve McMichael is crazy. It makes for a wild bunch."*

Questions asked and answered in New Orleans the week before Super Bowl XX:
To "Refrigerator" Perry: WHAT IS YOUR FAVORITE RESTAURANT IN THIS TOWN?
"I don't know, I don't notice names, I just browse."

To Dan Hampton: WHAT'S IN YOUR PLANS AFTER THE SEASON'S OVER?
"Cheese-sculpting."

To Mike Ditka: HOW WOULD YOU DESCRIBE YOUR RELATIONSHIP WITH JIM MCMAHON?
"Strange and wonderful. He's strange and I'm wonderful."

**Shaun Gayle, on Giant Sean Landeta's missed punt in the playoffs, which Gayle ran
in for what is probably the shortest punt return touchdown in history, 5 yards:**
"I don't know what you'd call it . . . a foul tip?"

Sportscaster Dick Enberg in the third quarter of Super Bowl XX:
"If it was a prizefight, they'd have to stop it."

Sunday at Soldier Field the Bears hosted the Tampa Bay Buccaneers, a team which posted a 6-10 record in 1984, and was considered a relatively easy opener. Only the Bucs scored 28 points in the first half and their key running back, James Wilder, gained 105 yards rushing. At the break, it was Tampa 28, Chicago 17. The Bear defense, which even Ronnie Lott respected, was embarrassed . . . but responded. To start the second half, defensive end Richard Dent tipped a pass into the hands of cornerback Leslie Frazier who ran the interception in for a touchdown.

The Bear offense reacted, too, with a touchdown pass and run from quarterback Jim McMahon. Chicago outscored the Bucs 21-0 in the second half for a 38-28 victory. The 28 points Tampa scored that hot afternoon was the second-highest total the Bears

would allow all year.

The rest of the regular season was one of relentless ascent, with significant highlights on the way.

NEW ENGLAND: The defense did the job, three interceptions and six sacks, and did not allow a single Patriot point until the final period. New England would not know until the Super Bowl how lucky they were escaping with just a 20-7 loss.

MINNESOTA: The famous Thursday night spectacle. An injured McMahon came off the bench in the third quarter with the Bears down 17-9 and dazzled a national television audience with three touchdown passes in the third quarter, a 70-yarder to Willie Gault and two for 25 and 43 yards to Dennis McKinnon. The first two scores came on consecutive passes. The final: Bears 33, Minnesota 24.

WASHINGTON: The Redskins were up 10-0 when

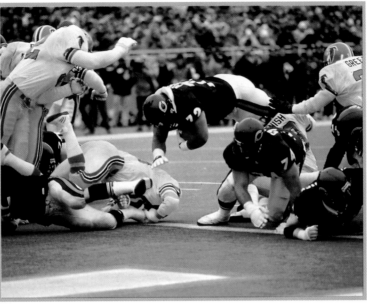
William Perry scores one of his three touchdowns in 1985.

Willie Gault returned a kickoff 99 yards for a touchdown, the longest in the NFL that year and the third longest in Bear history. McMahon added three touchdown passes to help the Bears to a 31-point second quarter. Two more touchdowns in the second half and an unyielding defense made the final 45-10.

TAMPA BAY: Walter Payton scored his 100th and 101st touchdowns to help the Bears overcome a 12-3 halftime deficit and beat the Buccaneers 27-19.

SAN FRANCISCO: The reigning Super Bowl champions hosted the Bears at Candlestick Park and this time the Bears heeded Ronnie Lott's advice and brought along their offense. Payton rushed for 132 yards and two touchdowns and Kevin Butler kicked four field goals, in a 26-10 Bears' win.

GREEN BAY: The 300-pound defensive tackle William "Refrigerator" Perry moved into the back-

Neal Anderson (35) has just scored, while Dennis McKinnon (85) and Emery Moorehead (87) head over to celebrate.

BEAR RECORDS SET IN 1985

INDIVIDUAL

Points, career	654	Walter Payton	(1975–1985)
Previous	629	Bob Thomas	(1975–1984)
Points, season	144	Kevin Butler	
Previous	132	Gale Sayers	(1968)
100-yard games rushing, career	73	Walter Payton	(1975–1985)
Previous	63	Walter Payton	(1975–1984)
100-yard games, rushing consecutive	9	Walter Payton	
Previous	6	Walter Payton	(1984)
Field goals, season	31	Kevin Butler	
Previous	25	Mac Percival	(1968)
Field goals, attempted, season	38	Kevin Butler	
Previous	36	Mac Percival	(1968)
Consecutive field goals,	12	Kevin Butler	(1985)
Previous	11	Bob Thomas	(1984)
Field goal %, season	81.6	Kevin Butler	(1985)
Previous	78.5	Bob Thomas	(1984)

TEAM

Most points, season	456	(16 games)
Previous	409	1965 (14 games)
Most yards gained, season	5,837	(16 games)
Previous	5,830	1983 (16 games)
Most first downs, season	343	(16 games)
Previous	297	1984 (16 games)
Most first downs, rushing, season	176	(16 games)
Previous	164	1984 (16 games)
Most first downs, passing, season	145	(16 games)
Previous	144	1954 (12 games)
Most field goals, season	31	(16 games)
Previous	25	1968 (14 games)
Most extra points, no misses, season	51	(16 games)
Previous	37	1955 (12 games)
Most safeties, season	3	(16 games)
Previous	2	5 times, last in 1976
Fewest yards allowed, passing, game	-22	11/24/85, vs. Atlanta
Previous	-12	11/4/74, vs. Green Bay
Most opponent kickoff returns, season	78	(16 games)
Previous	72	1965 (14 games)

Wish You Were Here...

Well, he was . . . George Halas marked his first NFL championship in 1921 when the Chicago Staleys went 9-1-1, only the second year of the National Football League's existence. At the time he was playing end, coaching the team and handling the administration of the franchise along with his partner Dutch Sternaman.

His last championship, and one he admitted was one of his all-time favorites, was the 14-10 victory over the New York Giants at Wrigley Field on a below-freezing December afternoon in 1963.

Well, he was not here to watch the Bears' next world championship. But that is arguable . . .

As his daughter, Virginia McCaskey, said when the Bears were in the final days of making their way to the Super Bowl: "Dad would relish this . . . And it was not just the excitement from people in Chicago but from all over the country . . . the world in fact. The night before we met people from Japan, England, France, people who might not know anything about American football, but suddenly they were all in love with the Chicago Bears.

"I've never had this much fun . . . . Dad would really have loved it all. The Bears were his life. Mugs, my brother, it was his life, too.

"But, Dad, he's upstairs, taking notes, cheerleading . . . . He's with us. You don't see him, but he's still with us."

field and provided a block heard round the world. Perry exploded into and flattened Packer linebacker George Cumby, enabling Walter Payton to plunge in for a score. Later Perry ran one in himself from the one-yard line to help in the 23-7 Chicago victory.

MINNESOTA: The Bears intercepted five Viking passes, one of which linebacker Otis Wilson one-handed and returned for a touchdown, Payton rushed for 118 yards, McMahon threw two touchdown passes . . . that was enough for a 27-9 win.

GREEN BAY: The Packers saw William Perry in the backfield again, but this time he didn't carry the ball in for a touchdown—he caught a McMahon touchdown pass. The questions swirled—when would he pass the football, kick field goals, return punts? Payton picked up 192 yards on the ground which equalled the yardage he gained against the Chiefs in 1977, and the third most productive rushing day of his career. Final: Bears 16, the Pack 10.

DETROIT: Both Walter Payton and Matt Suhey rushed for more than 100 yards, 107 and 102 respectively. The Bears possessed the ball for more than 41 minutes, the Lions just under 19; the Bears gained 360 yards, the Lions 106; the Bears earned 26 first downs, the Lions 8. The Bears won 24-3.

DALLAS: The worst day in Cowboy history, 44-0, the first time Dallas had been shut out in 218 games and the first time the Bears had defeated them since 1971 (when the Cowboys had a tight end named Mike Ditka). With a record of 11-0, the Bears now clinched the NFC Central title. Walter Payton also racked up his ninth 1,000-yard rushing season. Just so all the glory did not go to the offense, defensive end Richard Dent and cornerback Mike Richardson both scored touchdowns on interception returns and Otis Wilson led a punishing pass-rush.

ATLANTA: The Bear defense again decided not to let its opponent score a point. Walter Payton tied an NFL record with his seventh consecutive 100-yard rushing game. William Perry scored another touchdown and Payton dazzled with a 40-yard TD run in the 36-0 rout. At 12-0, the Bears became only the third team in NFL history to post that mark, joining the Bears of 1934 and the Miami

The scoreboard at Texas Stadium says it all.

Playoff Game 1

Chicago Bears vs. New York Giants — January 5, 1986
Soldier Field, Chicago — Attendance, 62,076

New York	0	0	0	0	0
Chicago	7	0	14	0	21

Scoring

Bears:	Gayle, 5 punt return (Butler kick)
Bears:	McKinnon, 23 pass from McMahon (Butler kick)
Bears:	McKinnon, 20 pass from McMahon (Butler kick)

Team Statistics

	Giants	Bears
Total yardage	181	363
Net rushing	32	147
Net passing	149	216
First downs	10	17
Rushing	1	9
Passing	8	8
By penalties	1	0
Interceptions	0	0
Sacks	0	6

Playoff Game 2

Chicago Bears vs. Los Angeles Rams — January 12, 1986
Soldier Field, Chicago — Attendance, 63,522

Los Angeles	0	0	0	0	0
Chicago	10	0	7	7	24

Scoring

Bears:	McMahon, 16 run (Butler kick)
Bears:	Butler, 34 FG
Bears:	Gault, 22 pass from McMahon (Butler kick)
Bears:	Marshall, 52 fumble return (Butler kick)

Team Statistics

	Rams	Bears
Total yardage	130	232
Net rushing	86	91
Net passing	44	141
First downs	9	13
Rushing	5	5
Passing	3	8
By penalties	1	0
Interceptions	0	1
Sacks	3	3

*Jim McMahon celebrates a touchdown in
the playoff game against the Rams.*

Dolphins of 1972.

MIAMI: Glitch. Something happened this Monday night. The Bears' celebrated defense allowed Dolphin quarterback Dan Marino to pass for 270 yards and three touchdowns. The score was Miami 31, Chicago 10 at the half and an astonished national television audience went on to watch the Bears lose their first game of the year 38-24. The only worthwhile part of the evening was Walter Payton rushing for 121 yards, setting an NFL record of

*After drubbing the Rams in the playoffs, Tom Andrews (left) and
Keith Van Horne let down in the locker room.*

eight consecutive 100-yard games.

INDIANAPOLIS: Payton made it nine straight, 111 yards on 26 carries, and the Bears got back on the winning track with a 17-10 triumph in a game they dominated even though the final score did not indicate that fact.

NEW YORK: The Jets managed to stop Payton's 100-yard-game rushing string, but they couldn't get past the Bear defense, scoring a mere 10 points while the Bears ran up 19 on four Kevin Butler field goals and a Jim McMahon touchdown pass into the hands of tight end Tim Wrightman.

DETROIT: The score was 6-3 at the half, the Bears barely ahead. Then Dennis Gentry ran back the kickoff to start the second half 94 yards for a touchdown and spark a 31-point surge which left the Lions on the short end of a 37-17 final score. Defensive tackle William Perry returned a fumble 59 yards but couldn't quite make it to the end zone (it was the fourth longest

Defensive stalwarts: Marshall, Fencik, Duerson, and Dent.

fumble return in club history).

And so the Bears closed out the regular season with a record of 15-1, the most games won in a single season in franchise history.

With by far the best record in the NFL, the Bears had home-field advantage and a week to rest up while the wild cards battled in the seventeenth week of the season.

The first test was against the New York Giants, who had defeated the defending Super Bowl champion 49ers in a wild card game. Coach Mike Ditka said of the Giants before the game, they were a team that "could be a real spoiler . . . loaded with talent . . . and no question on the upswing." Well, they had Lawrence Taylor, the

best outside linebacker in the league and maybe the best to ever play the position. They also had Phil Simms at quarterback, Joe Morris at running back, Mark Bavaro at tight end, and Leonard Marshall, among many outstanding players.

They brought them all to Soldier Field the first week in January and, Giant head coach Bill Parcells said before the game, "This is going to be the battle between the two best defenses in the league."

The Giants, it was said by more than one sportswriter, got off on the wrong foot. That was when punter Sean Landeta barely grazed the ball as he tried to punt deep in Giant territory in the first quarter. Bear safety Shaun Gayle scooped up the ball and ran it in for a touchdown. It was only 7-0 at the half, but the Bears had systematically shut down the Giants offense. When they came out for the second half, Chicago's offense struck, with Jim McMahon and Dennis McKinnon teaming for two touchdown passes in the third quarter. Parcells proved to be half right—there was no question the Bear defense, especially that day, was indeed the best in the NFL. They did not allow the Giants a single point. But the other statistics were equally awesome. The Bears did not allow a first down in the first 28 minutes of the first half. Their six sacks, costing the Giants 60 yards, were almost twice the 32 yards total the Bear defense gave up rushing all day. In 11 third-quarter plays, the Bears held New York to minus 11 yards.

Defensive end Richard Dent was credited with 3.5 sacks, one forced fumble, one knocked-down pass and three runs stopped behind the line of scrimmage.

The final score was: Bears 21, Giants 0.

The Los Angeles Rams, in that weekend's other NFC divisional playoff, were also posting a shutout, beating the Dallas Cowboys 20-0. The Rams had premier running back Eric Dickerson, who had rushed for 1,234 yards during the regular season, and had gained 234 yards rushing, an NFL playoff record, against the Cowboys. He would not find the Bear defense—the one defensive tackle Steve McMichael had taken to calling the "Take-no-prisoners-defense"—as receptive to his efforts. They held Dickerson to 46 yards and the entire Los Angeles offense to just 130.

The Bears scored on their first possession, a 66-yard drive which ended with Jim McMahon scrambling 16 yards for a touchdown. Kevin Butler added a field goal and the Bears led 10-0 at the half. The defense was as unbending in the second half as they had been in the first, even contributing a touchdown of their own when linebacker Wilber Marshall scooped up a fumble and ran 52 yards to score. That, along with a 22-yard pass from

SUPER BOWL XX STARTING LINEUPS

OFFENSE

Bears	Position	Patriots
Willie Gault	WR	Stanley Morgan
Jim Covert	LT	Brian Holloway
Mark Bortz	LG	John Hannah
Jay Hilgenberg	C	Pete Brock
Tom Thayer	RG	Ron Wooten
Keith Van Horne	RT	Steve Moore
Emery Moorehead	TE	Lin Dawson
Dennis McKinnon	WR	Stephen Starring
Jim McMahon	QB	Tony Eason
Walter Payton	RB	Tony Collins
Matt Suhey	RB	Craig James
Kevin Butler	PK	Tony Franklin

DEFENSE

Bears	Position	Patriots
Dan Hampton	LE	Garin Veris
Steve McMichael	LT/NT	Lester Williams
William Perry	RT/RE	Julius Adams
Richard Dent	RE/LOLB	Andre Tippett
Otis Wilson	LLB/LILB	Steve Nelson
Mike Singletary	MLB/RILB	Larry McGrew
Wilber Marshall	RLB/ROLB	Don Blackmon
Mike Richardson	LCB	Ronnie Lippett
Leslie Frazier	RCB	Raymond Clayborn
Dave Duerson	SS	Roland James
Gary Fencik	FS	Fred Marion
Maury Buford	P	Rich Camarillo
Mike Ditka	Coach	Raymond Berry

McMahon to Willie Gault, was more than enough.

The 24-0 shutout gave the Bears the distinction of being the first team to post back-to-back playoff shutouts since the Philadelphia Eagles who did it over two seasons, 1948 and 1949.

So for the first time in 22 years—since that bitterly cold day in 1963 when George Halas strode the sidelines—the Bears were going to the NFL championship game, Super Bowl XX.

The Bears were hoping for another shot at the Miami Dolphins, the only team they had lost to in 1985, but the New England Patriots deprived them of that opportunity when they upset the Dolphins 31-14 in the AFC title game.

The Bears took to New Orleans like kids to Disneyland. As owner Mike McCaskey later described it, "The entire week leading up to Super Bowl XX was like catching a wave and bodysurfing. It was just absolutely thrilling. I've seen others, when they got to Super Bowl week, get wound up so tight they can't enjoy it. . . . I didn't find it that way. None of us did. We had our share of fun and we felt the exhilaration heading to the Super Bowl. We also were feeling very good about our chances of winning."

All kinds of things were going on, ranging from Jim McMahon's antics—headbands, acupuncture and a press mooning—to rumors of defensive coordinator Buddy Ryan leaving for a head coaching job after this last game. The French Quarter heard the rap of the Super Bowl Shuffle mingle in the night air with the strains of Dixieland jazz. The Bear week

Dan Hampton on Going to the Super Bowl

All that season I used to ride with Ming (Steve McMichael) to practice, and every day we'd talk about going to the Super Bowl. After the last playoff game we got in the car and looked at each other, and we both said the same thing, "We're going!" It was a very moving moment.

I especially remember the night before the Super Bowl. It was an emotional time, we'd been ready for so long. We had meetings that night and were going to watch a game film, but by this time we were sick of game films. I said, "Hey, Ming, I cannot watch another roll of film. We got to do something."

I'm watching about the sixth play, and my heart's beating fast. I can't wait.

So I just got up and kicked the projector off the little table it was sitting on..

Ming, at that moment, leaped up and grabbed a chair and screamed some expletive about the Patriots and swung the chair at the chalkboard that had all these plays diagrammed on it. All four legs stuck into the chalkboard. Nobody said anything. Then I finally just said, "Let's get the hell out of here."

We all walked out of the room, no one saying anything, and went to our rooms and went to sleep. And everybody knows happened the next day!

was one of celebration, the exhilaration of just being there . . . and as the week spun on emotions and momentum were building.

It may not have been the playbook definition of preparing for what some call the "ultimate" game, but it worked.

Still it started out with a false first step. Walter Payton, the game's all-time leading rusher, fumbled on the second play of the game at the Chicago 19 yard-line and the Patriots recovered. The Bears stopped them on three passing downs but then gave up a field goal.

No more false steps.

The Bears responded with 23 unanswered points in the first half and the defense crushed New England's offense. Kevin Butler kicked two field goals to give Chicago the lead, the second coming after Richard Dent sacked New England quarterback Tony Eason, causing a fumble at the Patriot 13. Another New England fumble on the first play after the ensuing kickoff was gathered in by Mike Singletary. Two plays later Matt Suhey burst through on an 11-yard touchdown run. In the second quarter, Jim McMahon mounted a 59-yard drive and then carried it in from the two himself. The defense was a wall. Just before the half ended the Bears marched again, this time 72 yards, finishing it with Butler's third field goal and a 23-3 half-time lead.

New England fared no better after the intermission. The Bears came back out and scored three successive touchdowns in the third quarter. McMahon set up the first by passing from his own four-yard line, a 60-

yarder to Willie Gault. Eight plays later, McMahon carried it in from the one yard line. Three plays later, cornerback Reggie Phillips picked off a New England pass and ran it back 28 yards for another touchdown. Another New England fumble was recovered by Wilber Marshall. After a few blasts by Walter Payton and a 27-yard pass to Dennis Gentry the ball was at the Patriot one-yard line. Into the backfield came William "Refrigerator" Perry. There was not a betting man in the dome who would have wagered against it: Perry got the handoff and the Bears their third touchdown of the quarter. At the end of the third quarter, the score was 44-3, Bears.

In the final period, New England managed to score a touchdown on a Steve Grogan to Irving Fryar pass. But then the Bear defense added one more insult—reserve defensive tackle Henry Waechter broke through and sacked Grogan in the end zone for a safety and the last score of the game.

The Bear celebration, which began on the streets of downtown New Orleans and ended on the AstroTurf

McMahon and the incident

The Super Bowl was a ball . . . for the most part. Unfortunately, the first thing that comes to mind is that idiot from the TV station down in New Orleans coming on and saying I'd called all women sluts. Up to that time I'd been having a grand time in New Orleans . . . .

First he said I'd done a radio interview at six o'clock in the morning at some pizza place. Well, the reporters who knew me and the players knew damn well that I wasn't going to get up and do an interview at six in the morning. Well, this guy didn't check up on the story and he just went on the air with it.

Next thing I know, we've got women picketing outside our hotel. Men are calling my room and telling me I'm a dead man. . . .

I woke up to two callers who were yelling at me over the telephone. I didn't know what the hell was going on, so I went down to breakfast and the first guy I ran into was Jerry Vainisi (the Bears' general manager) who said, "You really did it this time, didn't you?"

Then Ditka came up to me and said, "Did you say that?" I said, "Say what?" Then he explained it to me. I couldn't believe what I was hearing.

My wife came down on Friday before the game and I spent the night with her at her hotel. On Saturday morning I got up and was walking back to the team hotel. I see all these cop cars and fire engines and all kinds of turmoil going on. I thought . . . they just bombed my roommate (offensive guard Kurt Becker).

As it turned out, it was in fact a bomb threat because of the crap on the news, but, no bomb, thank God.

After that, I was just glad to get the game over with and get the hell out of town.

of the Superdome, was over. Chicago had won 46-10, then the highest margin of victory in Super Bowl history.

Paul Zimmerman of *Sports Illustrated* summed it up best: "It will be many years before we see anything approaching the vision of hell that Chicago inflicted on the poor New England Patriots Sunday in Super Bowl XX. It was near perfect, an exquisite mesh of talent and system, defensive football carried to its highest degree. It was a great roaring wave that swept through the playoffs, gathering force and momentum, until it crashed home in New Orleans' Superdome in pro football's showcase game."

The season to remember was over. Several hundred thousand fans in Chicago were making plans to personally welcome the conquering heroes back into the city . . . several hundred million had watched and listened to it in cities and countries thousands of miles from New Orleans and Chicago. It was, in the words of defensive stalwart Steve McMichael, "one helluva kick!"

Bikers... an offense in their own way.
From the left: Keith Van Horne, Tom Thayer, Jay Hilgenberg,
Jim McMahon, Kurt Becker, Jim Covert.

1985: Ditka, Perry, Payton.

— SUPER BOWL SHUFFLE —

CHORUS

We are the Bears Shufflin' Crew
Shufflin' on down, doin' it for you.
We're so bad we know we're good.
Blowin' your mind like we knew we would.
You know we're just struttin' for fun,
Struttin' our stuff for everyone.
We're not here to start no trouble.
We're just here to do the Super Bowl Shuffle.

WALTER PAYTON

Well, they call me Sweetness,
And I like to dance.
Runnin' the ball is like makin' romance.
We've had the goal since training camp
To give Chicago a Super Bowl Champ.
And we're not doin' this
Because we're greedy.
The Bears are doin' it to feed the needy.
We didn't come here to look for trouble.
We just came here to do
The Super Bowl Shuffle.

WILLIE GAULT

This is Speedy Willie, and I'm world class.
I like runnin', but I love to get the pass.
I practice all day and dance all night,
I got to get ready for the Sunday fight.
Now I'm as smooth as a chocolate swirl,
I dance a little funky, so watch me girl.
There's not one here that does it like me,
My Super Bowl Shuffle will set you free.

MIKE SINGLETARY

I'm Samurai Mike, I stop 'em cold.
Part of the defense, big and bold,
I've been jammin' for quite a while,
Doin' what's right and settin' the style,
Give me a chance, I'll rock you good,
Nobody messin' in my neighborhood.
I didn't come here lookin' for trouble,
I just came to do the Super Bowl Shuffle.

(Repeat CHORUS)

JIM MCMAHON

I'm the punky QB, known as McMahon.
When I hit the turf, I've got no plan.
I just throw my body all over the field.
I can't dance, but I can throw the pill.
I motivate the cats, I like to tease,
I play so cool, I aim to please.
That's why you all got here on the double
To catch me doin' the Super Bowl Shuffle.

OTIS WILSON

I'm mama's boy, Otis, one of a kind.
The ladies all love me
For my body and my mind.
I'm slick on the floor as I can be
But ain't no sucker gonna get past me.
Some guys are jealous
Of my style and class,
That's why some end up on their—.
I didn't come here, lookin' for trouble.
I just get down to the Super Bowl Shuffle.

STEVE FULLER
They say Jimbo is our man,
If Jimmy can't do it, I sure can.
This is Steve, and it's no wonder
I run like lightnin', pass like thunder.
So bring on Atlanta, bring on Dallas,
This is for Mike and Papa Bear Halas.

I'm not here to feather his ruffle,
I just came here to do
The Super Bowl Shuffle.

MIKE RICHARDSON
I'm L.A. Mike, and I play it cool.
They don't sneak by me 'cause I'm no fool.
I fly on the field, and get on down.
Everybody knows I don't mess around.
I can break 'em, shake 'em,
Any time of day.
I like to steal it and make 'em pay,

So please don't try to beat my hustle
'Cause I'm just here to do
The Super Bowl Shuffle.

(Repeat CHORUS)

RICHARD DENT
The sackman's comin', I'm your man Dent,
If the quarterback's slow,
He's gonna get bent.
We stop the run, we stop the pass,
I like to dump guys on their—.
We love to play for the world's best fans,
You better start makin'
Your Super Bowl plans.
But don't get ready or go to any trouble
Unless you practice
The Super Bowl Shuffle.

GARY FENCIK
It's Gary here, and I'm Mr. Clean.
They call me "hit man,"
Don't know what they mean.
They throw it long and watch me run,
I'm on my man, one-on-one.
Buddy's guys cover it down to the bone,
That's why they call us the 46 zone.
Come on everybody, let's scream and yell,
We're goin' to do the Shuffle,
Then ring your bell.

WILLIAM PERRY
You're lookin' at the Fridge,
I'm the rookie.
I may be large, but I'm no dumb cookie.
You've seen me hit, you've seen me run,
When I kick and pass, we'll have more fun.
I can dance, you will see
The others, they all learn from me.
I don't come here lookin' for trouble,
I just came here to do
The Super Bowl Shuffle.

(Repeat CHORUS)

The Bears line up to give New England a taste of what's to come in this 20-7 midseason victory.

*The sign on the Bear charter flight to
New Orleans for Super Bowl XX.*

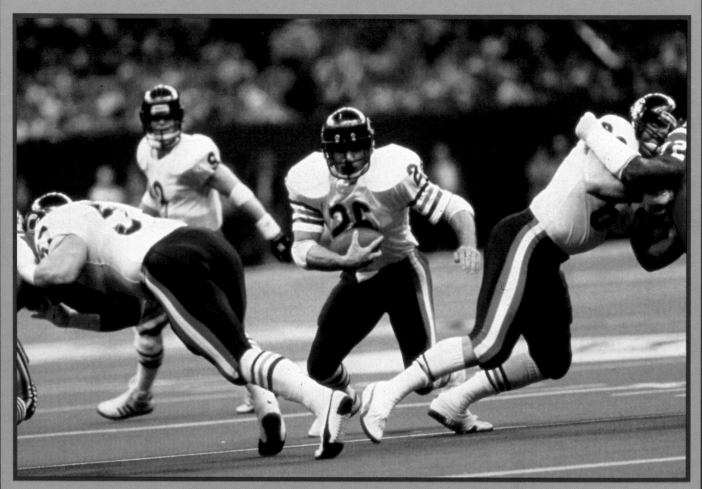

*Matt Suhey scores the first Bear touchdown in Super Bowl XX.
Opening the hole for him are Tom Thayer (left) and Jay Hilgenberg as Jim McMahon watches.*

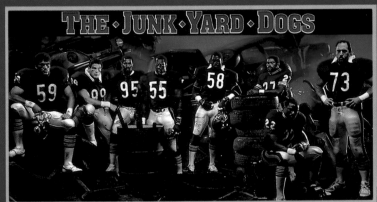

From the left: Ron Rivera,
Dan Hampton, Richard Dent, Otis Wilson,
Wilber Marshall, Mike Richardson,
Dave Duerson, and Mike Hartenstine.

Posing before Super Bowl XX at the Superdome
in New Orleans, Bear photogrpher
Mitch Friedman handling the camera.

The Super Year defense: Buddy Ryan along with
front four Richard Dent (95), William Perry (72),
Steve McMichael (76), Dan Hampton (99);
linebackers Wilber Marshall (58),
Mike Singletary (50), Otis Wilson (50);
defensive backs Leslie Frazier (21), Gary Fencik (45),
Dave Duerson (22), Mike Richardson 27).

The site, the Louisiana Superdome,
New Orleans, January 26, 1986.

Bear Super defense! (above) Dan Hampton sacks New England's Tony Eason. Also in the photo are Otis Wilson (55), Richard Dent (95) and Tyrone Keys (98).

Otis Wilson sacks Steve Grogan (right).

RECORDS SET BY THE CHICAGO BEARS IN SUPER BOWL XX

Most points, team	46
Largest victory margin	36
Most points, team, second half	23
Most points, team, third quarter	21
Most touchdowns, rushing	4

The celebration begins on the sideline: Gary Fencik (45) leading it. Also in the picture are Mike Richardson (27) and Dan Hampton (99).

Fencik and Wilson enjoy a world championship.

Jim McMahon triumphant.

Happy linebackers after having done their job so well: Wilber Marshall (58), Mike Singletary (50), and Otis Wilson (58).

Bear president Mike McCaskey shows off the Vince Lombardi Trophy, which only a Super Bowl champion can showcase.

Super Bowl XX MVP Richard Dent (left) is interviewed by Bob Costas of NBC after the game as William Perry awaits his turn.

Welcome home.

A championship moment.

Super Bowl XX

Chicago Bears vs. New England Patriots — January 26, 1986
Superdome, New Orleans, LA — Attendance, 73,818

Chicago	13	10	21	2	46
New England	3	0	0	7	10

Scoring

Patriots:	Franklin, 36 FG
Bears	Butler, 28 FG
Bears	Butler, 24 FG
Bears	Suhey, 11 run (Butler kick)
Bears	McMahon, 2 run (Butler kick)
Bears	Butler, 24 FG
Bears	McMahon, 1 run (Butler kick)
Bears	Phillips, 28 interception return (Butler kick)
Bears	Perry, 1 run (Butler kick)
Patriots:	Fryar, 8 pass from Grogan (Franklin kick)
Bears	Safety—Waechter sacked Grogan in end zone

Individual Statistics

Rushing

Bears   Payton 22 for 61; Suhey 11 for 52, 1 TD; Gentry 3 for 15; Sanders 4 for 15; McMahon 5 for 14, 2 TDs; Thomas 2 for 8; Perry 1 for 1, 1 TD; Fuller 1 for 1.

Patriots: Collins 3 for 4; Weathers 1 for 3; Grogan 1 for 3; C. James 5 for 1; Hawthorne 1 for -4.

Passing

Bears: McMahon, 12 of 20 for 246; Fuller 0 of 4.

Patriots: Grogan 17 of 30 for 177, 1 TD, 2 I; Eason, 0 of 6.

Receiving

Bears: Gault 4 for 129; Gentry 2 for 41; Margerum 2 for 36; Moorehead 2 for 22; Suhey 1 for 24; Thomas 1 for 4;

Patriots: Morgan 7 for 70; Starring 2 for 39; Fryar 2 for 24, 1 TD; Collins 2 for 19; Ramsey 2 for 16; C. James 1 for 6; Weathers 1 for 3.

Team Statistics

	Bears	Patriots
Total yardage	408	123
Net rushing	167	7
Net passing	241	116
First downs	23	12
Rushing	13	1
Passing	9	10
By penalties	1	1
Interceptions	2	0
Sacks	7	3

1985 CHICAGO BEARS - SUPERBOWL CHAMPIONS

FIRST ROW: (from left); Maury Buford(8), Jim McMahon, Steve Fuller(4), Kevin Butler(6), Kevin McMahon (9), Mike Tomczak(18), Thomas Sanders(20), Leslie Frazier(21), Dave Duerson(22), Shaun Gayle(23), Jeff Fisher(24)

SECOND ROW: Mike Richardson(27), Dennis Gentry, Jerry Vainisi, Matt Suhey(26), Mike Richardson(27), Dennis Gentry (29), Ken Taylor(31), Calvin Thomas(33), Walter Payton(34), Gary Fencik(45), Reggie Phillips(48), Mike Singletary(50), Jim Morrissey(51), Michael McCaskey

THIRD ROW: Pete McGame, Cliff Thrift(52), Dan Rains(53), Brian Cabral(54), Otis Wilson(55), Tom Thayer(57), Wilber Marshall(58), Ron Rivera (59), Tom Andrews(60), Mark Bortz(62), Jay Hilgenberg(63), Henry Waechter(70), Ray Earley

FOURTH ROW: William Perry(72), Mike Brian McCaskey, Andy Frederick(71), William Perry(72), Mike Hartenstine(73), Jim Covert(74), Stefan Humphries(75), Steve McMichael(76), Keith Van Horne(78), Kurt Becker(79), Tim Wrightman(80), James Maness(81), Gary Haeger

FIFTH ROW: Fred Caito, Willie Gault(83), Brian Baschnagel(84), Dennis Pete McGame, Cliff Thrift(52), Dan Rains(53), Brian Cabral(54), Otis McKinnon(85), Brad Anderson(86), Emery Moorehead(87), Pat Dunsmore(88), Mitch Krenk(89), Richard Dent(95), Kevin Okonigo (96), Tyrone Keys(98), Dan Hampton(99), Clyde Emrich

SIXTH ROW: Mike Ditka, Ted Plumb, Ed Hughes, Dale Haupt, Jim LaRue, Johnny Roland, Steve Kazor, Dick Stanfel, Buddy Ryan, Jim Dooley

Photo by Mitch Friedman

"*Without the Bears, there might as well not be an NFL!*"
—*Robin and Bryan Wilson*

ON BEING A BEAR FAN

They mirror the personality of the team they come to cheer, in that they are cut from the sturdy cloth George Halas wove so many years ago.

Butkus was tough, right? So are the guys who sit in the south end zone at Soldier Field with a December north wind sawing on their noses.

McMichael was durable, right? **ROBERT UNGER** has 365 ticket stubs from Bear games he's attended since 1943, and that doesn't count the 30 or so coupons he purchased beginning in 1939, until he turned 15. With the coupon, you could get into the games for a quarter.

Bears fans . . . what a remarkable story!

Fathers have passed their passion for the Bears to sons who, in turn, have passed it to their sons. And so on. Guys who carry lunch buckets during the week rub elbows with guys who eat breakfast in Chicago and dinner in Belgium. Over the years, the biggest change has to be the terrific growth in the number of female fans.

A number of Bear fans were asked to put into words what the Bears mean to them.

BONNIE BADER remembered games at Wrigley Field as a youngster, "wearing a battery pack around my waist with wires running down my pant legs to the latest invention, electric socks!" Her family has held tickets since 1941. "My Dad was still going to games the year he died (1989), and now my daughter has taken his place as an avid fan."

BILL KIRSCHTEN: "They are Chicago, a part of this community. I no longer live or die by them (I'm older now), but any time I travel people want to know about the Bears. They are still part of us all. . . ."

RON AND STAN BANAS, season ticket holders for more than 30 years, "We don't just go to the games, our offices are decorated in Bear memorabilia—plaques, prints, photos, everything. . . ."

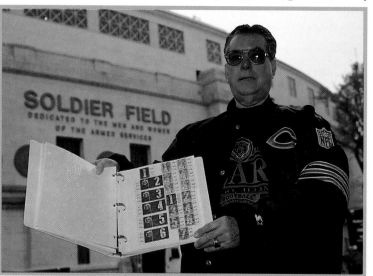

Robert Unger with his collection of 365 ticket stubs . . . and still growing.

"The Bears have been the most important part of my life," **PAT ROCKFORD,** says. "I recall long ago when, at the age of 12, I sneaked in to see my first Bear game at Wrigley Field. Most of the time after that I got caught. Later I can say that I missed my first Bear home game in 35 years in 1987 because of a heart attack. I'd gone to Bear games with three

broken ribs, a broken wrist, bone chips on my ankle, and a broken tail-bone. Sub-zero weather? Never missed a game because of the weather."

MARTIN GECHT observed, "It seems to me the coaches always meant for the Bears to be sportsmanlike but firm in their desire to demonstrate ability and perfection. The team has had its ups and downs, along with the fans, but we never had to be ashamed of the way they played the game — a l w a y s straight!"

DENNY HEBSON recollects being on the sidelines at Wrigley Field in the early 1950s. He was a member of a top grammar school football team and they were invited to a game. "I was in awe," he said. "When I got older we began organizing bus trips from our restaurants out in the suburbs to the games. We've had as many as five or six busloads on a given Sunday."

"A lifetime of good times, bad times, and something to look forward to," said **CHARLES MERIGOLD.**

PATRICK MCCARTHY has only missed two home games as a season ticket holder. One was when a Bob Thomas field goal to upset the Raiders hit the upright and bounced back, and the other was when . . . well, let Patrick tell it.

"It was December 7, 1980, and it was due to the birth of my son. We waited too long and I had to deliver the baby myself. Thank God it was our third, so I had some idea of what to do. He was born early in the morning and I stayed home with my family and missed seeing

the Bears destroy Green Bay 61-7! I don't regret it, though, because my son was born healthy."

RICK WEBBER has a survivor's view. "Being a fan means going to Soldier Field to freeze watching my team, whether they win or lose. It means dedication. No matter what the score, it means staying for 60 complete minutes, 10 games a year. For the time in between seasons, it means suffering the fact that I cannot hear helmets crack again until fall."

SHARON MARTY'S career as a fan has been a love story.

"On December 14, 1947, I saw my first Bears game and had my first date with Pete. He became my husband of 40 years until his death in 1989. We went to all games, and now our love of the Bears has been passed on to our children and grandchildren. The Bears have a special place in my heart."

JAMES STASZCUK doesn't have a least-favorite Bear.

"Any player who plays for an NFL team, especially the Bears, is a favorite with me. They possess a talent the average person can't appreciate. I salute all of them, and I would love to trade places with any one of them on any given Sunday."

"They are my most passionate 'other interest'," claims **PATRICK CARROLL.** "I can't wait each year for camp to open and I'm disappointed when the season is over. The best words: BEAR DOWN."

FRED GREENBERG shared his memories of being a Bear fan.

PETE WHITE

No fan got closer to the action than Pete White, to the occasional consternation of the NFL office.

"Who's that little guy out there on the sideline?" the league would bark. "He's not media, is he?"

"Not exactly," the Bears would reply.

"Doesn't work for the team, does he?"

"Not exactly," the Bears would reply.

When the heat got bad Pete would be warned to keep a low profile for a while, which shouldn't have been hard because he was jockey-sized at best and easily lost on the Bears' bench. But he'd only stay lost for five minutes or so, then he'd be back up there by the sideline, hollering encouragement to the players.

Pete was a shoeshine man. He got to know the Bears because he shined shoes in an office building on Jackson Boulevard where the Bears offices were. His first friendship was with Jim Finks, and it blossomed through the organization. It was simple . . . everybody liked Pete, including the players.

Dan Hampton would fuss over him to Pete's huge delight, and Noah Jackson would hear it when Pete told him to work harder. He could counsel Walter Payton or kid with Otis Wilson.

Yet, out there on the sideline, natty as could be in his pinstripes, Pete was all business . . . and television's big parabolic microphones would pick up that fierce little voice of his:

"Come on . . . Come on . . . You can do it!"

Pete died a while back. The sideline is poorer without him.

ON BEING A BEAR FAN

*From SATURDAY NIGH
Chris Farl*

"They were our t
ter given and none
watching Sid Luckr
Seeing Papa Bear st
"I'm sure," said
people call themse
so I don't want to
ments. But I will
more than I do,
attest to that."

HENRY PAULUS
blocks west of Wr
was on a rainy day
park and stood in
tickets. The park
before game time,
seats. They indicat
being there in the
as long as the seats
tle more comfortab
Halas' thought. In
ets and added twc
Soldier Field. Nov
pany me to the gai
One anonymous
to go to brunch bef
TODD SCHULTZ
zeal. "I grew up in
I guess I was brai
reason I can think
Lombardi years!"

They mirror the personality of the team they come to cheer, in that they are cut from the sturdy cloth George Halas wove so many years ago.

Butkus was tough, right? So are the guys who sit in the south end zone at Soldier Field with a December north wind sawing on their noses.

McMichael was durable, right? **ROBERT UNGER** has 365 ticket stubs from Bear games he's attended since 1943, and that doesn't count the 30 or so coupons he purchased beginning in 1939, until he turned 15. With the coupon, you could get into the games for a quarter.

Bears fans . . . what a remarkable story!

Fathers have passed their passion for the Bears to sons who, in turn, have passed it to their sons. And so on. Guys who carry lunch buckets during the week rub elbows with guys who eat breakfast in Chicago and dinner in Belgium. Over the years, the biggest change has to be the terrific growth in the number of female fans.

A number of Bear fans were asked to put into words what the Bears mean to them.

BONNIE BADER remembered games at

Wrigley Field as a youngster, "wearing a battery pack around my waist with wires running down my pant legs to the latest invention, electric socks!" Her family has held tickets since 1941. "My Dad was still going to games the year he died (1989), and now my daughter has taken his place as an avid fan."

BILL KIRSCHTEN: "They are Chicago, a part of this community. I no longer live or die by them (I'm older now), but any time I travel people want to know about the Bears. They are still part of us all. . . ."

RON AND STAN BANAS, season ticket holders for more than 30 years, "We don't just go to the games, our offices are decorated in Bear memorabilia— plaques, prints, photos, everything. . . ."

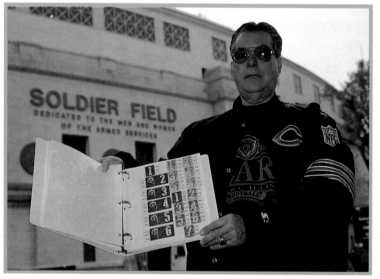

Robert Unger with his collection of 365 ticket stubs . . . and still growing.

"The Bears have been the most important part of my life," **PAT ROCKFORD,** says. "I recall long ago when, at the age of 12, I sneaked in to see my first Bear game at Wrigley Field. Most of the time after that I got caught. Later I can say that I missed my first Bear home game in 35 years in 1987 because of a heart attack. I'd gone to Bear games with three

broken ribs, a brok
and a broken tail
missed a game bec

MARTIN GECH
coaches always me
but firm in their c
to demonstrate a
and perfection.
team has had its up
downs, along wit
fans, but we neve
to be ashamed o
way they played
g a m e — a l w
straight!"

DENNY HE
recollects being o
sidelines at W
Field in the
1950s. He was a
ber of a top gra
school football
and they were in
to a game. "I w
awe," he said. "
I got older we
organizing bus
from our restai
out in the subu
the games. We'v
as many as five
busloads on a
Sunday."

"A lifetime of
times, bad time
something to lo
ward to,"

CHARLES MERIO

PATRICK MCC
games as a seaso
Thomas field goa
and bounced bac
let Patrick tell it.

"It was Decem
of my son. We w
baby myself. Tha
idea of what to c
and I stayed hor

Irv DuBoff

Toward the end of the long coaching tenure of George Halas, a northside drapery-cleaning establishment ran the following message on its marquee:

"Mr. Halas. Would you be the coach if you weren't the owner?"

The man who put that message up has missed just two home games in the last 51 seasons, and one road game since 1958. He was hospitalized during the 1985 Super Bowl season, missing home wins over Atlanta and Indianapolis and the season's only loss, at Miami. He had a stroke three years ago, so the road games get tougher, but he's shooting for one more season.

"I loved the Bears," said Irv DuBoff, referring to the time he put up the marquee message. "I still love them. I was frustrated—I thought the game was passing Mr. Halas by and I said so. Right or wrong, it was what I felt. I know Mr. Halas was mad. I am grateful, though, that in later years I saw him several times at games and he always said hello to me."

That 1985 problem came the day after the Bears beat Dallas 44-0. At DFW Airport returning to Chicago, Irv started hemorrhaging. He made it back to Chicago and was hospitalized with an intestinal problem.

"My first game back was the Jets on the road," DuBoff recalled. "I walked into the hotel and saw Don Pierson of the *Tribune,* Mike Adamle and Mike Singletary. They started talking about me breaking my string of Bears games. I said, 'Do I have to start over?'.

Mike Singletary laughed and said, 'No, Irv, we put you on injured reserve'."

Irv's gone to so many games, he and his wife Cyrille have earned free frequent-flyer trips to Hawaii and Europe.

"People say, 'You must have spent a fortune!' I don't drink, I don't smoke . . . the Bears are my vice. I have enjoyed, so much, getting to know players on the road trips. I say hello, but I don't bug them." Because he doesn't, the players accept him.

All those years, all those games . . . does Irv have a favorite Bear?

The answer was prompt in coming. "Ronnie Bull. He was a good athlete and he's a fine person."

born March 16, 1954, so when the season ticket application arrived we didn't renew on time due to the fact that we did not have anyone to stay with the baby when the games would be played. We wrote to Mr. George Halas and requested that we be allowed to renew even though we were late. To our great surprise we received a letter and a check for $5 as a gift for the addition to our family."

AL SAIA offered a profound assessment of his team.

"The Bears truly represent the cultural fiber of our great city and its character and personality. They symbolize the will of its fans and the people of Chicago. And, win or lose, like a member of the family, they can make you laugh or cry, and good or bad, you still love them in the end."

MIKE HAGEN likes the fact that the Bears personify toughness and tenacity while at the same time having fun. Mike has a favorite Bear moment, too. "I got Brian Piccolo's autograph as a kid. It was after the game when Sayers hurt his knee. Brian told me not to worry that Gale would be okay. How ironic."

MARK NEELY grew up in Chicago, but now lives in California.

"The Bears are a link to my life in Chicago. I left when I was 16 and through them . . . I return home."

Kevin gets his due.

Comedian George Wendt (left)
and WGN's Chuck Swirsky.

The Greatest Fans in the World!

Tailgating outside Soldier Field.

"We look for an edge."
—David McGinnis, linebacker coach

WHAT YOU DON'T SEE

Louise Johnson doesn't answer phones at home if she can help it, and Gary Haeger doesn't do laundry. They do that kind of thing all day long for the Bears.

And the three hours-worth of football you see on those exciting fall Sundays is—as they say—just the tip of the iceberg.

This is about what you don't see.

Sixty-one people work regularly in support of the Bears . . . a number that does not include the dozens of extras who pitch in on a part-time basis. Those range from team internists, orthopedists, foot doctors, dentists, and eye doctors; to cleaners, caterers and suppliers; to airline crews, stadium crews, and hotel staffs. And the hundred or so of Steve Zielke's eager-beavers who staff the summer training camp at Platteville, Wisconsin.

It is—to borrow another old chestnut—a big deal.

The focus here is on some of the people up in Lake Forest, a town of sophistication and charm, seemingly at odds with the bloody-nose business of

Max Swiatek, who came to work for the Bears when Bronko Nagurski was the chief running back in 1934 and is still a member of the staff, poses with one of his other favorite running backs, Walter Payton.

professional football. Not the case, though—Lake Forest likes the Bears and vice-versa. The team headquarters has been there since 1975 and now the whole operation is in that north shore town.

So what about Louise Johnson? Well, Louise runs the switchboard.

Lot of calls?

"At least one a minute from nine to five," she said. "We get the most calls after a loss. Guys will absolutely insist I relay their message to the coaches about who should play next week, or what play not to run. The calls I get after lunch are even more interesting. And by then, I'm kind of running out of steam. Sometimes I want to say, I don't know where you guys go for lunch, but I'll join you!"

Walter Payton used to relieve Louise on the switchboard. Kevin Butler does now.

And Gary Haeger's home laundry embargo?

Gary's the equipment manager. Tony Medlin's his able assistant. Between

On board the charter flight home, relaxing, Gary Fencik (left) and Mike Hartenstine.

them, they do about 20 75-pound loads of laundry every day. "More if it's muddy," said Haeger.

The Bears wear between 800 and 900 pairs of socks per year. One conspicuous consumer is kicker Butler, who wears one pair for pre-game warm-ups, another during the first half and a third for the second half. And all must be new. "That's 60 pairs a year right there," Haeger noted.

The NFL has a rule now that all visiting team equipment must be guarded by security while in a foreign locker room. Haeger was a key man in getting that rule made law. His inspiration?

"We played at Indianapolis and somebody stole Mike Singletary's helmet out of the locker room the night before the game. We could replace it, that wasn't the problem—we had the same helmet, the same mask, the same pads. But it wasn't

Longtime Bear business manager Rudy Custer on the sideline with mascot George Motyka.

210

LOOKING AFTER BUSINESS

Somebody had to do it, and Rudy Custer did from the time of World War II until Super Bowl XX.

George Halas met Rudy in the Pacific during World War II. They were both serving under Admiral Chester Nimitz. Rudy's job was to get things done for the more senior officers. One of them was Lieutenant Commander Halas. "He always had directives to write, and he hated doing it," Rudy explained. "My commander told Halas if he needed something done to go to me and I would do it. And I did.

"At the of the war, Halas held a party out there in the Pacific and I was invited. During the party, he said he wanted to talk to me and we went off to a separate room. He handed me a roll of bills. It was $500. I asked what it was for and he told me for the things I'd done for him while we were out there. I told him I couldn't accept it. He said, yes, I could, and that he wanted me to go to work for the Bears when we got out of the Navy."

There was a little back-and-forth regarding that. Halas said he would hire him as "Assistant to the President." Rudy thought that was maybe a little too much. He suggested "Business Manager."

Well, Rudy got out of the service before Halas and showed up in Chicago for his job. The only problem was that Halas had neglected to tell his secretary, Frances Osborn, and temporary business manager Ralph Brizzolara of the hiring. Rudy was sent to the backroom where, for the next three months he spent his time with Max Swiatek as they tried to figure out something constructive for him to do.

Halas returned from the war and got the situation worked out. Rudy became "Business Manager," the title Coach bestowed upon him. He handled everything Halas did not want to do anymore in Chicago than he had in the Pacific. Stadium matters, travel, business, advertising, promotions, broadcasting arrangements . . . you name it. Not to mention all those directives, memos, and reports. If you needed something from the Bears, you called Rudy.

He served for 40 years, and Halas appreciated it just as much in the Bear offices as he had on shipboard.

THE BOTTOM LINE

It's a competition . . . played on a green field, too, only this one's made of dollars.

Ted Phillips is the contract negotiator for the Chicago Bears. He spends millions.

How do you do that?

Patiently.

"Jim Finks told me something I try to keep in mind. . . 'Don't talk a lot. Listen. You'll learn more'. I try to be prepared, too. I look at a negotiation from our side, certainly, but I try to look at it from their side, too. I need to understand the alternatives available to both sides."

Ted's been the Bears' contract man since 1987. He also is the club's chief financial officer. Before joining the Bears in 1983 Phillips was a tax auditor and accountant with Ernst & Whinney. He's a Notre Dame graduate.

"I went through the 'Who's he?' period with the agents, but they know me now. What makes a negotiation work is when both sides make an effort to understand the other guy and where he's coming from."

How do you feel when a big one's done?

"Not really happy, but not really upset, either. Kind of edgy, I guess. If it went well, I think both sides feel good but they feel like they didn't get everything the way they wanted it. That's the way it's supposed to come out—it might not be exactly what you want, but both sides can live with it. I think that's negotiating."

KEEPING THINGS IN ORDER. . .

A few years ago there was a little framed sign hung in that area of the Bears dressing room used by the offensive linemen. The sign read: "Offensive line, Official Visitors seat."

The person who made the sign, hung it, and sat under it was Richard L. McMurrin.

Richard lives across the street from Halas Hall, the Bears' Lake Forest facility. He is the building custodian.

"Mr. Finks hired me, " he is fond of saying. "I have a lifetime contract."

And the official visitor's seat?

"Offensive linemen are pleasant fellows, " Richard explained. "They're intelligent and sensitive. They're fairly polite. Defensive players are less attractive. Otis Wilson used to slap the California Death-Lock on me, and Steve McMichael punched my arm so hard I couldn't lift it for a week. So I would sit with the offensive linemen. It was nice, I could have a cup of tea and visit with Van Horne or Hilgenberg or Jim Covert, or I could just sit and read if I wanted to. Sometimes I would share their lunch with them."

Richard occasionally went to dinner with Coach Ditka and his wife after Bear games at Soldier Field. During the game, he would sit behind the bench on a tarp roller and read. When the Bears were really going good in the Eighties, Richard was reading the collected works of Shakespeare right along with the collected works of Raymond Chandler.

Noting that Coach Wannstedt spent a lot of time dashing up and down the halls when he first arrived at Lake Forest, Richard cautioned. "You know, Rome wasn't built in a day, Coach."

When Jim Finks was the Bears general manager, he went out to his office one night, opening the door to find Richard sprawled on the sofa, smoking a cigar and watching television.

Finks, poker-faced, said "Oh, pardon me," and closed the door.

Richard smiled. "What a nice man. He gave me a lifetime contract, you know."

His favorite former Bear employee was Ted Haracz, public relations director in the 1970s.

"He kept a neat wastebasket," Richard explained.

Mike's helmet. I had to be the guy to go out there when he got off the bus and tell him his helmet had been stolen."

Caroline Guip manages the Soldier Field skyboxes, of which there are 116. Her Sunday crew numbers 86 employees. Prime Foods, the caterer, has 60 employees working on skybox service.

Bryan Harlan, the public relations director, and his assistant Doug Green are at Soldier Field by 7 a.m. on game day if it's a noon game. They close the pressbox at about 8 p.m. In between, they and their staff accommodate about 300 media representatives on the field, in the press box and in the TV trucks. The press box is in direct-line, "ring down" telephone contact with 30 different locations in the stadium on game day.

"It's a juggling job," said Harlan. "PR is trying to balance the interests of the owners, the coaches, the players and the media." After the season there's always next season—production of a year book, media guide, highlight film, fan news letters and news releases.

If you wanted to know who the really tough Bears have been, who would you ask?

Fred Caito, for 25 years the Bears trainer, would be a good choice.

"Payton would have to be high on the list, but so would other guys," said Caito. "Like Alan Page. He was only here four years, but he showed me how he was able to play so well for so long." It isn't just physically tough, those guys are mentally tough, too. The tough guys are there for the long haul, good days and bad. They're survivors."

Who else? Caito remembers Mike Hartenstine, Doug Buffone, Dan Hampton, Jim Osborne and Brian Baschnagel. "Brian broke a bone in his forearm," said Caito. "He never missed a practice, let alone a game." And there were others.

Are players different now? "They're better informed. It used to be, if a guy got hurt you just said, 'Now here's what we're going to do' and he did it. Now, you have to explain, really take time to discuss treatment with them. It's a good thing."

We, the fans—the watchers and listeners and readers—tend to think of healthy players more than hurt

continued on page 214

THE FINDER...

His name was Frank Korch, and he served the Bears well for 25 years until his untimely death in 1958. His scouting efforts were legendary. He found Bulldog Turner down at tiny Hardin-Simmons College in Texas and Willie Galimore at Florida A&M before most other NFL teams even knew the schools existed, much less had football programs.

Hall of Fame back and former Bear coach Paddy Driscoll said of him: "No American boy ever wandered into the five-and-dime to buy a 59-cent football without Korch rushing in to take the boy's name, address, and vital statistics for the Bears' card index."

George Halas claimed he was forever indebted to him and said after Korch died of a heart attack at age 45, "I brought Frank into our organization when he was just a budding sportswriter. His interest in pro football and his memory for the smallest details, prompted me to hire him to handle publicity and collect material on potential players. Korch dug in and amazed us with his ability to gather information on boys playing football at schools we had never heard of. His files were so comprehensive that for years we were able to come up with the 'sleeper' overlooked by all the other clubs.

"During World War II, when he was a sergeant at Fort Sill, Oklahoma, and I was with the navy in Norman, he would come over on every off day to talk football with me," said Halas. "Other servicemen thought it was strange to see an army sergeant and a navy commander so continually buddy-buddy. They didn't realize we had many bonds."

On Being Flexible.

For the better part of fifty years, success in professional football was measured in the wise drafting and patient development of college player talent.

As the old saying goes, the "cake" was baked from scratch.

But that was then . . . Free agency is now.

The tackle you planned on to anchor your offensive line through the turn of the century goes somewhere else, and probably will move again before we reach the year 2000. If you think you've got a chance to reach the playoffs—and with parity stalking the land, everybody does—you'll try to draft a quality tackle, but chances are you may go looking for a quick-fix veteran, just like the team that grabbed your guy.

Now the cake is more apt to be a box mix—add water and one egg, stir, and hope.

Rod Graves, the Bears chief scout and player personnel man, used to follow that scratch recipe, scouting college talent. Now he oversees that supply source as well as the several pools of available veteran talent.

Rod said the big change in the job, to his thinking, is the critical need to rely on others for input.

"My job is to gather and shape information, our product. I still watch film, but I can't watch all of it. So I have to rely on our staff. That's how I gather and shape."

Another change in the personnel game has a dollar sign in front of it—the salary cap. Graves and Ted Phillips, the Bears vice president of operations, have to work closely together. Graves knows who can help, Phillips knows if they can fit.

"We really do work closely," said Rod. "There's got to be trust and a mutual respect for it to work, and we have that. There's going to be times when one of us has to be willing to gamble on the other one being right."

Rod's dad, Jackie Graves, was a highly respected pro scout. Rod's remindful of Jackie—polite and proper. And more.

"He taught me to be my own man," said Rod. "He told me to do the job soundly then stand by my convictions. He said it was mostly about hard work."

Still is . . . just a different set of rules, now. Graves and the Bears' personnel staff can live with that.

INSIGHT: DOWN UNDER

"Down under" is where the stadium works, where all of those things happen that you really aren't aware of unless they don't happen.

Like the calm, unflappable guy who works the officials' dressing room. He's been doing it for years, long enough that he knows most of the officials by their first names and is at least on a nodding basis with the rest.

He pulls for the home team. He wouldn't be there, otherwise. There's a lot that's not very slick about standing around for hours before and after the game down in the cold concrete bottom of the ballpark. But he is more than a fan. A fan couldn't do what he does. A fan couldn't hide his disappointment and wrath after a tough loss, tending to the needs and safe-keeping of the crew. Never mind that their call killed what should have been a winning drive. The game is like cards; you play with what's dealt. The calls are the same way.

So the unflappable man sees to towels and sweet rolls and coffee and tape and crashers and dry socks on the bad days. He develops stone ears when they forget or get excited and talk in front of him. He doesn't ever say "good job" or "bad job" because he knows that, however it came out, it was their best job.

The stadium manager is less tranquil.

Just before 11 o'clock on a rainy game morning, standing in the tunnel at the south end, he's talking about water-removal. An overnight rain has left ankle-deep pools in the walkways of the upper level. He is speaking to a game-day roustabout who doesn't see much future in sweeping water on a rainy day.

"You'll squeegee it up, out of the passages, into the stadium."

"Yeah, but there's one hell of a lot of them passages! What if we sweep 'em out and it rains again?"

The stadium manager rests a hand on the shoulder of the non-believer.

"Then we'll sweep them again, won't we?"

The stadium manager's walkie-talkie bleeps in

---

ones. Caito doesn't. "I can get as excited about the progress an injured guy might make during the week as I do about the game. Every one of these guys is a spoke in the wheel."

Vice-president Tim McCaskey is Bear point-man on efforts to build a new stadium, one of the organization's top priorities.

Marketing director Ken Valdiserri knows about ratings points, make-goods, commercial tracking, shortfalls and all those things. The Bears package their own pre-season telecasts, coaches' show and fan show. Valdiserri, with John Bostrom and Jack Trompeter, keep those balls in the air along with some 70 local sponsors, special trips, stadium give-aways and a day-long fan bash centered around the first day of the college player draft.

Valdiserri also is the key contact with WGN, the club's flagship radio station.

Until fairly recently, most pro football teams had a laid-back approach to sponsorship and marketing. But not now. In a time when the competition with other sports just keeps on growing, Valdiserri and the Bears have taken a vigorous stance when it comes to developing promotional support and identification.

Patrick McCaskey has looked after team travel for

10 years and spearheads the highly successful Piccolo Golf Outing, a support group for research into the cancer that killed former Bear Brian Piccolo. McCaskey also oversees the Bears Learning Corps—an educational program of NFL-based geography for area schools, among other community activities.

Tim LeFevour, director of administration, sees to training camp, special projects, stadium use and club facilities.

Every Monday after a home game LeFevour meets with representatives of the Park District, the city, the ushering service, and the ticket office to review problems. "It's helping," said LeFevour. "If something's wrong, we let people know. It's not to berate, it's to make it work better."

LeFevour and groundskeeper Ken Mrock race the calendar each spring to get Halas Hall practice fields in shape. "Kenny doesn't believe in sod, he thinks seeding gives us a better field," said LeFevour. "He pre-germinates seed, so that we're sowing grass that's already rooted. With mini-camps, we have to get a running start."

George McCaskey, ticket manager, has a crew of twelve on game-day.

"We're busiest an hour before the game," he said.

interruption: water is backing up in the showers in the visiting team clubhouse.

By 11:15 it's raining again.

At the home team bench, the Telco man covers his head with a soggy towel and speaks into one of the coaches' headsets. Upstairs in the booth, his assistant responds.

"Yeah, I hear you good. Now come on down and wrap the junctions and the connections. It's raining again.

The backfield coach who uses the headset wanders out of the dressing room.

"Working okay?"

"Yes, it's fine. . . right now."

A club guy locates the man who operates the rig they use to remove water from the field. They are down under the bowl end and the guy has just parked his rig. He smiles at the club guy.

"Just got done. She's in good shape."

"But you didn't do the end zones."

The driver shrugs. "Did the field."

"Great, but we play in the end zones, too."

The man in charge of the chain crew cautions his first-down marker man as they dress under the north stand.

"We got another beef after the last game, Johnny. When they're measuring for first down, you've got to stand as far from the stick as you can so's the camera shot ain't blocked."

A club guy, the stadium public address man, and the television red-hat get out of the rain underneath to synchronize on television time. The public address reminds the club guy to remind the house band to quit playing over his spots in the first time out.

The stadium PA man wheezes into his booth just as the teams come out for warm-ups. He has a head cold and soaked feet from standing on the field checking visiting lineup changes. His wife's mad because she's sitting out in the rain and he's in a dry booth and she hadn't wanted to come to the game in the first place.

But he's a pro, so it doesn't show in his voice when he says, "Good afternoon, ladies and gentlemen."

"That's when people arrive at the stadium and realize they forgot their tickets. It doesn't seem like anybody ever thinks of it while they're backing out of the driveway."

And the tickets themselves? Artwork, first, must be approved. Then artists do design and layouts. The collector-appeal of a ticket is appreciated in the design.

Tickets are printed in early summer under secure conditions, then imprinted by the Bears computer department. About 90 percent of the tickets are mailed to season ticket customers.

Brian McCaskey, operations assistant and player liaison coordinator, helps players in such areas as family assistance, financial education, degree completion, and post-career internships.

Clyde Emrich, with more than two decades on the staff of the Bears, was one of the first NFL strength coordinators.

He used to teach big guys like Stan Jones and Joe Fortunato and smaller guys like Dave Whitsell how to get strong without sacrificing speed or movements. He did it on his own at first, at a YMCA in Chicago. Then the Bears hired him.

Clyde has been with the Bears ever since. When he arrived the team had a random set or two of dumbbells and weights in a corner of the locker room. Today there is an elaborate, well-equipped weight-training room in the basement of Halas Hall.

Emrich contributed that to the Bears . . . and he influenced other teams as well.

When a Bear player walks into the team weight-room in the off-season today, which he is encouraged to do four times a week, he is handed a card that tells him what exercises to do, how much weight to lift, how many reps, what to do on the stationary bike and what to do on the stairs.

"We tailor a program for every player," said physical development coordinator Russ Riederer. "The program is a result of input from the player, his position coach and myself.

Rod Graves

Ted Phillips

The programs are constantly evaluated and modified."

Riederer's efforts are pegged to the premise of increasing quickness and power.

What is power, anyway?

"Weight times distance divided by time," he answered. "An easier way to think of it is strength in motion."

Dean Pope is director of video services. The advent of free agency has added to the workloads of many club employees, including Pope.

"We have tapes of all the games played by all 28 teams, in case our people want to study someone."

The Bears film—tape, actually—a game from a midfield sideline location and from the end zone, giving the tapes of offense, defense and special team plays as seen from the two vantage points. They also shoot two cameras at every practice. During the season, Pope and his staff will run through 500 30-minute Beta tapes. The big difference between Pope's pictures and what you see on television is that he must get all 22 players in the picture.

Jim Parmer
ON SCOUTING THE FRIDGE . . .

We didn't have agreement he (defensive tackle William Perry) was a first-round player and a couple of us had to talk like hell to get (Michael) McCaskey to take him. You see a lot of times the kids in the, say, twentieth to twenty-eighth picks have really second-round grades, but if you take them in the first round then you have to pay them first-round wages.

A number of the people weren't super-high on him. Ditka liked him. Some others didn't. He was awfully tough to grade. I'd been over to Clemson and talked to his position coach there, a fella I knew from when he was at Oklahoma State. He told me about Perry.

"The biggest thing you're going to have to watch about him is his appetite, which is enormous," he said. "One day we had a real hard two-a-day workout and we just worked his ass off. Well, he went home and had his wife go out and buy six chickens, and he ate every piece."

I said that's got to be a goddam lie, nobody can eat six chickens. But it wasn't a lie.

He also had a deal with McDonald's down there (Clemson, South Carolina). You see, he was easily the most visible person in town. So McDonald's would let him come in at night, just when they were closing, and what they hadn't sold they'd give to him. Sometimes he'd eat as many as twenty hamburgers a night.

tapes, he brings video players for team and coaches meetings.

Greg Gershuny directs the team's information systems. The Bears, like the rest of the NFL, are increasingly computer-driven.

The breaking down or "take off" of each running of a certain play used to be done manually. Now the computer does it. The computer categorizes game tapes for use in preparing for an opponent and it permits the Bears to scout themselves—to search for tendencies other teams might pick up and exploit.

"The scouting department has a wall covered with magnetic cards identifying every player in the league and showing our evaluation of him," Gershuny said. "We still have the wall, but now Rod Graves, director of scouting, carries the wall around in his computer. He can be on the road scouting and Coach Wannstedt can call him for an opinion. All Rod does is turn on his computer and he's got the wall."

Coaches coach more than you might expect. David McGinnis, linebacker coach, says the 2

When the Bears travel, Pope has twelve cases of equipment. In addition to cameras, tools, tripods and 1/2 hours a player spends on the practice field is supported by about 10 hours' work by the coaches.

Max

He joined the Bears in 1934. George Halas hired him as a "staff assistant," whatever that meant. What it meant was total dedication to a man and his football team. Over the years, Max Swiatek worked as equipment manager, trainer, traveling secretary, purchasing agent . . . and whatever other special chores Halas would come up with.

Sixty years later, Max is still with the Bears. His title, officially, purchasing agent; unofficially, dean of the front office staff.

During all those years—when Bronko Nagurski might wander into the office . . . or Bulldog Turner would be looking for a new pair of cleats . . . or Butkus or Payton or Singletary needed something special, Max was always there, and he managed to get things done for all of them.

At the same time, he was George Halas' friend and confidante. After a long practice and all the administrative details were done for the day, Halas would come up to Max and clap him on the shoulder and say, "Max, let's you and I go have a little talk."

They would go to Halas' office and have a glass of wine together. "Irv Kupcinet used to send it to him," Max explained. "We would just sit down and talk about things in general. He still had calls to make, to the league office or other teams or some other things to attend to, but we just sat down and talked. He wanted to relax. So we would sip and talk."

Max had another job during the season. After a game, Halas would have to go up to the Pink Poodle in Wrigley Field to meet with the press and celebrated guests. "He would tell me, Max, I want you to be up there and I want you to get me out of there at some point. I'll give you a sign. Then you just step in and mention I've got to be somewhere and we'll get the hell out of there.'"

Which he did. Then he drove Coach home.

What would they talk about in those private sessions? Sometimes, according to Max, "Halas would unload about something that was bothering him in regard to the team, but most times it was just talk, a half-hour, maybe an hour, a glass of wine, a little relaxation."

George Halas is gone today. Max is still with the Bears. He misses the boss—Max just called him Halas—and he misses the little get-togethers at the end of the day. But even now, in the 1990s, he doesn't miss a day at the office or his stint as doorkeeper at the Soldier Field locker room on game day.

Max remembers when the helmets he used to hand out were leather and that some players, like Hewitt and Plasman, didn't even bother to wear one.

"The defensive staff meets, you do your preparation work as an individual, you meet with your players and you're on the field."

Off-season doesn't slow down much.

"You start on the new season right away," said McGinnis. "We evaluate the free agents. We work to upgrade ourselves technically. We study our games of last year, not just to see how we played, but how we adjusted to change. We look for a pattern. Did we adjust to innovation? We look at the notes we took during the season and see if we should be incorporating them into next year. We look at and evaluate potential players coming up in the draft and we concern ourselves with the off-season conditioning and development of the players we already have. If you boiled it down, you'd say we look at league talent, at college talent, at our talent . . . and we look for an edge. We stay busy."

The personnel or scouting staff, headed by Rod Graves, checks and rechecks college seniors. Scouts work players in their given area, then cross-check, switching areas for a new view.

National combine scouting reports are added to the mix and then Graves makes his report on the top prospects. Once the Bears season is over, the coaches participate in evaluation of the upcoming draftees. Mike McCaskey, Coach Dave Wannstedt, Graves, and Ted Phillips participate in the bottom-line decisions made in the draft room.

Once the draft choice is made or the free agent target-

FEEDING TIME

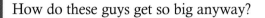

How do these guys get so big anyway?

Following is one day's menu from the Bears' training camp at the University of Wisconsin-Platteville.

Breakfast:

Eggs to order
Bacon or sausage patties
Pancakes & syrup
Cornbread
Danish pastries and bagels
Cereal
Grits
Hash-brown potatoes
Oatmeal
Steamed rice
Fresh fruit (served salad bar)

Lunch

Beef barley soup
French dip sandwiches
Sliced cold meats and cheeses
French-fried potatoes
Steamed rice
Corn on the cob, whole tomatoes
Salad bar
Assorted breads
Ice cream

Dinner

Pork and shrimp egg rolls
Rib-eye steak, 12-ounce
Carved ham
Assorted vegetables
Steamed rice
Au gratin potatoes
Beets
Cauliflower with cheese sauce
Salad bar
Fresh fruit bar
Assorted sliced breads
Cookie trays
Pecan pie
Ice cream bar

. . . What's on the salad bar? Fresh mushrooms, sliced cucumbers, tomatoes, croutons, red onions, bacon bits, chopped eggs, diced ham, diced turkey, shredded cheddar cheese, cottage cheese, tuna fish, carrot sticks, celery sticks, broccoli buds, radishes, macaroni shells, pasta salads, yogurt salad, peas . . . and sunflower seeds.

The fresh fruit bar?

Apples, bananas, cantaloupe, cherries, peaches, honeydew melon, plums, nectarines, oranges, strawberries, watermelon , kiwi fruit, grapes . . . and Casaba melon.

Better question: How come they're not bigger?

ed or the unsigned veteran deemed a need for the future, responsibility swings to Phillips, vice president of operations and club's contract negotiator. While player salaries have risen sharply in recent years, the growth of free agency and the addition of a salary cap for all clubs has made Phillips' job enormously challenging.

And that's just a quick look at the rest of the iceberg.

Even Walter Payton can suffer. Tending to him is longtime trainer Fred Caito (left), and strength coordinator Clyde Emrich (right).

"... we will do things that make the wearing of the
Chicago Bear uniform a point of special pride for the players."
—Mike McCaskey

TWENTY-FOUR

WHAT'S AHEAD

A Conversation with CEO Mike McCaskey and Coach Dave Wannstedt

The Bears and the National Football League face a new world in the 1990s. The game has changed considerably, although not nearly so much as the business which supports it. It has become an enormous enterprise. And that, in the evolutionary scope of things, is just the way it is going to be . . . en route to the next century.

Gone are the guys who played the game during the season and worked another job in the off-season just to make ends meet. Franchises that once could be bought for hundreds of thousands of dollars are now valued in the hundreds of millions. The days when a team relied on 30,000 showing up on a particular Sunday in order to make payroll and costs are gone, too. Now television dollars and licensing rights and endorsements and ancillary market promotions are the integral bottom-line factors.

George Halas was an innovator in the game of professional football and a constant force in guiding the league he helped to create back in 1920. He was there when it was an acorn, and he helped it grow into a towering, splendid oak tree. That legacy has been passed to his heirs. The Bears of the 1990s have to follow his lead if they want to survive in the significantly changing world of professional football.

The present rests in their hands, owner and coach alike, both of whom must pick up the old cudgel and mill and shape it into a workable and successful tool to satisfy Chicago Bear fans.

The present is in the hands of CEO Mike McCaskey and Coach Dave Wannstedt, and the two men sat down to answer questions pertaining to the game, the business, and the Bears.

QUESTION: What do you really want to accomplish in the 1990s . . . besides going to the Super Bowl again and getting a state-of-the-art stadium?

McCASKEY: Those are foremost, but only part of the answer. The game is different today; we have to make major adjustments to compete and keep up with the changes.

QUESTION: What do you think is the biggest change affecting the 1990s?

McCASKEY: The new collective bargaining agreement. It's changed the whole landscape. It's something all of us in the NFL must adjust to. We're aware here; we're trying to be among the leaders in working under the new system.

QUESTION: How does that change from 1983, when you became president of the ballclub?

McCASKEY: Everything has changed dramatically. We are implementing a new system, we have a new coach, and everything is based on building. That's where we feel Dave will carry the load for the new Bears.

WANNSTEDT: The game is so different today. The Bears have to face the 1990s. I'm looking for players who can help us accomplish that end. It's a new world out there.

QUESTION: How do you go about doing that?

McCASKEY: Dave's got what we call "The Board."

It's in his office. It's got the names of our players on magnetic cards at each position. There are some blank cards where we think our needs are. We talk about whether we're going to try and satisfy those needs through the draft or through free agency or through trades. The evaluation of the board must be done in concert with the salary cap, where you're pulling together the financial information as well as the player personnel information, and the coaching evaluation of where our strengths and weaknesses as a team are right now.

QUESTION: And so, obviously, Ted Phillips, your financial man, has got to be involved in player decisions, too.

McCASKEY: He is very much involved. So is Rod Graves, our scouting director.

QUESTION: You have to be constantly assessing talent but you're also assessing that talent in terms of what you can afford and what you can do under the salary cap?

McCASKEY: Right. You might love to have that wide receiver and be certain that he would help the team, but the price tag he's carrying may be too expensive relative to your priorities which might be defensive end or linebacker or some other position.

QUESTION: This is true, too, in terms of maintaining people that you already have, isn't it?

McCASKEY: Absolutely.

WANNSTEDT: Everybody's in the same boat these days. If a guy's a free agent, no matter if you're dealing with a player that's currently on your team or a guy you're pursuing, they really all go into the same basket. We signed Mark Bortz because we had an offensive line need and he was the man we wanted. You have to look at it that way. You can't just count your players apart from others who are out there. The tough thing at this point in dealing with this new free agency system—and we'll need to have a few years under our belt—is to set the market price for different positions. Right now it's very difficult because you see extremes on each team. There are different philosophies among teams as far as what's important to them to be successful. We sit down now and between Mike and myself and Rod (Graves) and Ted (Phillips), we face a whole new agenda. It's a little bit difficult right now because we're in the early stages of a major change.

QUESTION: Weren't there certain things that went on last year, like Reggie White, the defensive end at Green Bay who got the huge salary just before the salary cap?

McCASKEY: In anticipation of the salary cap.

QUESTION: Do you fight that kind of thing, what went on just before the cap?

McCASKEY: As a result of something like Reggie White's contract, players in this first capped year may have overly high expectations of what their salary could be because they look at last year, and expect that it will be a little bit more than that. But, it's not. Because the new system has come in place.

QUESTION: In regard to that, are we getting into a rent-a-player deal?

WANNSTEDT: We would hope not.

McCASKEY: I hope not, too, but it's too early to say, really. We still want to have guys like Mark Bortz play with us for twelve years. We hope that we will have the ability to pay those players commensurate with their performance on the field, and that we will do a terrific job as an organization providing the coaching environment, the work environment, and the family environment that they find attractive.

WANNSTEDT: We're at a point where we've got real young players and we've got some older players who are finishing out their careers. The older players obviously aren't going to be with us for another five or ten years. On the other hand, our younger players are just beginning to develop. I think we'll have some young players in key positions. But as Mike said, we want the seasoned, dedicated players to finish their careers in Chicago. So, right now we just have to handle both situations, the older and the young.

McCASKEY: And we're trying to create an organization that will keep them, but, it'll become more difficult because of free agency.

QUESTION: Jim Finks used to say, "Coaches coach. Players play. Scouts scout. Owners own. That's the way the game is played." If that was true when Finks was general manager here, has it changed now?

McCASKEY: I think it has changed noticeably. There has to be a much tighter coordination between the business and the coaching and the personnel aspects of the game today. It's a result of the new collective bargaining agreement for one thing, but also the changing nature of the game.

QUESTION: Isn't there an irony in this whole thing? The game is returning to the way it was when George Halas was coaching. Halas was the owner, the coach

and at one time a player. In the really old days, you did everything, even through the 1940s and 50s and much of the 60s. Then Jim Finks' philosophy kicked in, but today, it seems, management has reverted to the Halas era.

WANNSTEDT: I think a lot of the teams have had success that way in recent years. If you look at the way teams are being managed now, the owners are so much more involved on a daily basis. They have to be right there because the money's gone up so much. And if you look at the coaching end of it, with these free agencies, it's a whole new ballgame.

Coaches used to be done at the end of a season. They'd take two months off and come back before the draft and do a little bit there, but then they really weren't concerned until just before training camp. I mean now it's a 12-month-a-year job. It doesn't stop anywhere along the way. On March 14th we had close to 35 players in our weight room who flew in from all over the country. So it's a 12-month-a-year job for the players, too. If you have free agents, they have to come in, they have to see you, and you see them. They have to understand our system.

McCASKEY: This is an interesting comparison. When my grandfather was playing and coaching and owning, he would pass the hat to collect enough money to make good on the promises he'd made to the players. If he'd promised them 50 bucks a game, then he'd count it out after the game, and sometimes if the crowd wasn't good enough, well, then he'd have to pass out an I.O.U. or something like that.

He was also very concerned about the entertainment aspect of it, too. Ray Berry, the great end for the Colts, tells a story, and I'll squeeze it down some. It was a game that was clearly in the hands of the Bears, and the other team had to punt. They punted and my grandfather, then on the sidelines as a coach, ran onto the field and caught the punt and the referee came charging over and yelled "George, George, what the hell are you doing?"

And he said, "Look over my shoulder, you see those empty seats?" The referee said, "Yeah." Coach Halas said, "Next year they won't be empty." He was not beyond doing some crazy things if it helped to promote the game. True story.

QUESTION: Well, at least a head coach today doesn't have to write the press releases.

McCASKEY: True. My grandfather wrote the press releases in the '20s and would carry them around to the Chicago papers after the game trying to get them into print. He had that drive. At the same time, as Dave was talking about, once the season was over he and the players went on to some other job because football didn't pay the freight. It didn't pay enough money to live on for an entire year. So my grandfather went off to the dry cleaning business or the sports wholesaling business. He had to have another job, and so did the players and so did the other coaches. So that part has changed now; it's moved to this very intense year-round effort. And because of the very nature of the business of pro football today, the owner, the coach, the financial person, the player personnel guy, all have to work closely to make it succeed. In my grandfather's day, he was all of them. Now it's a collective effort.

QUESTION: Coach, you played and you've coached with different teams over the years. How has it changed from your perspective?

WANNSTEDT: Well, the things that Mike talked about, on the professional level have changed considerably in just the few years I've been around. I saw it in Dallas and elsewhere around the league. The game itself really goes through trends. I hate to use the word change—it goes through trends as far as the different things that are done football-wise: offense, defense, the kicking game. It moves around. So much of it depends on who's winning and how a team's winning. What's the hot trend? I think the trends come and go, but I don't know how much lasting effect they have. I think a lot of the game now is done for the interest of the fan, from the entertainment end of it with the emphasis on scoring.

McCASKEY: There are different philosophies. Tex Schramm (longtime president of the Dallas Cowboys until the team was sold in 1989) always thought, and a bunch of supporters thought, that the fans were mainly interested in scoring. I think in Chicago the fans have been interested in great defense. One of the greatest games we ever had here in the last ten years was a 10-9 victory over San Francisco on a Monday night in 1988. A tremendous game. Knock-out, drag-out, defensive battle, heavyweights slugging at each other, and the number of points wasn't important. The fans loved that game. It was just one hell of a game.

QUESTION: Like the 1963 championship game where the New York Giants had the best offense in the

league and the Bears had the best defense? This was probably the classic confrontation: offense versus defense. And it was a fantastic game, although a low scoring one (14-10, Bears).

McCASKEY: People remember that game. They come up to me and pull out their wallet and they've got a ticket stub to show that they attended the '63 championship game.

QUESTION: You mention Tex Schramm. The succeeding regime under Jerry Jones and Jimmy Johnson brought about a much closer relationship between owner and coach. Although that particular owner/coach relationship is now severed, did it set a precedent? Are the Bears fashioning themselves after the new Dallas Cowboys or is this just the trend in general?

WANNSTEDT: My only comment on that would be there are so many things that are changing in the NFL, and we are trying to be as aggressive and progressive as we possibly can to get back on top. Whether it's Dallas or some other team it doesn't matter. We have our own philosophy here in Chicago for achieving this. I don't see how, without Mike and I communicating daily, anything could get done effectively in the new scheme of things. It was a very important consideration in my decision to come to Chicago, to be able to have a relationship where we could talk on a daily basis, where it wouldn't take two weeks to make a decision. We have to act quickly and decisively or we could lose out on an opportunity. I couldn't imagine this working without close communication.

McCASKEY: I was looking for a man with whom I could have free and easy communication. That was one of many strengths in Dave that appealed to me. I had the deep feeling that we would be able to talk and work on this thing, that we would both be devoted to making the Bears a Super Bowl champion, and that we would be able to talk and work well together trying to achieve that. I believed if we made mistakes, as we inevitably will, we would have the ability to assess them and not kill ourselves over having made them. We just have to go on to the next decision and try to be right about that one. And over the course of time we expect to be more right than wrong, and therefore start piling up those trophies.

QUESTION: Mike Ditka, said, "In Bear history, it was always something very substantial that you were a Bear." Is that still going to be possible, given the changing NFL?

McCASKEY: We're going to try our darndest to maintain that. It's going to be harder, though. Just look at what's happening in American society in the 1980s and '90s. There has been a weakening of loyalty to the company, and company loyalty to the employee or player. This latest bargaining between the union and the league has left us with a system of free agency. The players said they wanted it. And so it will be more on a year to year basis, how you assemble a team, which is not how it was before.

But I continue to hope that we will do things that make the wearing of the Chicago Bear uniform a point of special pride for the players.

WANNSTEDT: The tradition that the Bears have is one that can kindle pride. It's a great tradition. How do you get it? By winning games, and we're going to win games. By support from the fans, and we've got the best fans here in Chicago that a team could hope for. That's how you generate success, how you kindle a great feeling about where you're at, and, I feel, how you could go to a Super Bowl.

McCASKEY: You have to have success. That's the key. Everything else, every effort, feeds into that—the history, the tradition, the past successes, the great games along the way. People look at those and say that's our team, they did it. And you have that great pride.

QUESTION: When you took over as CEO, Mike, and when you took over as head coach, Dave, did you realize it was going to be quite like it is today?

McCASKEY: Well, I took over back in 1983, and it was very different. Nancy, my wife, and I had to think long and hard before moving from the academic/consulting world into professional football. One of the people I talked to was Jim Finks, and he painted a picture of running an NFL team that was vastly different from how it turned out to be several years later. Things change, that's part of life. The pace of change in the NFL has been dramatically rapid. Back in the middle '80s the off-season was a time that was very busy, much busier than it had been five years earlier. It's changes like that which just continue at an amazing pace, and we have to keep up with them.

QUESTION: What about you, Dave, you played and you obviously had your sights set, at some point, on running the whole show.

WANNSTEDT: I just believe that you surround yourself with good people, you make sure that you know as much or more about the business than your competi-

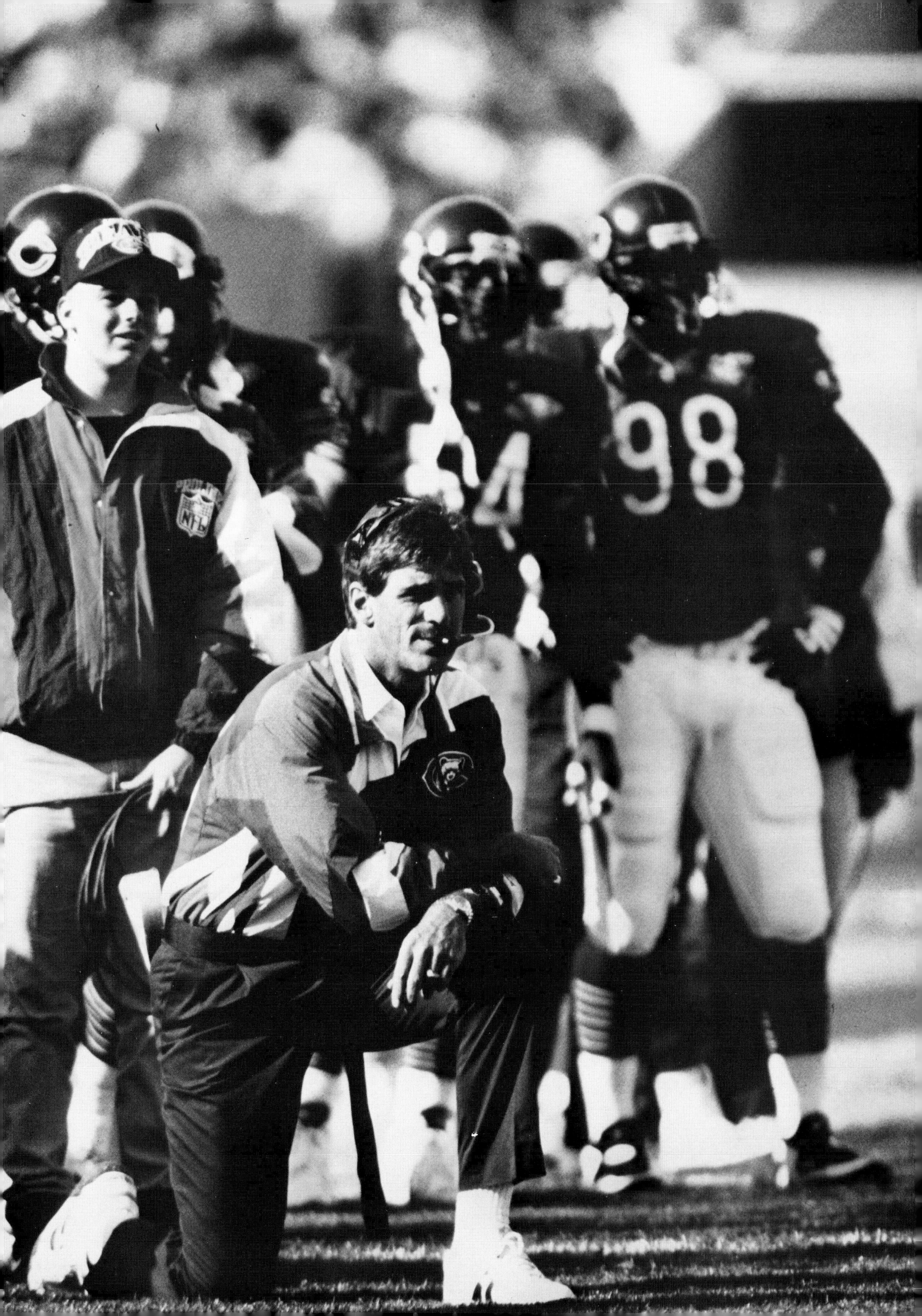
98
NFL

tor, and you are willing to put in the time and work to get the job done. The changes, whether we had a salary cap, or no salary cap, or we had a hundred players on the team or fifty players on the team—we have to work through those things, we really do. That can't be the focus on whether you're going to win or you're going to lose.

McCaskey: The teams that are appalled by the number of changes and resist them, those that hang back and moan about how good it used to be, or how pure it used to be, or how football-oriented it used to be . . . . I think they are the teams that will fall behind.

The changes come and you say "Okay, where are the opportunities in there?" That's what we're trying to do, Dave and I and everybody else at the Bears. We're trying to find the opportunities in the new system and go at them with relish. We don't spend a lot of time bemoaning the changes, we accept the new system and ask how can we make this work for the Bears. Where are the opportunities?

Question: Did you think that head coaching was going to be as complex a thing when you first started out in your coaching career?

Wannstedt: Oh, I think so, no question. I feel fortunate that I started my coaching career under Johnny Majors at Pittsburgh. He was such a detail man. Every assistant coach, I mean everyone, had everything specified, down to who was responsible for turning the lights in the locker room on and who was responsible for turning them off. So, I learned, from an early age, the importance of detail. I think coaching in college helped prepare me for what's happening now in the NFL. With the advent of free agency this year, I have spent a lot of nights downtown with free agents, taking them to dinner and selling them on the Bears. I was selling them on our organization. I was picking guys up at the airport, all the kinds of things you did on the college level when you were recruiting.

McCaskey: I see as a great advantage for the Bears that Dave is so familiar with this aspect of the job. Someone who had just been an assistant coach in the NFL might say, "That's not the job I signed up to do! That's college stuff." But now recruiting is a big part of it. We're trying to get the player who has a choice to make excited about coming to the Bears. All of us share in this important task. If Rod Graves can do a good job of that when he's out scouting, that's terrific; and if Ted Phillips can also create that same sense

when he's dealing with agents, that's a great advantage. This is the pro football environment of today, and it's the way it's going to be in the future.

Question: It is going to be difficult. Can you share with Bear fans how it's going to be from the inside?

Wannstedt: Well, to take it a step farther from what Mike said, when we have a guy come in here, he'll visit with Bryan Harlan, our public relations man; Russ Riederer, the physical development coordinator; and a whole lot of other people. Our trainers, in fact, are picking guys up at the airport; our doctors are adjusting their schedules to give them physicals. They visit with Brian McCaskey about furthering their education. It's a lot more than just what I'm doing, and Mike is doing.

McCaskey: It's everybody in the organization conveying that feeling to our existing players, to our new players, or to potential Bears—that this organization is interested in them. We talked to Mark Bortz and we interacted with him day by day. He became a free agent, and he had a choice whether to stay with the Bears or go someplace else. We wanted him to stay with the Bears.

Wannstedt: The other thing that's going to be interesting is how teams, coaches, and owners deal with this new system. So we say to ourselves everyday, you better surround yourself with good people. I'm talking about players, good players, those who feel football is truly important to them and winning is truly important to them.

Question: Do you think the players will be as committed as they should be under the new structure?

Wannstedt: Sure. They better be . . . or they won't be playing for the Bears. That part of it can't change. Because there's always somebody waiting out there to take their place. They've got to produce.

McCaskey: Football has always been an emotional sport and a team sport and we'll be looking for those guys who treat it that way, and if they don't we'll move on to the next guy.

Question: It seems you will face difficult decisions. There could be players who are popular with the fans who won't fit in your plans. Is this accurate?

McCaskey: That's the tough part. We'll keep them as long as they can perform at a championship level, whereas in the past we might have kept a player for sentimental reasons or because of past performance a year beyond when he was truly performing. We can't

do that now. That's cheating the team, that's cheating our fans. And the coaches will know sooner than the fans will about a falling off in performance. We'll have to act on that and explain it as best we can in order to keep the team successful.

WANNSTEDT: To back up what Mike was saying, we've got to look at a player and say, "Is he the best guy and where does he fit into the plans?" So, it's tough. It's difficult, particularly to teams like the Bears that are sensitive to the players who have done a great job for them. It's not an easy situation.

McCASKEY: I believe one of the clearest messages to come out of the pre-free-agency era was just how important performance is. Dave has cut several players who had all the potential in the world, but they were not performing. I think the other players got the message. We're going to support you and teach you, and encourage you to be the best possible player you can be, but we can't and won't wait forever. The performance has to be there and, if it's not, then we will have to make the decision and try somebody else. It's clearly what is going to characterize how personnel decisions are made for the Bears over the forthcoming years.

QUESTION: Where do you think the Bears will be in the year 2000?

McCASKEY: If I imagine myself to be in the year 2000, and look back at how the last seven or so years have gone, I'd hope that we could have created an organization that's a model in professional sports on all fronts. It will be something people would say, "Gee, the Bears have good people, they work really well together, and they've achieved great success together." I hope to see several Super Bowl trophies, and a new stadium that is state of the art, one that is set apart from all the other football stadiums in the country, one that is distinctively a Chicago Bears' stadium, not a cookie-cutter kind of thing. At the same time, we have training facilities and offices that really help get the job done. I want an environment that everybody likes to come to. If we can do these things, then we'll have accomplished a lot.

QUESTION: One last question: Would both of you give me your opinion of what you think it will be like on a fall afternoon in the year 2000, playing the Green Bay Packers. . . .

McCASKEY: In the year 2000 I think it will still be one of the special rivalries in the National Football League. People will get up that morning and be really excited to be going to the game. They will know they're going to see two teams go at it hard and strong, and it'll be a great football game.

WANNSTEDT: I would like to think that we will be heavily favored going into the game, that we've done our job in that area. I don't see all that much changing between now and then. I haven't seen those locker rooms change much in twenty years. There's still the same excitement, the intensity. That's not going to change. But in the year 2000, playing Green Bay, I would like us to have the division clinched, playoff-bound, we're winning, and we're going to clear the bench and let everybody play.

McCASKEY: It all comes back to how emotional a game football is. If the team doesn't have that devotion, that sense of intensity before the game, they're not going to play very well. It doesn't matter how big the Jumbo-Tron screen might be in the stadium, it's those guys facing each other across the line, opposed to each other, where one's going to be able to put the other guy down on the ground. And that's the team that will win. That's what it was in the Halas era, what it's about now, and what it will be in the year 2000.

And, yes, in the year 2000, we're planning to win that Packer game!

BEAR HALL OF FAMERS

Player	Position	Years with Bears	Year Inducted
Red Grange	Halfback	1925, 1929–1934	1963*
George Halas	End / Coach	1920–1983	1963*
Bronko Nagurski	Fullback / Tackle	1930–1937, 1943	1963*
Ed Healey	Tackle	1922–1927	1964
Link Lyman	Tackle	1926–1934	1964
George Trafton	Center	1920–1932	1964
Paddy Driscoll	Halfback	1920, 1926–1929	1965
Danny Fortmann	Guard	1936–1943	1965
Sid Luckman	Quarterback	1939–1950	1965
George McAfee	Halfback	1940–1941, 1945–1950	1966
Bulldog Turner	Center / Linebacker	1940–1952	1966
Joe Stydahar	Tackle	1936–1942, 1945–1946	1967
Bill Hewitt	End	1932–1936	1971
Bill George	Linebacker	1952–1965	1974
George Connor	Tackle / Linebacker	1948–1955	1975
Gale Sayers	Running Back	1965–1971	1977
Dick Butkus	Linebacker	1965–1973	1979
George Blanda	Quarterback, Placekicker	1949–1958	1981
Doug Atkins	Defensive End	1955–1966	1982
George Musso	Tackle	1933–1944	1982
Mike Ditka	Tight End	1961–1966	1988
Stan Jones	Guard/Defensive Tackle	1954–1965	1991
Walter Payton	Running Back	1975–1987	1993

*Charter Member

BEAR RETIRED JERSEY NUMBERS

Number	Player	Position
3	Bronko Nagurski	Fullback / Tackle
5	George McAfee	Halfback
7	George Halas	End
28	Willie Galimore	Halfback
34	Walter Payton	Running Back
40	Gale Sayers	Running Back
41	Brian Piccolo	Running Back
42	Sid Luckman	Quarterback
51	Dick Butkus	Linebacker
56	Bill Hewitt	End
61	Bill George	Linebacker
66	Bulldog Turner	Center / Linebacker
77	Red Grange	Halfback

BEAR HONOR ROLL

The following is a list of players who have been on the Chicago Bears' active roster for at least one NFL game between 1920 and 1993.

* indicates deceased players / coaches
( ) indicates number of seasons with the Bears
Year indicates first Bear season

· A ·

Abbey, Joe (North Texas State)	E	(2)	1948
Adamle, Mike (Northwestern)	RB	(2)	1975
Adams, John (LSU)	B	(4)	1959
Adickes, John (Baylor)	C	(2)	1987
Adkins, Roy* (Millikin & Bethany)	G	(2)	1920
Age, Louis (SW Louisiana)	T	(1)	1992
Akin, Len (Baylor)	G	(1)	1942
Albrecht, Ted (California)	T	(5)	1977
Allen, Duane (Santa Ana)	E	(2)	1966
Allen, Eddie (Pennsylvania)	FB	(1)	1947
Allen, Egypt (TCU)	DB	(1)	1987
Allman, Robert (Michigan State)	E	(1)	1936
Althoff, Jim (Winona State)	DT	(1)	1987
Amsler, Marty (Evansville)	DE	(2)	1967
Anderson, Art (Idaho)	T	(2)	1961
Anderson, Brad (Arizona)	WR	(2)	1984
Anderson, Ed* (Notre Dame)	E	(1)	1923
Anderson, Henry (Northwestern)	G	(1)	1931
Anderson, Hunk* (Notre Dame)	G	(6)	1922
Anderson, Marcus (Tulane)	WR	(1)	1981
Anderson, Neal (Florida)	RB	(8)	1986
Anderson, Ralph* (Los Angeles St.)	E	(1)	1958
Anderson, William (Compton JC)	HB	(2)	1953
Andrews, Tom (Louisville)	C	(2)	1984
Antoine, Lionel (Southern Illinois)	T	(6)	1972
Apolskis, Charles* (DePaul)	E	(2)	1938
Ardizzone, Tony (Northwestern)	C	(1)	1979
Armstrong, Trace (Florida)	DT	(5)	1989

Arnett, Jon (USC)	HB	(3)	1964
Arp, John (Lincoln)	T	(1)	1987
Artoe, Lee (California)	T	(4)	1940
Ashburn, Clifford (Nebraska)	T	(1)	1930
Asher, Bob (Vanderbilt)	T	(4)	1972
Ashmore, M. Roger* (Gonzaga)	T	(1)	1927
Aspatore, Edward* (Marquette)	T	(1)	1934
Atkins, Doug (Tennessee)	E	(12)	1955
Atkins, Kelvin (Illinois)	LB	(1)	1983
Autrey, Billy (SF Austin)	C	(1)	1953
Auzenne, Troy (California)	T	(2)	1992
Avellini, Bob (Maryland)	QB	(10)	1975
Aveni, John (Indiana)	E	(2)	1959

· B ·

Babartsky, Al (Fordham)	T	(3)	1943
Babinecz, John (Villanova)	LB	(1)	1975
Badaczewski, J. (Western Reserve)	G	(1)	1953
Bailey, Johnny (Texas A & I)	WR	(2)	1990
Baisi, Al (West Virginia)	G	(3)	1940
Baker, Myron (Louisiana Tech)	LB	(1)	1993
Banks, Fred (Liberty)	WR	(1)	1993
Barker, Richard* (Iowa State)	G	(1)	1921
Barnes, Erich (Purdue)	HB	(3)	1958
Barnes, Gary (Clemson)	E	(1)	1964
Barnes, Joe (Texas Tech)	QB	(1)	1974
Barnes, Lew (Oregon)	WR	(1)	1986
Barnett, Steve (Oregon)	T	(1)	1963
Barnhardt, Tom (North Carolina)	P	(1)	1987
Barwegan, Richard* (Purdue)	G	(3)	1950
Baschnagel, Brian (Ohio State)	WR	(9)	1976
Bassi, Dick* (Santa Clara)	G	(2)	1938
Battles, Bill (Brown)	E	(1)	1939
Bauman, Alf (Northwestern)	T	(3)	1948
Bausch, Frank* (Kansas)	C	(4)	1937
Baynham, Craig (Georgia Tech)	RB	(1)	1970
Becker, Dave (Iowa)	S	(1)	1980
Becker, Doug (Notre Dame)	LB	(1)	1978

Becker, Kurt (Michigan)	G	(8)	1982
Becker, Wayland (Marquette)	E	(1)	1934
Bell, Bob (Missouri)	LB	(1)	1987
Bell, Kay (Washington State)	T	(1)	1937
Bell, Todd (Ohio State)	S	(6)	1981
Bennett, Ben (Duke)	QB	(1)	1987
Benton, Jim (Arkansas)	E	(1)	1943
Bergerson, Gilbert* (Oregon State)	G	(2)	1932
Berry, Connie, M. (NC State)	E	(5)	1942
Berry, Royce (Houston)	DE	(1)	1976
Best, Art (Kent State)	RB	(2)	1977
Bettis, Tom (Purdue)	LB	(1)	1963
Bettridge, John (Ohio State)	HB	(1)	1937
Bingham, Don (Sul Ross)	HB	(1)	1956
Bishop, Bill (North Texas)	T	(9)	1952
Bishop, Don (Los Angeles City)	E	(1)	1959
Bivins, Charles* (Morris Brown)	HB	(7)	1960
Bjork, Del* (Oregon)	T	(2)	1937
Blackburn, JA	T	(1)	1923
Blacklock, Hugh* (Michigan State)	T	(6)	1920
Blackman, Lennon (Tulsa)	HB	(1)	1930
Blackwell, Kelly (TCU)	TE	(1)	1992
Blair, Paul (Oklahoma State)	T	(2)	1986
Blanda, George (Kentucky)	QB	(10)	1949
Blaylock, Anthony (Winston-Salem)	CB	(1)	1993
Boden, Lynn (South Dakota State)	G	(1)	1979
Bolan, George* (Purdue)	FB	(4)	1921
Bonderant, JB* (DePaul)	C	(1)	1922
Boone, JR (Tulsa)	HB	(4)	1948
Bortz, Mark (Iowa)	G	(11)	1983
Boso, Cap (Illinois)	TE	(5)	1987
Bowers, Sam (Fordham)	TE	(1)	1987
Brackett, ML (Auburn)	T	(2)	1956
Bradley, Chuck (Oregon)	TE	(1)	1977
Bradley, Ed (Wake Forest)	G	(2)	1950
Bradley, Steve (Indiana)	QB	(1)	1987
Braidwood, Charles* (Chattanooga)	E	(1)	1932
Bramhall, Art (DePaul)	HB	(1)	1931
Bratkowski, Zeke (Georgia)	QB	(6)	1954
Bray, Ray* (Western Michigan)	G	(10)	1939
Brewers, Chris (Arizona)	RB	(1)	1987
Brink, Larry (Northern Illinois)	E	(1)	1954
Britton, Earl* (Illinois)	FB	(1)	1925
Brockman, Edward (Oklahoma)	B	(1)	1930
Brooks, Anthony (E. Texas St.)	WR	(1)	1993
Brown, Charley (Syracuse)	DB	(2)	1966
Brown, Ed (San Francisco)	QB	(8)	1954
Brown, Kevin (W Texas State)	P	(1)	1987
Brown, William (Illinois)	FB	(1)	1961
Bruer, Bob (Mankato State)	TE	(1)	1976
Brumbaugh, Carl* (Florida)	QB	(8)	1930
Brupbacher, Ross (Texas A&M)	LB	(4)	1970
Bryan, Johnny* (Chicago)	HB	(4)	1922
Bryant, Waymond (Tennessee St.)	LB	(4)	1974
Buck, Arthur (John Carroll)	HB	(1)	1941
Buckler, William "Bill"* (Alabama)	G	(6)	1926
Buffone, Doug (Louisville)	LB	(14)	1966
Buford, Maury (Texas Tech)	P	(5)	1985
Buivid, Ray* (Marquette)	QB-HB	(2)	1937
Bukich, Rudy (USC)	QB	(9)	1958
Bull, Ronnie (Baylor)	B	(9)	1962
Burdick, Lloyd* (Illinois)	T	(2)	1931
Burgeis, Glenn (Tulsa)	T	(1)	1945

Buger, Todd (Penn State)	G	(1)	1993
Burks, Randy (SE Oklahoma St.)	WR	(1)	1976
Burman, George (Northwestern)	T	(1)	1964
Buss, Arthur (Michigan State)	T	(2)	1934
Bussey, Young* (LSU)	QB	(2)	1940
Butkus, Dick (Illinois)	LB	(9)	1965
Butler, Gary (Rice)	TE	(1)	1975
Butler, Kevin (Georgia)	K	(9)	1985
Buzin, Rich (Penn State)	T	(1)	1972

· C ·

Cabral, Brian (Colorado)	LB	(5)	1981
Cadile, James (San Jose State)	G	(11)	1962
Caffey, Lee Roy* (Texas A&M)	LB	(1)	1970
Cain, Joe (Oregon Tech)	LB	(1)	1993
Calland, Lee (Louisville)	CB	(1)	1969
Cameron, Jack (Winston-Salem)	WR	(1)	1984
Campana, Al (Youngstown)	HB	(4)	1950
Campbell, Gary (Colorado)	LB	(7)	1977
Campbell, Leon (Arkansas)	FB	(3)	1952
Canady, James (Texas)	HB	(2)	1948
Carrier, Mark (USC)	S	(4)	1990
Carey, Bob* (Michigan State)	E	(1)	1958
Carl, Harland (Wisconsin)	HB	(1)	1956
Carlson, Jules "Zuck"* (Oregon St.)	G	(8)	1929
Caroline, JC (Illinois)	HB	(10)	1956
Carter, Virgil (BYU)	QB	(4)	1968
Casares, Rick (Florida)	FB	(10)	1955
Casey, Tim (Oregon)	LB	(1)	1969
Castete, Jesse (McNeese State)	HB	(1)	1956
Chamberlin, Guy* (Nebraska)	E	(2)	1920
Chambers, Wally (E Kentucky)	DT	(5)	1973
Chapura, Dick (Missouri)	DT	(3)	1987
Chesley, Al (Pittsburgh)	LB	(1)	1982
Chesney, Chester "Chet"* (DePaul)	C	(2)	1939
Childs, Clarence (Florida A&M)	DB	(1)	1968
Christian, Bob (Northwestern)	FB	(2)	1992
Cifers, Ed (Tennessee)	E	(2)	1947
Clark, Daryl (Texas)	RB	(1)	1987
Clark, Gail (Michigan State)	LB	(1)	1973
Clark, Greg (Arizona State)	LB	(1)	1988
Clark, Harry (West Virginia)	HB	(4)	1940
Clark, Herman* (Oregon State)	G	(5)	1952
Clark, Phil (Northwestern)	DB	(1)	1970
Clarkson, Stuart* (Texas A&I)	G	(7)	1942
Clemons, Craig (Iowa)	S	(6)	1972
Coady, Rich (Memphis State)	C/E	(5)	1970
Cobb, Mike (Michigan State)	TE	(4)	1978
Cody, Ed (Purdue)	FB	(2)	1949
Coia, Angelo (USC)	HB	(4)	1960
Cole, Emerson (Toledo)	FB	(1)	1952
Cole, Linzy (TCU)	WR	(1)	1970
Coley, James (Clemson)	TE	(1)	1990
Concannon, Jack (Boston College)	QB	(5)	1967
Conkright, Bill* (Oklahoma)	C	(2)	1937
Connor, George (Notre Dame)	T	(8)	1948
Conway, Curtis (USC)	WR	(1)	1993
Conzelman, Jim* (Washington)	HB	(1)	1920
Cooke, Ed (Maryland)	E	(1)	1958
Copeland, Ron* (UCLA)	WR	(1)	1969
Corbett, George* (Millikin)	HB	(7)	1932
Cornish, Frank (Grambling)	DT	(4)	1966
Corzine, Lester (Davis & Elkins)	HB	(1)	1938

Richard Dent, defensive end, 1983–1993

Matt Suhey leads interference for Walter Payton.

Rickey Watts returns a kickoff 83 yards for a TD to help Bears defeat Cardinals in 1979 and clinch a playoff berth.

Cotton, Craig (Youngstown)	TE	(1)	1973
Covert, Jim (Pittsburgh)	T	(8)	1983
Cowan, Les (McMurry)	T	(1)	1951
Cox, Ron (Fresno State)	LB	(4)	1990
Crawford, Fred (Duke)	T	(2)	1934
Crawford, James "Mush" (Illinois)	G	(1)	1925
Croft, Abe* (SMU)	E	(2)	1944
Croftcheck, Don (Indiana)	G	(1)	1967
Cross, Bob* (SF Austin State)	T	(2)	1952
Culver, Alvin (Notre Dame)	T	(1)	1932
Cunningham, Harold (Ohio State)	E	(1)	1929
Curchin, Jeff (Florida State)	T	(2)	1970

· D ·

Daffer, Ted (Tennessee)	E	(1)	1954
Damore, John (Northwestern)	C	(2)	1957
Daniell, Jim (Ohio State)	T	(1)	1945
Daniels, Dick (Pacific-Oregon)	S	(2)	1969
Davis, Art (Alabama State)	T	(2)	1953
Davis, Fred (Alabama)	T	(6)	1946
Davis, Harper (Mississippi State)	HB	(1)	1950
Davis, John (Missouri)	DB	(1)	1970
Davis, Roger (Syracuse)	G	(4)	1960
Davis, Wendell (LSU)	WR	(6)	1988
Dean, Fred (Texas Southern)	G	(1)	1977
DeCorrevont, Bill (Northwestern)	HB	(2)	1948
DeLong, Steve (Tennessee)	DE	(1)	1972
Deloplaine, Jack (Salem)	RB	(1)	1979
Dempsey, Frank (Florida)	G	(4)	1950
Denney, Austin (Tennessee)	E	(3)	1967
Dent, Richard (Tennessee St.)	DE	(11)	1983
Devlin, Chris (Penn State)	LB	(1)	1978
Dewveall, Willard (SMU)	E	(2)	1959
Digris, Bernie (Holy Cross)	T	(1)	1943
Dimancheff, Boris Babe (Purdue)	HB	(1)	1952
Ditka, Mike (Pittsburgh)	TE	(6)	1961
Dodd, Al (NW Louisiana)	DB	(1)	1967
Doehring, John "Bull"*	FB	(6)	1932
Doerger, Jerry (Wisconsin)	T	(1)	1982
Donchez, Tom (Penn State)	RB	(1)	1975
Dooley, Jim (Miami U.)	E	(9)	1952
Dottley, John (Mississippi)	FB	(3)	1951
Douglas, Merrill (Utah)	FB	(3)	1958
Douglass, Bobby (Kansas)	QB	(7)	1969
Douglass, Maurice (Kentucky)	DB	(7)	1986
Douthitt, Earl (Iowa)	S	(1)	1975
Dreher, Ferd (Denver)	E	(1)	1938
Dressen, Charley*	QB	(1)	1920
Drews, Ted (Princeton)	E	(1)	1928
Dreyer, Wally (Wisconsin)	HB	(1)	1949
Driscoll, Paddy* (Northwestern)	HB	(5)	1926
Drulis, Chuck* (Temple)	G	(6)	1942
Drury, Lyle (St. Louis)	E	(2)	1930
Drzewiecki, Ron (Marquette)	HB	(2)	1955
Duarte, George (N Arizona)	CB	(1)	1987
Duerson, Dave (Notre Dame)	S	(6)	1983
Dugger, Jack (Ohio State)	E	(1)	1949
Dunlap, Bob (Oklahoma)	QB	(1)	1935
Dunsmore, Pat (Drake)	TE	(2)	1983
Dyko, Chris (Washington St.)	T	(1)	1989

· E ·

Earl, Robin (Washington)	RB-TE	(6)	1977

Ecker, Ed* (John Carroll)	T	(1)	1947
Edwards, Cid (Tennessee State)	RB	(1)	1975
Ellis, Allan (UCLA)	CB	(7)	1973
Elnes, Leland* (Bradley)	QB	(1)	1929
Ely, Harold (Iowa)*	G	(1)	1932
Ely, Larry (Iowa)	LB	(1)	1975
Engebretsen, Paul* (Northwestern)	G	(1)	1932
Englund, Harry	E	(4)	1920
Epps, Tory (Memphis State)	DT	(1)	1993
Erickson, Harold* (Wash. & Jeff.)	HB	(1)	1925
Evans, Earl (Harvard)	T	(4)	1926
Evans, Fred (Notre Dame)	HB	(1)	1948
Evans, Vince (USC)	QB	(7)	1977
Evey, Dick (Tennessee)	T	(6)	1964

· F ·

Fada, Rob (Pittsburgh)	G	(2)	1983
Fain, Richard (Florida)	CB	(1)	1992
Falkenberg, Herb* (Trinity)	FB	(1)	1952
Famiglietti, Gary* (Boston U.)	FB	(8)	1938
Fanning, Stan (Idaho)	T	(3)	1960
Farmer, George (UCLA)	WR	(6)	1970
Farrington, John* (Prairie View)	E	(4)	1960
Farris, Tom (Wisconsin)	QB	(2)	1946
Feathers, Beattie* (Tennessee)	HB	(4)	1934
Febel, Fritz* (Purdue)	G	(1)	1935
Federovich, John (Davis & Elkins)	T	(2)	1941
Feichtinger, Andy*	E	(2)	1920
Fencik, Gary (Yale)	S	(12)	1976
Fenimore, Bob (Oklahoma A&M)	HB	(1)	1947
Ferguson, JB	T	(1)	1932
Ferguson, Jim (South Carolina)	C/LB	(1)	1969
Fetz, Gus*	FB	(1)	1923
Figner, George (Colorado)	HB	(1)	1953
Finzer, Dave (DePauw)	P	(1)	1984
Fisher, Bob (SMU)	TE	(2)	1980
Fisher, Jeff (USC)	CB	(4)	1981
Fitzgerald, Greg (Iowa)	DT	(1)	1987
Flaherty, Pat* (Princeton)	E	(1)	1923
Flanagan, Dick (Ohio State)	G	(2)	1948
Flanagan, Latham (Carnegie Tech)	E	(1)	1931
Fleckenstein, Bill (Iowa)	G	(6)	1925
Floyd, Bobby Jack (TCU)	FB	(1)	1953
Flutie, Doug (Boston College)	QB	(1)	1986
Fontenot, Albert (Baylor)	DE	(1)	1993
Fontenot, Jerry (Texas A&M)	G	(5)	1989
Ford, Charlie (Houston)	CB	(3)	1971
Fordham, Jim* (Georgia)	FB	(2)	1944
Forrest, Tom (Cincinnati)	G	(1)	1974
Forte, Aldo (Montana)	G	(4)	1939
Fortmann, Dan (Colgate)	G	(8)	1936
Fortunato, Joe (Mississippi State)	LB	(12)	1955
Francis, Sam (Nebraska)	FB	(2)	1937
Franklin, Paul* (Franklin)	E	(5)	1930
Frazier, Leslie (Alcorn State)	CB	(5)	1981
Frederick, Andy (New Mexico)	T	(3)	1983
Frump, Milton (Ohio Wesleyan)	G	(1)	1930
Fuller, Steve (Clemson)	QB	(3)	1984
Furrer, Will (Virginia Tech)	QB	(1)	1992

· G ·

Gagnon, Dave (Ferris State)	RB	(1)	1974
Gaines, Wentford (Cincinnati)	CB	(3)	1978

Galimore, Willie* (Florida A&M)	HB	(7)	1957	Harley, Charles "Chic"* (Ohio State)	RB	(1)	1921
Gallagher, Dave (Michigan)	DE	(1)	1974	Harper, LaSalle (Arkansas)	LB	(1)	1989
Gallarneau, Hugh (Stanford)	HB	(5)	1941	Harper, Roland (Louisiana Tech)	RB	(8)	1975
Gardocki, Chris (Clemson)	P/K	(3)	1991	Harris, Al (Arizona State)	DE	(9)	1979
Garrett, Carl (New Mexico H'lands)	RB	(2)	1973	Harris, Chuck (West Virginia)	T	(1)	1987
Garrett, T. (Oklahoma A&M)	C	(2)	1947	Harris, Frank (NC State)	RB	(1)	1987
Garrett, WD (Mississippi State)	T	(1)	1950	Harris, Richard (Grambling)	DE	(2)	1974
Garvey, A. "Hec" (Notre Dame)	E	(4)	1922	Harris, Willie (Mississippi State)	WR	(1)	1993
Garvey, Ed* (Notre Dame)	HB	(1)	1925	Harrison, Jim (Missouri)	RB	(4)	1971
Gault, Willie (Tennessee)	WR	(5)	1983	Hart, Tommy (Morris Brown)	DE	(2)	1978
Gayle, Shaun (Ohio State)	S	(10)	1984	Hartenstine, Mike (Penn State)	DE	(12)	1975
Gedney, Chris (Syracuse)	TE	(1)	1993	Hartman, Fred (Rice)	T	(1)	1947
Gentry, Curtiss (Maryland State)	DB	(3)	1966	Hartnett, Perry (SMU)	G	(2)	1982
Gentry, Dennis (Baylor)	WR	(11)	1982	Haselrig, Clint (Michigan)	WR	(1)	1974
George, Bill* (Wake Forest)	G/LB	(14)	1952	Hatley, John (Sul Ross)	G	(1)	1953
Gepford, Sid* (Millikin & Bethany)	B	(1)	1920	Hazelton, Major (Florida A&M)	DB	(2)	1968
Gersbach, Carl (West Chester St.)	LB	(1)	1975	Healey, Ed* (Dartmouth)	T	(6)	1922
Geyer, Bill (Colgate)	HB	(3)	1942	Healy, Don (Maryland)	G	(2)	1958
Gibron, Abe (Purdue)	G	(2)	1958	Heardon, Tom* (Notre Dame)	QB	(1)	1929
Gilbert, Kline* (Mississippi)	G	(5)	1953	Heileman, Charles* (Iowa State)	E	(1)	1939
Gilliam, John (South Carolina St.)	WR	(1)	1977	Heimuli, Lakei (BYU)	RB	(1)	1987
Glasgow, Brian (N Illinois)	TE	(1)	1987	Helwig, John (Notre Dame)	G	(4)	1953
Glenn, Bill (E Illinois)	QB	(2)	1944	Hempel, Bill (Carroll)	T	(1)	1942
Glueck, Larry (Villanova)	B	(3)	1963	Henderson, Reuben (San Diego St.)	CB	(2)	1981
Goebel, Paul (Michigan)	E	(1)	1925	Hensley, Dick (Kentucky)	E	(1)	1953
Goodnight, Owen* (Hardin-Sims)	QB	(1)	1946	Herron, Bruce (New Mexico)	LB	(5)	1978
Gordon, Dick (Michigan State)	HB	(7)	1965	Hester, Jim (North Dakota)	TE	(1)	1970
Gordon, Lou* (Illinois)	T	(1)	1938	Hewitt, Bill* (Michigan)	E	(5)	1932
Gorgal, Ken (Purdue)	HB	(2)	1955	Heyward, Craig (Pittsburgh)	FB	(1)	1993
Grabowski, Jim (Illinois)	RB	(1)	1971	Hibbs, Jesse (USC)	T	(1)	1931
Graham, Conrad (Tennessee)	DB	(1)	1973	Hicks, Tom (Illinois)	LB	(5)	1976
Grandberry, Ken (Wash. St.)	RB	(1)	1974	High, Lennie	HB	(1)	1920
Grange, Garland "Gardie"* (Illinois)	E	(3)	1929	Hilgenberg, Jay (Iowa)	C	(11)	1981
Grange, Harold "Red"* (Illinois)	HB	(8)	1925	Hill, Harlon (Florence St. Tchrs)	E	(8)	1954
Green, Bobby Joe* (Florida)	P	(12)	1962	Hill, Ike (Catawba)	WR	(2)	1973
Green, Mark (Notre Dame)	RB	(4)	1989	Hintz, Mike (Wis-Platteville)	DB	(1)	1987
Green, Robert (William & Mary)	RB	(1)	1993	Hoban, Mike (Michigan)	G	(1)	1974
Greenwood, Glen* (Iowa)	HB	(1)	1924	Hobscheid, Fred* (Chicago)	G	(1)	1927
Grim, Bob (Oregon State)	WR	(1)	1975	Hodgins, Norm (LSU)	S	(1)	1974
Grosvenor, George (Colorado)	HB	(2)	1935	Hoffman, Jack (Xavier)	E	(5)	1952
Grygo, Al* (South Carolina)	HB	(2)	1944	Hoffman, John (Hawaii)	DE	(1)	1971
Gudauskas, Pete (Murray State)	G	(2)	1943	Hoffman, John* (Arkansas)	E	(8)	1949
Gulyanics, George* (Ellisville JC)	HB	(6)	1947	Hohensee, Mike (Minnesota)	QB	(1)	1987
Gunn, Jimmy (USC)	LB	(6)	1970	Hoke, Jonathan (Ball State)	CB	(1)	1980
Gunner, Harry (Oregon State)	DE	(1)	1970	Holloway, Glen (N Texas State)	G	(4)	1970
				Holman, Willie (South Carolina St.)	DE	(6)	1968
· H ·				Holmer, Walter* (Northwestern)	FB	(2)	1929
Haddon, Aldous (Wash. & Jeff.)	B	(1)	1928	Holovak, Mike (Boston College)	FB	(2)	1947
Haines, Kris (Notre Dame)	WR	(3)	1979	Hoptowit, Al (Washington State)	T	(5)	1941
Halas, George* (Illinois)	E	(10)	1920	Horton, Larry (Iowa)	DT	(2)	1972
Hale, Dave (Ottawa)	DE	(3)	1969	Howley, Charles (West Virginia)	C	(2)	1958
Haluska, Jim (Wisconsin)	HB	(1)	1956	Hrivnak, Gary (Purdue)	DT	(4)	1973
Hamity, Lewis (Chicago)	HB	(1)	1941	Huarte, John (Notre Dame)	QB	(1)	1972
Hamlin, Gene (Western Michigan)	C	(1)	1971	Huff, Gary (Florida State)	QB	(4)	1973
Hammond, Henry (Southwestern)	E	(1)	1937	Huffine, Ken* (Purdue)	FB	(1)	1921
Hampton, Dan (Arkansas)	DE	(12)	1979	Hugasian, Harry (Stanford)	HB	(1)	1955
Hanke, Carl* (Minnesota)	G	(1)	1922	Hughes, Billy* (Texas)	C	(2)	1940
Hanny, Frank* (Indiana)	E	(5)	1922	Hull, Mike (USC)	FB	(3)	1968
Hansen, Clifford (Luther)	HB	(1)	1933	Hultz, Don (Southern Miss.)	DT	(1)	1974
Hansen, Wayne* (Texas Western)	C	(10)	1950	Humphries, Stefan (Michigan)	G	(3)	1984
Harbaugh, Jim (Michigan)	QB	(7)	1987	Hunsinger, Chuck (Florida)	HB	(3)	1950
Hardy, Cliff (Michigan State)	CB	(1)	1971	Hunt, Jackie (Marshall)	HB	(1)	1945
Hardy, John (California)	DB	(1)	1991	Hurst, William (Oregon)	G	(1)	1924

Hutchison, Anthony (Texas Tech)	RB	(2)	1983
Huther, Bruce (New Hampshire)	LB	(1)	1982
Hyche, Steve (Livingston)	LB	(1)	1989
Hyland, Bob (Boston College)	C	(1)	1970

· I ·

Ingwerson, Burt* (Illinois)	G	(2)	1920
Ippolito, Anthony* (Purdue)	G	(1)	1943
Ivlow, John (Colorado State)	RB	(1)	1993

· J ·

Jackson, Bobby (Alabama)	HB	(1)	1961
Jackson, Noah (Tampa)	G	(9)	1975
Jackson, Randy (Florida)	T	(8)	1967
Jackson, Vestee (Washington)	CB	(5)	1986
Jagade, Chick* (Indiana)	FB	(2)	1954
James, Dan (Ohio)	T	(1)	1967
Janata, John (Illinois)	T	(1)	1983
Janet, Ernie (Washington)	G	(3)	1972
January, Mike (Texas)	LB	(1)	1987
Jarmoluk, Mike (Temple)	T	(2)	1946
Jecha, Ralph (Northwestern)	G	(1)	1955
Jeffries, Eric (Texas)	CB	(1)	1987
Jencks, Robert (Miami, OH)	E	(2)	1963
Jennings, Keith (Clemson)	TE	(3)	1991
Jensvold, Leo* (Iowa)	QB	(1)	1931
Jeter, Bob (Iowa)	CB	(3)	1971
Jeter, Perry (California Poly Tech)	RB	(2)	1956
Jewett, Bob (Michigan State)	E	(1)	1958
Jiggetts, Dan (Harvard)	T	(7)	1976
Joesting, Herb* (Minnesota)	FB	(2)	1931
Johnson, Albert (Kentucky)	FB	(1)	1938
Johnson, Bill* (SMU)	G	(2)	1946
Johnson, Greg (Florida State)	DT	(1)	1977
Johnson, Jack (Miami)	B	(3)	1957
Johnson, John (Indiana)	T	(6)	1963
Johnson, Keshon (Arizona)	CB	(1)	1993
Johnson, Leo (Millikin)	HB	(1)	1920
Johnson, OG	FB	(1)	1924
Johnson, Pete (VMI)	B	(1)	1959
Johnson, Troy (Oklahoma)	LB	(2)	1988
Johnson, Will (NE Louisiana)	LB	(1)	1987
Johnsos, Luke* (Northwestern)	E	(9)	1929
Jones, Bob (San Diego State)	E	(1)	1967
Jones, Dante (Oklahoma)	LB	(6)	1988
Jones, Edgar (Pittsburgh)	HB	(1)	1945
Jones, Jerry* (Notre Dame)	G	(2)	1920
Jones, Jimmy (Wisconsin)	E	(3)	1965
Jones, Stan (Maryland)	T	(12)	1954
Jordan, Donald (Houston)	RB	(1)	1984
Juenger, Dave (Ohio U.)	WR	(1)	1973
Jurkovic, Mirko (Notre Dame)	G	(1)	1992

· K ·

Karr, William* (West Virginia)	E	(6)	1933
Karras, Ted (Indiana)	G	(5)	1960
Karwales, Jack (Michigan)	E	(2)	1946
Kassel, Chuck* (Illinois)	E	(1)	1927
Kavanaugh, Ken (LSU)	E	(8)	1940
Kawal, Ed* (Illinois)	C	(6)	1931
Keane, Jim (Iowa)	E	(6)	1946
Keefe, Jerry* (Notre Dame)	G	(1)	1920
Kelly, Elmo (Wichita U.)	E	(1)	1944

Kelly, Jim (Tennessee State)	TE	(1)	1974
Kendricks, Jim (Texas A&M)	T	(1)	1924
Keriasotis, Nick (St. Ambrose)	G	(3)	1942
Keys, Tyrone (Mississippi St.)	DE	(3)	1983
Kiesling, Walter* (St. Thomas)	G	(1)	1934
Kilcullen, Bob (Texas Tech)	T	(9)	1957
Kilgore, Jon (Auburn)	P	(1)	1968
Kindt, Don (Wisconsin)	HB	(9)	1947
Kindt, Don Jr. (Wis-LaCrosse)	TE	(1)	1987
King, Ralph (Chicago)	T	(1)	1925
Kinney, Steve (Utah State)	T	(2)	1973
Kirk, Ken (Mississippi)	C	(1)	1960
Kissell, Adolph (Boston College)	FB	(1)	1942
Klawitter, Dick* (S. Dakota State)	C	(2)	1956
Klein, Dick (Iowa)	T	(2)	1958
Knapczyk, Ken (Northern Iowa)	WR	(1)	1987
Knopp, Oscar* (Illinois)	FB	(6)	1923
Knox, Bill (Purdue)	DB	(3)	1974
Knox, Ron (UCLA)	QB	(1)	1957
Koehler, Robert* (Northwestern)	FB	(2)	1920
Kolman, Ed* (Temple)	T	(5)	1940
Konovsky, Bob* (Wisconsin)	G	(1)	1960
Kopcha, Joe* (Chattanooga)	G	(5)	1929
Kortas, Kenneth (Louisville)	T	(1)	1969
Kosins, Gary (Dayton)	RB	(3)	1972
Kozlowski, Glen (BYU)	WR	(6)	1987
Kreamcheck, John (Wm. & Mary)	T	(3)	1953
Kreitling, Rich (Illinois)	E	(1)	1964
Kreiwald, Doug (West Texas State)	G	(2)	1967
Krenk, Mitch (Nebraska)	TE	(1)	1984
Krumm, Todd (Michigan State)	S	(1)	1988
Kuechenberg, Rudy (Indiana)	LB	(3)	1967
Kunz, Lee (Nebraska)	LB	(3)	1979
Kurek, Ralph (Wisconsin)	FB	(6)	1965

· L ·

LaFleur, Joe* (Marquette)	FB	(3)	1922
LaForest, W.	FB	(1)	1920
Lahar, Harold (Oklahoma)	G	(2)	1941
Lamb, Walter (Oklahoma)	E	(1)	1946
Landry, Greg (Massachusetts)	QB	(1)	1984
Lanum, R. "Jake"* (Ill & Millikin)	QB	(5)	1920
Larson, Fred* (Notre Dame)	C	(1)	1922
Lashar, Tim (Oklahoma)	K	(1)	1987
Lasker, Greg (Arkansas)	S	(1)	1988
Latta, Greg (Morgan State)	TE	(6)	1975
Lawler, Allen (Texas)	HB	(1)	1948
Lawson, Roger (W. Michigan)	RB	(2)	1972
Layne, Bobby (Texas)	QB	(1)	1948
Leahy, Bernie (Notre Dame)	HB	(1)	1932
Leclerc, Roger (Trinity)	K/LB	(7)	1960
Lee, Buddy (LSU)	QB	(1)	1971
Lee, Herman (Florida A&M)	T	(9)	1958
Leeuwenburg, Jay (Colorado)	G	(2)	1992
Leeuwenburg, Rich (Stanford)	T	(1)	1965
Leggett, Earl (LSU)	T	(10)	1957
Lemon, Clifford* (Centre)	T	(1)	1926
Leonard, James (Colgate)	T	(1)	1924
Lesane, James (Virginia)	HB	(2)	1952
Lewis, Darren (Texas A & M)	RB	(3)	1991
Lick, Dennis (Wisconsin)	T	(6)	1976
Lincoln, Jeremy (Tennessee)	CB	(2)	1992
Line, Bill (SMU)	DT	(1)	1972

Name	Pos		Year
Lintzenich, Joseph* (St. Louis)	FB	(2)	1930
Lipscomb, Paul* (Tennessee)	T	(1)	1954
Lisch, Rusty (Notre Dame)	QB	(1)	1984
Livers, Virgil (W. Kentucky)	CB	(5)	1975
Livingston, Andy (Phoenix JC)	B	(2)	1964
Livingston, Howie (Fullerton JC)	DB	(1)	1953
Logan, James (Indiana)	G	(2)	1942
Long, Harvey (Detroit)	T	(1)	1929
Long, Johnny* (Colgate)	QB	(2)	1944
Lowe, Lloyd (North Texas State)	HB	(2)	1953
Luckman, Sid (Columbia)	QB	(12)	1939
Lujack, Johnny (Notre Dame)	QB	(4)	1948
Lusby, Vaughn (Arkansas)	CB	(1)	1980
Lyle, Garry (G. Washington)	CB	(7)	1968
Lyman, Roy "Link" (Nebraska)	T	(9)	1926
Lynch, Lorenzo (Cal St.-Sac.)	DB	(3)	1987
Lyon, George (Kansas State)	T	(1)	1929

· M ·

Name	Pos		Year
MacLeod, Robert (Dartmouth)	HB	(2)	1939
Macon, Ed (College of Pacific)	HB	(2)	1952
MacWherter, Kile* (Bethany)	FB	(1)	1920
Magnani, Dante* (St. Mary's)	HB	(3)	1942
Maillard, Ralph (Creighton)	T	(1)	1929
Malone, Charles (Texas A&M)	E	(1)	1933
Manders, Jack* (Minnesota)	HB	(8)	1933
Maness, James (TCU)	WR	(1)	1985
Mangum, John (Alabama)	CB	(4)	1990
Maniaci, Joe (Fordham)	RB	(4)	1938
Manning, Pete (Wake Forest)	E	(2)	1960
Manske, Edgar (Northwestern)	E	(4)	1937
Marconi, Joe (West Virginia)	FB	(5)	1962
Margarita, Bob (Brown)	HB	(3)	1944
Margerum, Ken (Stanford)	WR	(4)	1981
Marshall, Wilber (Florida)	LB	(4)	1984
Martin, Bill (Georgia Tech)	E	(2)	1964
Martin, Billy* (Minnesota)	HB	(3)	1962
Martin, Dave (Notre Dame)	LB	(1)	1969
Martin, Frank (Alabama)	HB	(1)	1941
Martinovich, P. (College of Pacific)	G	(1)	1940
Maslowski, Matt (San Diego U.)	WR	(1)	1972
Mass, Wayne (Clemson)	OT	(3)	1968
Masters, Bob* (Baylor)	FB	(2)	1943
Masterson, Bernie* (Nebraska)	QB	(7)	1934
Masterson, Forest (Iowa)	C	(1)	1945
Mastrogany, Gus* (Iowa)	E	(1)	1931
Matheson, Jack (W. Michigan)	E	(1)	1947
Mattes, Ron (Virginia)	T	(1)	1991
Matthews, Shane (Florida)	QB	(1)	1993
Mattson, Riley (Oregon)	T	(1)	1965
Matuza, Al (Georgetown)	C	(4)	1941
May, Chester*	G	(1)	1920
May, Walter O. "Red"*	G	(1)	1920
Mayes, Rufus (Ohio State)	T	(1)	1969
Maznicki, F. (Boston College)	HB	(2)	1942
McAfee, George (Duke)	HB	(8)	1940
McClendon, Willie (Georgia)	RB	(4)	1979
McColl, Bill (Stanford)	E	(8)	1952
McCray, Bruce (W Illinois)	CB	(1)	1987
McDonald, Lester* (Nebraska)	E	(3)	1937
McElwain, Bill (Northwestern)	HB	(1)	1925
McEnulty, Doug (Wichita)	FB	(2)	1943
McGee, Tony (Bishop College)	DE	(3)	1971

Name	Pos		Year
McGuire, Gene (Notre Dame)	C	(1)	1993
McInerney, Sean (Frostburg State)	DT	(1)	1987
McKinnely, Phil (UCLA)	T	(1)	1982
McKinney, Bill (West Texas)	LB	(1)	1972
McKinnon, Dennis (Florida State)	WR	(6)	1983
McLean, Ray* (St. Anselm)	HB	(8)	1940
McMahon, Jim (BYU)	QB	(7)	1982
McMichael, Steve (Texas)	DT	(13)	1981
McMillen, Jim* (Illinois)	G	(6)	1924
McMullen, Daniel* (Nebraska)	G	(2)	1930
McPherson, Forrest (Nebraska)	G	(1)	1935
McRae, Bennie (Michigan)	HB	(9)	1962
McRae, Franklin (Tenn. State)	DT	(1)	1967
Meadows, Ed* (Duke)	E	(3)	1954
Mellekas, John (Arizona)	T	(5)	1956
Merkel, Monte (Kansas)	G	(2)	1942
Merrill, Mark (Minnesota)	LB	(1)	1979
Meyers, Denny* (Iowa)	T	(1)	1931
Meyers, Jerry (N Illinois)	DE-DT	(4)	1976
Michaels, Edward* (Villanova)	G	(1)	1935
Mihal, Joe* (Purdue)	T	(2)	1940
Miller, Charles "Ookie" (Purdue)	C	(6)	1932
Miller, Milford (Chadron)	T	(1)	1932
Milner, Bill (Duke)	G	(3)	1947
Milton, Eldridge (Clemson)	LB	(1)	1987
Miniefield, Kevin (Arizona State)	CB	(1)	1993
Minini, Frank (San Jose State)	HB	(3)	1947
Minter, Barry (Tulsa)	LB	(1)	1993
Mintum, John F. "Jack"*	C	(2)	1921
Mitchell, Charley (Tulsa)	HB	(1)	1945
Mohardt, John* (Notre Dame)	HB	(1)	1925
Molesworth, Keith* (Monmouth)	HB	(7)	1931
Montgomery, Randy (Weber State)	CB	(1)	1974
Montgomery, Ross (TCU)	FB	(2)	1969
Mooney, Jim* (Georgetown)	E	(1)	1935
Mooney, Tip* (Abilene Christian)	HB	(3)	1944
Moore, Albert (Northwestern)	QB	(1)	1932
Moore, Jerry (Arkansas)	S	(2)	1971
Moore, Joe (Missouri)	RB	(2)	1971
Moore, McNeil (Sam Houston)	HB	(3)	1954
Moore, Rocco (Western Michigan)	G	(1)	1980
Moorehead, Emery (Colorado)	TE	(8)	1981
Morgan, Anthony (Tennessee)	WR	(3)	1991
Morgan, Mike (Wisconsin)	RB	(1)	1978
Morris, Francis (Boston U.)	HB	(1)	1942
Morris, Johnny (Santa Barbara)	FL	(10)	1958
Morris, Jon (Holy Cross)	C	(1)	1978
Morris, Larry (Georgia Tech)	LB	(7)	1959
Morris, Ray (UTEP)	LB	(1)	1987
Morris, Ron (SMU)	WR	(6)	1987
Morrison, Fred (Ohio State)	FB	(4)	1950
Morrissey, Jim (Michigan State)	LB	(9)	1985
Morton, John (Missouri)	HB	(1)	1945
Moser, Robert* (Pacific)	C	(3)	1951
Mosley, Anthony (Fresno State)	RB	(1)	1987
Mosley, Henry (Morris Brown)	HB	(1)	1955
Mucha, Charles (Washington)	G	(1)	1935
Mucha, Rudy (Washington)	G	(2)	1945
Muckenstrum, Jerry (Arkansas St.)	LB	(7)	1976
Mudd, Howard (Hillsdale)	G	(2)	1969
Mullen, Verne* (Illinois)	E	(3)	1923
Mullins, Don R. (Houston)	HB	(2)	1961
Mullins, Noah (Kentucky)	HB	(4)	1946

Quarterback Mike Tomczak scrambles.

Walter Payton receives a portrait from Ed and Virginia McCaskey on the occasion of the last home game of his career in 1987. His number 34 was also retired that day.

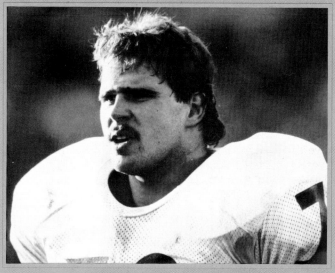

Tackle John Wojciechowski (73).

Roland Harper (35) carries, Ted Albrecht (64) blocks.

Center Jay Hilgenberg (63) and guard Mark Bortz (62) block as Jim McMahon drops back to pass.

Guard Tom Thayer

Mundee, Fred (Notre Dame)	C	(3)	1943	Percival, Mac (Texas Tech)	K	(7)	1967
Murray, Richard* (Marquette)	T	(1)	1924	Perez, Peter (Illinois)	G	(1)	1945
Murry, Don* (Wisconsin)	T	(8)	1924	Perina, Bob* (Princeton)	HB	(2)	1949
Musso, George (Millikin)	G	(12)	1933	Perini, Pete (Ohio State)	FB	(2)	1954
Musso, Johnny (Alabama)	RB	(3)	1975	Perkins, Don (Platteville)	FB	(2)	1945
Muster, Brad (Stanford)	FB	(5)	1988	Perrin, Lonnie (Illinois)	RB	(1)	1979
Myslinski, Tom (Tennessee)	OL	(1)	1993	Perry, Todd (Kentucky)	OL	(1)	1993
				Perry, William (Clemson)	DT	(9)	1985
				Petitbon, Richie (Tulane)	HB	(10)	1959

· N ·

Nagurski, Bronko* (Minnesota)	FB	(9)	1930	Petty, John* (Purdue)	FB	(1)	1942
Neacy, Clement* (Colgate)	E	(1)	1927	Petty, Ross* (Illinois)	G	(1)	1920
Neal, Dan (Kentucky)	C	(9)	1975	Phillips, Loyd (Arkansas)	DE	(3)	1967
Neal, Ed (LSU)	G	(1)	1951	Phillips, Reggie (SMU)	CB	(3)	1985
Neck, Tommy (LSU)	HB	(2)	1962	Phipps, Mike (Purdue)	QB	(5)	1977
Negus, Fred (Wisconsin)	C	(1)	1950	Piccolo, Brian* (Wake Forest)	RB	(4)	1966
Neidert, John (Louisville)	LB	(1)	1970	Pickens, Bob (Nebraska)	T	(2)	1967
Nelson, Everett (Illinois)	T	(1)	1929	Pickering, Clay (Maine)	WR	(1)	1986
Nesbitt, Dick* (Drake)	HB	(4)	1930	Pifferini, Bob (UCLA)	LB	(4)	1972
Newsome, Billy (Grambling)	DE	(1)	1977	Pinder, Cyril (Illinois)	RB	(2)	1971
Newton, Bob (Nebraska)	G	(5)	1971	Plank, Doug (Ohio State)	S	(8)	1975
Nickla, Ed (Maryland)	G	(1)	1959	Plasman, Dick* (Vanderbilt)	E	(6)	1937
Nielsen, Hans (Michigan State)	K	(1)	1981	Podmajersky, Paul* (Illinois)	G	(1)	1944
Nix, Kent (TCU)	QB	(2)	1970	Polisky, John* (Notre Dame)	G	(1)	1929
Nolting, Ray (Cincinnati)	HB	(8)	1936	Pollock, Bill (Penn. Military Acdy.)	HB	(2)	1935
Norberg, Hank (Stanford)	E	(1)	1948	Pool, Hampton (Stanford)	E	(4)	1940
Nordquist, Mark (Pacific)	G-C	(2)	1975	Potter, Kevin (Missouri)	S	(2)	1983
Nori, Reino* (DeKalb)	HB	(1)	1938	Preston, Pat (Wake Forest)	G	(4)	1946
Norman, Dick (Stanford)	QB	(2)	1961	Price, Terry (Texas A & M)	DT	(1)	1990
Norman, Tim (Illinois)	G	(1)	1983	Pride, Dan (Jackson State)	LB	(2)	1968
Norris, Jon (American Int'l.)	DE	(1)	1987	Proctor, Rex (Rice)	HB	(1)	1953
Norvell, Jay (Iowa)	LB	(1)	1987	Pruitt, Mickey (Colorado)	LB	(3)	1988
Novoselsky, Brent (Penn)	TE	(1)	1988	Purnell, James (Wisconsin)	LB	(5)	1964
Nowaskey, Bob* (G Washington)	E	(3)	1940	Pyle, Mike (Yale)	C	(9)	1961

· O ·

· R ·

O'Bradovich, Ed (Illinois)	DE	(10)	1962	Rabold, Mike* (Indiana)	G	(3)	1964
O'Connell, JF* (Penn State)	C	(1)	1924	Rains, Dan (Cincinnati)	LB	(4)	1982
O'Connell, Tom (Illinois)	QB	(1)	1953	Rakestraw, Larry (Georgia)	QB	(4)	1964
O'Quinn, John (Wake Forest)	E	(2)	1950	Ramsey, Frank (Oregon State)	G	(1)	1945
O'Rourke, Charles (Boston College)	QB	(1)	1942	Rather, Bo (Michigan)	WR	(5)	1974
Obee, Terry (Oregon)	WR	(1)	1993	Reader, Russ (Michigan State)	HB	(1)	1947
Oech, Verne (Minnesota)	G	(1)	1936	Reese, Lloyd* (Tennessee)	FB	(1)	1946
Oelerich, John* (St. Ambrose)	HB	(1)	1938	Reilly, Mike (Iowa)	LB	(5)	1964
Ogden, Ray (Alabama)	TE	(3)	1969	Rentie, Caesar (Oklahoma)	T	(1)	1988
Oliver, Jack (Memphis State)	T	(1)	1987	Rentner, Ernest Pug* (N'western)	HB	(2)	1936
Ortego, Keith (McNeese State)	WR	(3)	1985	Reppond, Mike (Arkansas)	WR	(1)	1973
Osborne, Jim (Southern)	DT	(13)	1972	Reynolds, Tom (San Diego State)	WR	(1)	1973
Osmanski, Bill (Holy Cross)	FB	(7)	1939	Rice, Andy (Texas Southern)	DT	(2)	1972
Osmanski, Joe (Holy Cross)	FB	(4)	1946	Richards, Golden (Hawaii)	WR	(2)	1978
				Richards, Ray (Nebraska)	T	(4)	1933
				Richardson, Mike (Arizona State)	CB	(6)	1983

· P ·

				Richman, Harry* (Illinois)	G	(1)	1929
Pagac, Fred (Ohio State)	TE	(1)	1974	Rivera, Ron (California)	LB	(9)	1984
Page, Alan (Notre Dame)	DT	(4)	1978	Rivera, Steve (California)	WR	(1)	1977
Parsons, Bob (Penn State)	P-TE	(11)	1972	Rivers, Garland (Michigan)	DB	(1)	1987
Patterson, Billy (Baylor)	QB	(1)	1939	Rives, Don (Texas Tech)	LB	(6)	1973
Paul, Markus (Syracuse)	S	(4)	1989	Roberts, Tom* (DePaul)	G	(2)	1943
Pauley, Frank Don (Wash. & Jeff.)	T	(1)	1930	Roberts, Willie (Houston)	CB	(1)	1973
Payton, Sean (E Illinois)	QB	(1)	1987	Rodenhauser, Mark (Illinois State)	C	(2)	1987
Payton, Walter (Jackson State)	RB	(13)	1975	Roder, Mirro	K	(2)	1973
Pearce, W. "Pard"* (Penn.)	QB	(3)	1920	Roehlk, Jon (Iowa)	G	(1)	1987
Pearson, Madison* (Kansas)	C	(6)	1929	Roehnelt, William* (Bradley)	G	(2)	1958
Pederson, Jim (Augsburg)	HB	(1)	1932	Rogers, Mel (Florida A&M)	LB	(1)	1977
Peiffer, Dan (SE Missouri State)	C	(3)	1975				

Roggeman, Tom (Purdue)	G	(2)	1956
Romanik, Steve (Villanova)	QB	(4)	1950
Romney, Milton* (Chicago)	QB	(5)	1925
Ronzani, Gene* (Marquette)	QB	(8)	1933
Roper, John (Texas A&M)	LB	(4)	1989
Rosequist, Ted* (Ohio State)	T	(3)	1934
Rothschild, Doug (Wheaton)	LB	(1)	1987
Rouse, James (Arkansas)	RB	(2)	1990
Roveto, John (SW Louisiana)	K	(2)	1981
Rowden, Larry (Houston)	LB	(1)	1971
Rowell, Eugene (Dubuque)	DT	(1)	1987
Rowland, Brad (McMurry)	HB	(1)	1951
Rowland, Justin (TCU)	HB	(1)	1960
Rubens, Larry (Montana State)	C	(1)	1986
Rupp, Nelson* (Dennison)	QB	(1)	1921
Russell, Reginald (Northwestern)	E	(1)	1928
Ryan, John (Detroit)	T	(1)	1929
Ryan, Rocky (Illinois)	E	(1)	1958
Ryan, Tim (USC)	DT	(4)	1990
Rydalch, Ron (Utah)	DT	(6)	1975
Rydzewski, Frank* (Notre Dame)	C	(1)	1923
Rykovich, Julie* (Illinois)	HB	(3)	1949

· S ·

Sacrinty, Nick (Wake Forest)	QB	(1)	1947
Saldi, Jay (South Carolina)	TE	(2)	1983
Sanders, Glenell (Louisiana Tech)	LB	(1)	1990
Sanders, Thomas (Texas A&M)	RB	(5)	1985
Sanderson, Reggie (Stanford)	RB	(1)	1973
Savoldi, Joe* (Notre Dame)	FB	(1)	1930
Sayers, Gale (Kansas)	HB	(7)	1965
Schiechl, John* (Santa Clara)	C	(2)	1945
Schmidt, Terry (Ball State)	S	(9)	1976
Schreiber, Larry (Tenn. Tech)	RB	(1)	1976
Schroeder, Gene (Virginia)	E	(6)	1951
Schubert, Steve (U Mass.)	WR	(5)	1975
Schuette, Paul* (Wisconsin)	G	(3)	1930
Schwantz, Jim (Purdue)	LB	(1)	1992
Schweda, Brian (Kansas)	DE	(1)	1966
Schweidler, Dick (St. Louis)	HB	(3)	1938
Scott, James (Henderson JC)	WR	(7)	1976
Scott, Ralph* (Wisconsin)	T	(5)	1921
Seals, George (Missouri)	G	(7)	1965
Seibering, Gerald (Drake)	FB	(1)	1932
Senn, Bill* (Knox)	HB	(6)	1926
Serini, Washington (Kentucky)	G	(4)	1948
Sevy, Jeff (California)	T-DE	(4)	1975
Seymour, Jim (Notre Dame)	WR	(3)	1970
Shank, JL	HB	(1)	1920
Shanklin, Ron (N Texas State)	WR	(2)	1975
Shannon, John (Kentucky)	DT	(2)	1988
Shaw, Glenn (Kentucky)	HB	(1)	1960
Shearer, Brad (Texas)	DT	(3)	1978
Shellog, Alec* (Notre Dame)	T	(1)	1939
Sherman, Saul (Chicago)	QB	(2)	1939
Shipkey, Jerry (UCLA)	FB	(1)	1953
Shoemake, Hub (Illinois)	G	(2)	1920
Shy, Don (San Diego State)	RB	(3)	1970
Siegal, John (Columbia)	E	(5)	1939
Sigillo, Dom* (Xavier)	T	(2)	1943
Sigmund, Arthur W.	G	(1)	1923
Simmons, David (North Carolina)	LB	(1)	1983
Simmons, J. (Bethune-Cookman)	WR	(1)	1969

Simpson, Carl (Florida State)	DT	(1)	1993
Singletary, Mike (Baylor)	LB	(12)	1981
Sisk, John* (Marquette)	HB	(5)	1932
Sisk, John Jr. (Miami)	B	(1)	1964
Skibinski, John (Purdue)	RB	(4)	1978
Smeja, Rudy (Michigan)	E	(2)	1944
Smith, Clarence (Georgia)	E	(1)	1942
Smith, Eugene (Georgia Tech)	G	(1)	1930
Smith, H. Allen* (Mississippi)	E	(2)	1947
Smith, JD (N Carolina A&T)	FB	(1)	1956
Smith, James (Compton JC)	HB	(1)	1961
Smith, Quintin (Kansas)	WR	(1)	1990
Smith, Ray Gene (Midwestern)	HB	(4)	1954
Smith, Ron (Wisconsin)	S	(4)	1965
Smith, Russell* (Illinois)	T	(3)	1921
Smith, Sean (Grambling)	DT	(2)	1987
Smith, Vernice (Florida A & M)	G	(1)	1993
Smith, Vinson (East Carolina)	LB	(1)	1993
Snow, Percy (Michigan State)	LB	(1)	1993
Snyder, Bob (Ohio U.)	QB	(5)	1939
Sorey, Revie (Illinois)	G	(8)	1975
Spellman, Alonzo (Ohio State)	DL	(2)	1992
Spivey, Mike (Colorado)	CB	(3)	1977
Sprinkle, Ed (Hardin-Simmons)	E	(12)	1944
Stachowicz, Ray (Michigan State)	P	(1)	1983
Stahlman, Dick* (DePaul)	T	(1)	1933
Staley, Bill (Utah State)	DT	(2)	1970
Standlee, Norm* (Stanford)	FB	(1)	1941
Stautberg, Gerald (Cincinnati)	G	(1)	1951
Steinbach, Larry* (St. Thomas)	G	(2)	1930
Steinkemper, Bill* (Notre Dame)	T	(2)	1942
Stenn, Paul (Villanova)	G	(4)	1948
Sternaman, Edward* (Illinois)	HB	(11)	1920
Sternaman, Joe (Illinois)	HB	(8)	1922
Steuber, Bob (Missouri)	HB	(2)	1942
Stickel, Walt* (Penn)	T	(4)	1946
Stillwell, Roger (Stanford)	DE-DT	(3)	1975
Stinchcomb, Pete* (Ohio State)	QB	(2)	1921
Stinson, Lemuel (Texas Tech)	CB	(5)	1988
Stoepel, Terry (Tulsa)	G	(1)	1967
Stolfa, Anton* (Luther)	HB	(1)	1939
Stone, Billy (Bradley)	HB	(4)	1951
Stonebreaker, Michael (Notre Dame)	LB	(1)	1991
Stoops, Mike (Iowa)	DS	(1)	1987
Streeter, George (Notre Dame)	DB	(1)	1989
Strickland, Larry* (North Texas)	C	(6)	1954
Sturtridge, Dick (DePaul)	HB	(2)	1928
Stydahar, Joe* (West Virginia)	T	(9)	1936
Suhey, Matt (Penn State)	RB	(10)	1980
Sullivan, Frank* (Loyola, NO)	C	(5)	1935
Sumner, Charles (Wm & Mary)	HB	(4)	1955
Sweeney, Jake (Cincinnati)	T	(1)	1944
Swisher, Bob* (Northwestern)	HB	(5)	1938
Szymanski, Frank (Notre Dame)	C	(1)	1949

· T ·

Tabor, Paul (Oklahoma)	C	(1)	1980
Tackwell, CO* (Kansas State)	E	(3)	1931
Taft, Merrill* (Wisconsin)	FB	(1)	1924
Tate, David (Colorado)	S	(5)	1988
Tate, Lars (Georgia)	RB	(1)	1990
Taylor, Brian (Oregon State)	RB	(1)	1989
Taylor, Clifton (Memphis State)	RB	(1)	1974

Name	Pos		Year
Taylor, Joe (N. Carolina A&T)	DB	(8)	1967
Taylor, JR "Tarz"* (Ohio State)	G	(2)	1921
Taylor, Ken (Oregon St.)	CB	(1)	1985
Taylor, Lionel (NM Highland Univ.)	E	(1)	1959
Taylor, Roosevelt (Grambling)	DB	(8)	1961
Thayer, Tom (Notre Dame)	G	(8)	1985
Thomas, Bob (Notre Dame)	K	(10)	1975
Thomas, Calvin (Illinois)	FB	(6)	1982
Thomas, Earl (Houston)	WR	(3)	1971
Thomas, Stan (Texas)	T	(2)	1991
Thompson, Russ (Nebraska)	T	(4)	1936
Thornton, James (Cal St.-F'ton)	TE	(5)	1988
Thrift, Cliff (E Central Oklahoma)	LB	(1)	1985
Thrower, Willie (Michigan State)	QB	(1)	1953
Tom, Mel (San Jose State)	DE	(3)	1973
Tomczak, Mike (Ohio State)	QB	(6)	1985
Torrance, Jack* (LSU)	T	(2)	1939
Trafton, George* (Notre Dame)	C	(13)	1920
Trimble, Steve (Maryland)	DB	(1)	1987
Trost, Milt (Marquette)	T	(5)	1935
Tucker, Bill (Tennessee State)	RB	(1)	1971
Turner, Cecil (California Poly)	FL	(6)	1968
Turner, Clyde (Hardin-Simmons)	C	(13)	1940

· U ·

| Ulmer, Mike (Doane) | CB | (1) | 1980 |
| Usher, Lou* (Syracuse) | T | (1) | 1920 |

· V ·

Vactor, Ted (Nebraska)	CB	(1)	1975
Vallez, Emilo (New Mexico)	TE	(2)	1968
Van Horne, Keith (USC)	T	(13)	1981
Van Valkenburg, Pete (BYU)	RB	(1)	1974
Veach, Walter*	HB	(1)	1920
Venturelli, Fred*	T	(1)	1948
Vick, Ernie* (Michigan)	C	(3)	1925
Vick, Richard (Wash. & Jeff.)	QB	(1)	1925
Vodicka, Joe (Lewis Institute)	HB	(3)	1943
Voss, Walter "Tillie" (Detroit)	E	(2)	1927
Vucinich, Milt (Stanford)	G	(1)	1945

· W ·

Waddle, Tom (Boston College)	WR	(5)	1989
Wade, Charles (Tennessee St.)	WR	(1)	1974
Wade, William (Vanderbilt)	QB	(6)	1961
Waechter, Henry (Nebraska)	DE	(4)	1982
Wager, Clinton (St. Mary's)	E	(2)	1942
Wagner, Barry (Alabama A & M)	WR	(1)	1992
Wagner, Bryan (Cal St.-Northridge)	P	(2)	1987
Wallace, Bob (UTEP)	E	(5)	1968
Wallace, John (Notre Dame)	E	(1)	1928
Wallace, Stan (Illinois)	HB	(4)	1954
Walquist, Laurie* (Illinois)	QB	(10)	1922
Walterscheid, Len (S Utah)	S	(6)	1977
Ward, John (Oklahoma State)	C-G	(1)	1976
Washington, Fred* (TCU)	DT	(1)	1990
Washington, Harry (Colorado St.)	WR	(1)	1979

Watkins, Bobby (Ohio State)	HB	(3)	1955
Watts, Rickey (Tulsa)	WR	(5)	1979
Weatherly, Gerald (Rice)	C	(3)	1950
Wetnight, Ryan (Stanford)	TE	(1)	1993
Wetoska, Bob (Notre Dame)	T	(10)	1960
Wetzel, Damon (Ohio State)	HB	(1)	1935
Wheeler, Ted (W Texas State)	G	(1)	1970
Wheeler, Wayne (Alabama)	WR	(1)	1974
Whitaker, Danta (Miss. Valley St.)	TE	(1)	1993
White, Lawrence (Dana)	WR	(1)	1987
White, Roy* (Valparaiso)	FB	(5)	1923
White, Wilford (Arizona State)	HB	(2)	1951
Whitman, SJ (Tulsa)	HB	(2)	1953
Whitsell, Dave (Indiana)	DB	(6)	1961
Whittenton, Jesse (West Texas)	HB	(1)	1958
Wightkin, Bill (Notre Dame)	DE	(8)	1950
Williams, Bob (Notre Dame)	QB	(3)	1951
Williams, Brooks (N Carolina)	TE	(2)	1981
Williams, Broughton (Florida)	T	(1)	1947
Williams, Dave (Colorado)	RB	(3)	1979
Williams, Fred (Arkansas)	T	(12)	1952
Williams, James (Cheyney St.)	DT	(3)	1991
Williams, Jeff (Rhode Island)	G	(1)	1982
Williams, Oliver (Illinois)	WR	(1)	1983
Williams, Perry (Purdue)	RB	(1)	1974
Williams, Walt (New Mexico St.)	CB	(2)	1982
Willis, Peter Tom (Florida St.)	QB	(4)	1990
Wilson, George* (Northwestern)	E	(11)	1937
Wilson, Nemiah (Grambling)	CB	(1)	1975
Wilson, Otis (Louisville)	LB	(8)	1980
Wojciechowski, John (Mich. St.)	T	(7)	1987
Wolden, Allan (Bemidji State)	RB	(1)	1987
Woods, Tony (Oklahoma)	DT	(1)	1989
Woolford, Donnell (Clemson)	CB	(5)	1989
Worley, Tim (Georgia)	RB	(1)	1993
Wright, Eric (Stephen F. Austin)	WR	(2)	1991
Wright, Steve (Alabama)	T	(1)	1971
Wrightman, Tim (UCLA)	TE	(2)	1985
Wynne, Elmer* (Notre Dame)	FB	(1)	1928

· Y ·

Youmans, Maury (Syracuse)	T	(4)	1960
Young, Adrian (USC)	LB	(1)	1973
Young, Randolph* (Millikin)	T	(1)	1920
Youngblood, George (LSU)	S	(1)	1969
Yourist, Abe	E	(1)	1923

· Z ·

Zanders, Emanuel (Jackson State)	G	(1)	1981
Zarnas, Gust (Ohio State)	G	(1)	1938
Zawatson, Dave (California)	T	(1)	1989
Zeller, Joe (Indiana)	G	(1)	1938
Zizak, Vince* (Villanova)	G	(1)	1934
Zorich, Chris (Notre Dame)	DT	(3)	1991
Zorich, George* (Northwestern)	G	(3)	1944
Zucco, Vic (Michigan State)	HB	(3)	1957

COACHES OF THE CHICAGO BEARS

		Years	Overall W-L-T	(Pct.)	Regular W-L-T	Post-season W-L-T
1	George Halas	1920–1929				
		1933–1942				
		1946–1955				
		1958–1967	324-151-31	(.681)	318-148-31	6-3-0
2	Mike Ditka	1982–1992	112-68-0	(.622)	106-62-0	6-6-0
3	Neill Armstrong	1978–1981	30-35-0	(.462)	30-34-0	0-1-0
4	Ralph Jones	1930–1932	24-10-7	(.706)	23-10-7	1-0-0
5	Hunk Anderson / Luke Johnsos (co-coaches)	1942–1945	24-12-2	(.657)	23-11-2	1-1-0
6	Jack Pardee	1975–1977	20-23-0	(.465)	20-22-0	0-1-0
7	Jim Dooley	1968–1971	20-36-0	(.357)	20-36-0	None
8	Paddy Driscoll	1956–1957	14-10-1	(.583)	14-9-1	0-1-0
9	Abe Gibron	1972–1974	11-30-1	(.268)	11-30-1	None
10	**Dave Wannstedt**	**1993–**	**7- 9-0**	**(.438)**	**7-9-0**	**None**
	TOTALS	1920–1993	586-384-42	(.607)	572-371-42	14-1

Coaches George Halas, Hunk Anderson, Luke Johnsos, Paddy Driscoll